BASIC GENETICS:
A HUMAN APPROACH

 The Center for Education in Human and Medical Genetics

 A Continuing Program of the BSCS

W9-CGV-330

**KENDALL/HUNT
PUBLISHING COMPANY**
Dubuque, Iowa

CONTENTS

ON OUR COVER

The cover of *Basic Genetics: A Human Approach* shows what this magazine is all about. This magazine is about people. People come in all sizes and shapes. They are of different colors and different ages. They have different interests and different ideas. But people also have some things in common. For one thing, all have a genetic heritage. Each person is unique. But each person is also, at least in part, a product of the hereditary material that has been transmitted from generation to generation over millions of years.

In general, this magazine is about people. But specifically, this magazine is about you, about your parents and relatives, and about the children you may have someday. In part, you are a unique individual because of the genes you inherited from your mother and father. This inheritance has been acted on by your environment and your experiences. An important aim of education is to have you understand yourself, your capacities, and your limitations. These are, in part, genetically determined. This magazine will try to give you new insights into yourself as a product of past heredity, present capability, and future potential.

To help you uncover these ideas about yourself, we will be dealing with genetics as a discipline to give you an understanding of the inherited instructions that make you what you are. Genetics, for the most part, has been taught using organisms other than humans. But the principles of genetics can be illustrated by human beings as well as by any other organism. The use of the human as an example provides the benefits of immediately applied biology. You will come to understand what a pedigree is and how certain human characteristics are determined. The laws of probability and their effect on you and children you may have can be very important for your future and the future of your family.

Not all human inheritance is positive. People inherit characteristics for normal human operation, but they also may inherit defects. Disorders that are genetically determined frequently are more serious because they are longer lasting than the infectious diseases we spend so much time combatting. Even genetic disorders, however, can sometimes be anticipated. In some cases, they can be prevented or made less severe. But the medical interest in genetic disorders and diseases leads quickly to social, moral, and legal problems.

We are living at a time when new knowledge in genetics and medicine provides new power. And along with this power comes new responsibility. Simply because we know *how* to do something does not mean that we *ought* to do it. The rapid growth of information and technology means that all of us will incur responsibility for decisions that previous generations never had to face. The range of choices that human beings must make grows ever wider.

Our new knowledge can and should be used to benefit individuals and society. But how are such benefits to be determined? The study of human genetics leads to many issues that are outside the realm of scientific inquiry. Furthermore, the study of human genetics has a practical and applied value, but this practical application may well be different for each person. Perhaps no two individuals, after studying these materials, will come to exactly the same conclusions. Each of us is different, and our backgrounds make us feel differently about certain issues.

This particular area of biology is of great importance to the lives of each and every one of us. A knowledge of genetics will give you a better understanding of how to cope with what is, while giving you an understanding of your capacities to change what might be.

We are eager to hear how you have used the material and what effect it has had on you. Your comments and suggestions are solicited. Please send them to the BSCS at the address below. Only by knowing what you think and how you have reacted can we further improve this magazine.

Jay Barton II
Chairman of the Board of
  Directors, BSCS
Office of the President
University of Alaska
Fairbanks, Alaska 99701

Jack L. Carter, Director
BSCS
The Colorado College
Colorado Springs,
Colorado 80903

LOOKING AHEAD

It is often true that learning is easier and more enjoyable if we can relate new information to ourselves. All of us need to see some relationship between new facts and our own lives or the lives of our families and friends. Since this entire magazine is devoted to the topic of human genetics, it is probably wise to take a moment to think about what is included. You should also consider how the new ideas you will encounter here relate to things you have learned in the past.

Most people have heard something about genetics at one time or another. Usually, genetics is presented in the context of plants and animals other than human beings. Most books emphasize the genetics of pea plants and fruit flies and sometimes other living things such as cows, mice, or certain flowering plants.

In this magazine, genetics is explained in a very different way. The big ideas are similar, but the organism that is examined here most often is *Homo sapiens.* It is important to remember that much of our present knowledge of genetics actually came from the study of plants and nonhuman animals. But it is also important to understand that the same genetic principles apply broadly to all living things. Furthermore, our knowledge of the genetics of human beings is growing very rapidly. No one should be surprised if some of the things scientists now think are true turn out to be wrong later on.

Anyone who studies this magazine for any time at all should be able to master some of the basic principles of genetics. But don't stop there. Nearly every section of this magazine opens the door for more extensive examination of the principles of genetics and of moral, ethical, and legal issues that arise from new knowledge and technology in genetics. These latter issues are unique to human beings, for human beings are the only organisms that can anticipate the long-term consequences of choices made today. The future will demand that you—as an individual and as a member of society—make some complex and difficult choices. The authors of this magazine hope that your experience in thinking through such decisions now will help you when you face difficult choices later on.

A Magazine, Not a Book

Basic Genetics: A Human Approach is a magazine, not a book. By magazine, we do not mean that it comes out every week or every month. Instead, it has the *form* of a magazine. It includes articles, stories, editorials, letters, interviews, and other features. Although this magazine makes sense if read from front to back, it does not have to be used that way. You can skip around. You may also find that you will spend more time with some parts than others.

But this magazine is like a book in one way. The authors had certain goals in mind when they wrote it. They settled on some things they thought everyone should gain from reading the stories and articles that are included here. To get an idea of what is in this magazine and to assess your own prior knowledge, complete the "inventory" provided by your teacher. Rate yourself before you read anything in this magazine. Rate yourself again after you have completed your studies. Your score should improve dramatically.

FAMILIES: LIVING WITH CYSTIC FIBROSIS

"What is the most common, lethal, inherited disorder in the Caucasian population?" This question was asked of 124 persons on the streets and in the stores of Helena, Montana. None was able to give the right answer. When they were told it is cystic fibrosis (CF), most said they had heard of it and many had contributed to the Cystic Fibrosis Foundation.

Only one actually knew a person with the condition. This is not surprising. Only five people with the disorder are known to be living in Lewis & Clark, Powell, Jefferson, and Broadway counties, which have a population of 59,600.

The description of CF by the Cystic Fibrosis Foundation as "the most common, lethal, inherited disorder in the Caucasian population" raised eyebrows everywhere. But then people were told that this means an occurrence at birth of 1 in 1,800. To this, most replied with relief, "Well, then, it can't really happen to me."

---

1 But it can happen to you.

The number 1 in 1,800 means that there is 1 chance in 1,800 chances of inheriting the genetic disorder, CF. One out of 1,800 is small and may seem of no consequence. But, in fact, people with CF are born and die every day.

Actually, the chance figures are different for different groups in the population. The chance of 1 in 1,800 applies to all live births in the U. S. The chance for whites is greater, about 1 in 1,600.

In this story, we will hear mostly from a Helena family to whom cystic fibrosis did happen, the Laxalts of North Prospect. Theirs is a 16-year journey through agony and triumph, pain and joy, despair and hope. This journey finally ended at acceptance, courage, and strength in the face of continuing uncertainties.

The blue-and-white trucks of the Laxalt Construction Company are well known in and around Helena. Bob Laxalt became company president ten years ago, when his father retired. Bob is regarded by many people as the most progressive member of the school board. He was recently elected to the board for a third term.

Mary and Bob have been married for 18 years. Mary has been a nurse at St. Peter's Hospital for almost 19 years. She met Bob there when she cared for him after a truck accident. Over the years, Mary's cheerful and gentle competence has earned her the love and respect of hundreds of citizens. Very few of these people ever knew of her private anguish.

It began with the long-awaited birth of their first child, John, years ago. At that time, the Laxalts were not doing very well financially. They had planned on only two children. Baby John was greeted by his father with pride and joy as his possible successor in the family business. The infant was a hefty eight-pounder. But shortly after birth, he was not passing any stool and his abdomen was swelling alarmingly. Immediate surgery was indicated. At the time of the operation, almost 12 inches of intestine were removed because of a severe intestinal obstruction. The baby recovered slowly from the surgery. He was almost two months old before Mary and Bob could take him home.

Though his wound had healed, he was not well. Mary worried because he continued to pass large, greasy, foul-smelling waste materials and failed to gain weight. At first, the doctors thought that too long a segment of intestine had been removed. They thought that the infant was unable to absorb all the nourishment he received. "It's something he's going to have to live with the rest of his life—it's nothing we can treat," the doctors said. Then the doctors thought the baby might be allergic to his food. But many changes of formula only seemed to make matters worse.

At that time, the first signs of strain in their marriage began to appear. Mary's frustrations took her from one doctor to another. She seemed to be involved in the baby's care day and night. She didn't trust her infant to baby-sitters. When the child began to have attacks of pneumonia, she had him sleep with her at night so she could watch him at all times.

"That was to be the last straw that drove me out of the house," said Bob somewhat sheepishly when this reporter interviewed the Laxalt family recently.

"It was an awful time in our lives," Mary explained sadly. "During the first six months of his life, John was in the hospital five times. What savings we had were gone in no time. We could not keep up the payments on the house and the car and had to move into a trailer. The doctors were unable to tell us anything about John's condition or what was going to become of him. I was totally frustrated. I got angry at Bob for being unable to help, or seeming not to care, or not wanting to help with John's care. When he moved out, I was so lonely and angry I started to overeat, and smoke, and drink too much. I gave up my job at St. Peter's. But it seemed that I was spending all my time there, anyhow, with John. I was just not getting paid for it.

2 CF can strain family relationships.

Many families learn to deal effectively with CF and some even find that facing difficulties together strengthens family ties. Dealing with the psychological and social (we use the word "psychosocial" to describe this interaction) aspects of CF for both the family and the affected person is as important as dealing with the physical aspects. A major factor in dealing successfully with CF, or any other genetic condition, is a thorough understanding by everybody involved. At this stage in our story, Mary and Bob do not know the cause of John's physical problems.

Some families solve their problems with CF more easily than others. It is common in CF families for the mother-child relationship to become overly close and exclusive. Often the father is driven away from the care of the CF child. The mother becomes overwhelmed by the burden of care. And she may resent her husband's seeming lack of interest and involvement. The stage is set for marital conflict.

In one group of 99 families with CF children, the divorce rate was 9.5 times greater than would be expected. Another study of 214 CF families turned up a rate 5.5 times greater than anticipated. This is still significantly higher than expected, but it is 42% lower than the rate of the other sample. We cannot know for sure how much higher the rate actually is. But it is fair to say that, for CF families, the divorce rate is significantly higher than the average rate.

"And then, one morning in February, when John was seven months old—he had just gotten out of the hospital after another bout with pneumonia and bad liver disease—Bob came home. He wrapped up the baby and said, 'I've found a doctor in Spokane who thinks he knows what's wrong with the kid and I'm taking him. If you want to come along you'd better hurry up!'"

Her tears began to flow as she recalled: "Bob drove like a madman, muttering under his breath all the time about not having taken John earlier. In Idaho it started to snow. When we got to Fourth of July Pass, we could hardly see. We didn't see the sign that said the pass was closed. We almost made it to the top. But then we slid off into the ditch. We were stuck for almost six

hours. A snow plow finally got us out, but we had to turn back.

"We only got to Kellogg in Idaho before it got dark and started to snow again. The only motel room we were able to find wasn't heated. The baby was burning with fever, but no doctor was

able to come. When the snow let up a little, we started to drive back home. Outside Missoula, the baby started to choke and turn blue. He died in the hospital emergency room in Missoula. When he died, he weighed only one pound more than he did at birth. We refused to have an autopsy done and we took his little body home to be buried."

At this point Bob went on: "That really was the low point in our lives. Each of us blamed the other for John's death. But our grief finally brought us back together. What was left was a great bitterness at the doctors. They didn't make a correct diagnosis and didn't refer us to someone who could have started the right treatment.

"When we asked them what would happen if we had another child, they said, 'Lightning never strikes twice.' And when Sarah was born a year later and was normal, we believed them. We thought we had put that agony behind us for good. But then..." Here Bob Laxalt's voice trailed off, but Mary, with renewed strength, continued:

"Then, almost 15 years ago, our Lisa was born. Things went well in the hospital and on the sixth day we came home. Lisa loved her bottle and had a good appetite. About two weeks after we were at home, I started to notice that her stools were not normal. It wasn't as bad as with John, and for a long time I tried to hide the fact from Bob. But then one day I did tell our new **pediatrician**. She took one look at Lisa and had a **stool fat test** done. She told me Lisa had **steatorrhea**. This means too much fat in the stool because not enough fat-digesting enzymes are produced by the pancreas. The doctor noticed Lisa was not gaining weight as she should. In fact, she was losing weight. When I told the doctor about John, she put two and two together. She told me Lisa might have cystic fibrosis.

"I was so frightened that I came close to fainting. The doctor told me that the outlook was not necessarily as bad as it had been for John. The missing pancreatic enzymes could be replaced in a pill or a capsule. This would relieve the steatorrhea and Lisa would grow. Also, her lungs could be cared for so she would be less likely to get an infection or pneumonia. The doctor said that children with cystic fibrosis are doing better now than they did before doctors knew much about the disease."

3 Variability of CF

The difference in the severity of CF between John and Lisa illustrates an important aspect of genetic conditions. The degree of severity of some genetic conditions runs from a few, like John, who die at a very young age to a few who may have a normal life expectancy.

The life expectancy of individuals affected with CF has improved markedly since John's death. Of all the CF patients born in 1955, 50% were expected to live to at least age 17. Of those born today, 50% are expected to live to the age of 20. Some of these patients will live until their 30s, and a very few will live into their 40s. The reasons for this dramatic increase in life expectancy since 1955 are many. A few of the most important ones are:

1. Diagnosis early in life, before irreversible changes can take place.

2. Daily pulmonary therapy to help clear the lungs of mucus.

3. Use of antibiotics to manage lung infections.

4. Use of special diets and enzymes to manage digestive problems.

5. Better understanding of the psychological and social effects on the CF patient and family.

Mary poured another cup of coffee for all. Then she went on: "Telling Bob was the worst part of it. I got so upset thinking he might leave us again that I did not tell him everything. I only said, 'Lisa has a mild case of the same condition John had.' But I think Bob had suspected that something was wrong for some time. When I told him that, he got so angry he knocked a great big hole in the wall with his fist. He cursed so loudly the neighbors came running, thinking we were having a fight.

"But he really had changed since John died. He calmed down right away and put a bandage on his cut hand. Then he went and got the doctor out of bed and had a long talk with her. And she was really good to him. Although she hadn't seen very many cases of the disease herself, she knew enough to tell him about the causes and symptoms of the disorder. Of course, all of John's symptoms were just as she described.

"When Bob came home that night, he was calm. He went over to the cradle and picked up the baby. He sat down with her in that rocking chair over there and held her in his arms a long time, trying not to cry. He kept saying, over and over again, 'Don't worry, Missy Lisa'—that's his nickname for her—'we'll take good care of you.'

"And the next morning the pediatrician called a doctor who was an expert on cystic fibrosis—Dr. Becker, at the University in Madison, Wisconsin. He wasn't in, but his co-worker, Dr. John Morgan, answered the phone. The two discussed Lisa's case. They concluded that she probably had cystic fibrosis, but the diagnosis should be confirmed through a test of the baby's sweat. So we went to St. Peter's hospital here in Helena, where they told us that they did not have the equipment or trained personnel to do a sweat test. They referred us to a CF center in Denver where a reliable sweat test could be performed."

4 "Sweat test"

Almost 30 years ago, doctors discovered that the salt content in the sweat from patients with CF was abnormally high. This knowledge resulted in a diagnostic method called the "sweat test." As of now, it is not applicable as a screening method at birth. It's not that the method is complicated, it's just that newborn babies usually don't sweat enough to provide a sample.

A sweat test, when properly performed and analyzed by trained personnel, is more than 98% reliable. The excretion of high amounts of salt in the sweat of a CF baby is the reason the family and friends experience a salty taste when kissing the baby. Many times, when parents are aware of this symptom, they are the first to detect the possibility of CF in their infant.

Early treatment resulting from early detection of some genetic conditions will greatly improve the chances of a long life expectancy and a fairly normal existence. Many genetic conditions such as PKU, sickle-cell anemia and CF can be detected early if the proper tests are given. Others like Huntington disease are still in the research stage, and early detection is not possible at this time.

"Boy, I tell you, that trip was a far cry from the last one we had taken with a CF baby," Bob cut in vigorously. "My dad, who was still living then, gave us the money for the airplane and room and board at a motel near the university hospital. Within a few hours after we got there, the sweat test was done. Soon Missy was getting her pancreatic enzymes and vitamins. She also had a diet suited to her nutritional needs. In a few days, she was already gaining weight. Another thing that helped was that there was a big CF clinic there. For the first time, we met many other parents of kids with CF."

"It's such a relief to know you are not alone in this world with your problems and that others have gone the same road before you," Bob went on. "Why, we saw CF kids of all ages there, some 18 years old, some just newborn babies. Some of them were really sick, but many of them were in better shape than we would have expected. The social worker and Dr. Collins, who runs that clinic, took a lot of time to tell us about CF. They gave us pamphlets and a lot of other reading material. I tell you, it was quite an education!

"For me, the most helpful thing they told us was that—if the lung infections are treated—most CF kids can lead a more or less normal life. They can go to school, you know, and even do some sports! Of course, there is a wide variability among affected people."

5 Cystic Fibrosis Centers

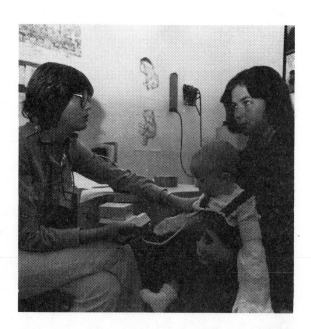

The Laxalts took Lisa to a Cystic Fibrosis Center. These centers receive partial support from the Cystic Fibrosis Foundation. There are over 125 such centers in 45 states, the District of Columbia, and Puerto Rico. The main functions of the centers are care of patients, research, education for CF families, teaching, and providing resources to conduct research.

A number of genetic disorders have similar foundations and similar centers. Groups of people, including doctors, nurses, and families, participate in organizing volunteer groups and foundations. Many people work together in centers that have all or some of the same functions as do the CF Centers.

6 Disease vs. Condition

Why did Lisa's mother say disease and then say condition? Psychologically, the patient and the family are better able to cope with CF when they think about it as a condition due to an inborn (genetic) error of metabolism. It was not something caught or caused by bacteria, viruses, or other microscopic organisms. It is not contagious. If the symptoms caused by the genetic error are treated, the patient can live a fairly normal life.

With infectious diseases, doctors often can treat the cause, not just the symptoms. They can give a patient medicine that will destroy the organism that causes a disease. But genetic conditions cannot be treated in the same way. Genetic conditions can be treated, but not "cured."

The use of the word condition, rather than disease, to describe genetic abnormalities is not universally accepted. Because CF and other genetic problems demand an ongoing regimen of medical care, the use of the term "disease" is appropriate in the opinion of many in the health care field. However, there is evidence that dealing with the problem as a condition, rather than a disease, has a higher success rate among some families and affected individuals.

Mary then added, "It was really wonderful the way Bob rose to the challenge of this disease...or perhaps I should say condition."

"While I took a little vacation," Mary continued, "Bob read and read and read. He kept bugging the doctors and nurses to explain things to him. Why, he even started to teach me at night in the motel and to tell me about all of the research work that was going on.

"While Lisa was getting good care, we spent a few days seeing the sights of Denver and the surrounding Rocky Mountain area," she added. "It really was our first vacation since we got married."

"Well, a lot of water has gone over the dam since then," Bob said. "If we had known then all that we know now, perhaps we would not have come home from Denver in such an optimistic mood. One thing we did agree on, though, was that we were not going to have another child. We found out in Denver that CF is an inherited condition and there is a 25% chance of CF in any child we might have. Sarah and Lisa have kept us plenty busy. We really could not have handled another child.

"At the present time, CF can't be diagnosed before birth. So each time you conceive, you don't know until the baby is born whether it is normal or not. And even though a 25% chance means that the odds are in your favor 3-to-1, Mary and I both felt a one-fourth probability is too high a risk to take. Two CF kids are enough!"

To this Mary added: "Amen."

7 Probability

How did the Laxalts know that if they were to have another child its chance of having CF would be 25%? To understand the answer to this, you need some background information on a branch of mathematics called probability. Much of what happens in genetics seems to follow certain laws of probability. These laws allow us to make predictions about the occurrence of CF in the Laxalt family. The basic question in probability is "How often should we expect a particular event to occur in a given number of events?" You can answer this question if you learn how to use the following formula.

$$\text{Probability} = \frac{\text{number of chances for a particular event}}{\text{number of possible, equally likely events}}$$

Now follow the directions of your teacher.

The afternoon sun was declining. For a moment, no one spoke. Sleeper, the family's dog, dozed before the fireplace.

Almost immediately, the clock chimed. It was three o'clock. Sleeper bounded toward the front door, wagging his tail. Together, Bob and Mary said, "Time for the kids to come home from school."

At that instant, the girls burst in, leaving a trail of mittens, scarfs, jackets, books, boots, and snow on their way to the refrigerator. Lisa stuck her head around the corner. "Oh, it's Alex—you are the reporter, aren't you? Come, join us for a glass of milk and some cookies."

I joined Sleeper and the girls in the kitchen for their after school snack. And although this reporter doesn't like milk, we had a delightful time. Lisa seemed to be breathing a little faster than Sarah, but that may have been my imagination. The only unusual thing that caught my attention was how often Lisa coughed.

8 Special treatment for CF patients

All CF patients receive special treatment based on their individual conditions. Each treatment has something to do with the extremely thick mucus that is the central aspect of CF. The cause of the thick mucus is unknown. Treatment generally includes:

Bronchial drainage or postural drainage. This is a form of physical therapy that helps to loosen mucus from the lungs. It keeps lung passages open. The method Lisa uses may be accompanied by a chest-clapping and vibration procedure done by a physical therapist or by a family member who has learned the procedure. The procedure loosens the mucus, and the patient is encouraged to cough up as much of it as possible.

Antibiotic therapy. CF patients may take drugs regularly to fight respiratory infections. Or, they may take them only when there is an indication of a lung infection. Why CF patients are more prone to lung infections is not known. One possibility is that the mucous accumulation in the lungs may act as a "breeding ground" for bacterial growth. The prime bacteria infection is caused by *Pseudomonas aeruginosa*. This infection is difficult to treat with the oral antibiotics that are available. CF patients often require hospitalization while they receive intravenous antibiotic treatment.

Dietary management. In CF patients, thick, sticky mucus blocks the ducts that carry enzymes from the pancreas and other digestive glands. As a result, much of their food is not digested and is excreted. This is treated by a well-balanced diet with extra quantities of high-protein, high-calorie food. Vitamins, pancreatic enzyme replacements, and a variety of nutritional supplements are often prescribed. Some CF patients take as many as 40 to 60 pills a day. The individual cost of the treatment outlined above plus any hospitalization can range from $6,000 to $12,000 per year.

"It feels good to be home," Lisa explained, "because our house is humidified. I can breathe and sleep easier. I take enzyme capsules before supper," she went on, "and vitamins with my supper. I'm still taking an antibiotic since my last chest infection, and every morning and night I do postural drainage." She explained that this involved positioning her body in various ways to permit the force of gravity to assist in draining the mucus from her bronchial tubes. Having to

9 Coping With CF

Lisa talks of her condition and treatment as very ordinary, everyday matters. Apparently, through her knowledge and understanding, she has learned to live with CF in a very positive way. But we must remember that each time Lisa is forced into the hospital could be the last. Death from a severe infection, pulmonary or heart failure is always possible. It will happen to Lisa. She will die from her condition at a relatively young age. People affected by many kinds of genetic conditions must face the possibility of early death every day. Many, like Lisa, seem to adjust; but there are others who do not adjust well. They require special counseling and support to cope with their problems.

take her enzyme capsules before lunch at school is the main thing that makes her different from her schoolmates.

Lisa is in the tenth grade and takes a full load of courses. She also swims, jogs, is the timer of the girls' basketball games, and plays drums in the band. Three days each week, she works as a volunteer at Shodair Children's Hospital after school.

"I might as well," she quipped, "since I am one of their favorite consumers." But she went on more seriously. "No, I really am not. In the last ten years, I've been hospitalized only five times, the last time three weeks ago. When my chest gets too full, I have to do additional pulmonary therapy or have help from a physical therapist. And the technicians in the lab periodically do

throat and sputum cultures to keep track of the bacteria in my system. The physicians want to know whether the bacteria are becoming resistant to the antibiotic I am taking. When I get fever and my cough gets worse, the physicians request X rays to be taken of my chest.

"I know pretty nearly everyone at Shodair, and they all have been very nice to me. Every now and then, I have a soda with the new geneticist there. She has been teaching me all about the genetics of CF, since we don't get much human genetics in our high school biology class."

Lisa was happy to share her knowledge with me. "CF is recessively inherited. This means that carriers, like my mom and dad, who have only *one* CF gene, are perfectly normal. Most carriers never have affected children because they don't marry another carrier. Since a *pair* of CF genes (she called them CF "alleles") are required for a child to have CF, *both* parents must be carriers. And since both parents also have the non-CF form of the gene (allele), their normal children each have a 2-in-3 chance of being carriers."

I gave up at that point and told Lisa she'd lost me.

---

10 The discovery of genes

And maybe Lisa's explanation has lost you, too. But the following information should help you understand the basic genetics involved in CF.

Our story starts with Gregor Mendel, an Austrian monk, who among other things tended a garden at the monastery. While working in his garden, he noticed how different some of the pea plants were from one another. He had planted what seemed to be the same kind of seeds. But the plants had different stem lengths; some were short and others were long. The peas they produced were different in color and texture. Some plants had flowers at the ends of their stems (terminal flowers), while others had them in the angles formed by the stems (axial flowers). These variations puzzled Mendel. He set out to find what caused them.

What Mendel discovered and explained to the world in 1865 became the foundation for the science of genetics. All living processes are controlled by factors (we now call them genes) that express themselves during the development and life of the individual. These genes are inherited from parents and transmitted to offspring. Human genes distinguish human beings from nonhuman beings. Genes also characterize certain groups of humans (races), certain families, or certain individuals—like Lisa with her CF condition.

Mendel spent several years raising plants that always produced offspring that showed the same form of a trait. He produced pure varieties of pea plants. For example, one variety always produced wrinkled seeds. Another variety always produced round seeds.

Mendel then began experiments involving crosses of the *pure varieties* of pea plants. He made hundreds of crosses to study a particular trait. One was a cross between pea plants whose seeds were always round and plants whose seeds were always wrinkled. When a cross is made between two varieties, the parent generation is called the P_1 *generation*. The offspring of the P_1 cross are the *first filial*, or F_1, *generation*.

In every case, Mendel found that all the F_1 plants had round seeds. When only one form of a trait (in this case, round seeds) appeared in the F_1 generation of a cross of pure varieties, Mendel called this the *dominant* trait. The trait that did not show was called the *recessive* trait. The offspring in all of Mendel's first crosses were exactly like one of the parents. There were never any in-between types nor any that showed a mixture of the parents' traits.

Mendel then crossed many of the F_1 plants by allowing self-pollination to occur. In the next generation, the F_2, the dominant trait (round seeds) appeared in 75% of the offspring. In 25%, the recessive trait (wrinkled seeds) reappeared. This gives a ratio of three dominant traits to one recessive trait in the F_2 generation. Mendel observed the same results in crosses involving other traits.

Mendel looked for a hypothesis to explain these results. He assumed that some part of the reproductive cell carried something that transmitted traits to offspring. We now call these "parts" genes, and we know they are carried on chromosomes. Mendel assigned letters to stand for the genes that caused each trait. For example, he used a capital **R** to stand for the gene that caused the dominant trait— round seeds. A small **r** stood for the gene that caused the recessive trait—wrinkled seeds.

In this example, we are assuming that the appearance of round seeds is caused by a certain gene, **R**. To characterize the trait itself, we use the word *phenotype*.

Continued on next page

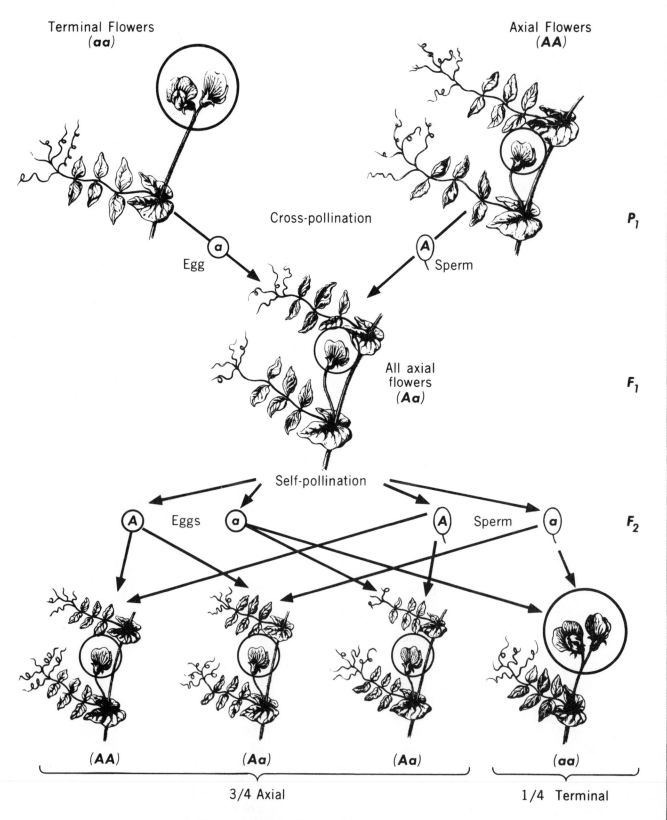

Figure 1. Inheritance of terminal and axial flowers in peas

Continued on next page

We use the word *genotype* to refer to the combination of genes that causes the phenotype. The egg and sperm that combine to produce the offspring may be genetically different. Each male or female reproductive cell contains only one of each kind of gene. When the two cells combine, the new cell contains two of each kind of gene—one from the mother and one from the father.

Mendel suggested that the reproductive cells of a pure, round-seed plant would carry only **R** genes. Thus, its genotype would be **RR**. And those of a pure, wrinkled-seed plant would carry only the **r** genes (genotype **rr**). We describe these individuals as *homozygous* because both *alleles* are the same—**RR** or **rr**.

The result of a cross between pure, round-seed plants and pure, wrinkled-seed plants would be an F_1 generation of plants that had both **R** and **r** genes. The genotype of those plants would be **Rr**. When the alleles are different (**Rr**), the individual is said to be *heterozygous*.

Because the **R** gene exerts a dominant effect, the phenotype of the F_1 generation would be round seeds. But we know that the **r** gene was present in the F_1 plants, because the wrinkled-seed trait reappeared in the F_2 generation. Figure 1 shows how this works for another set of characteristics in peas.

Gathering knowledge about, and developing an understanding of, the genetics of nonhuman life has been going on since before recorded history. Understanding human genetics is in some ways more difficult. In the laboratory, geneticists prefer to work with pure lines of organisms whose offspring will always show the same form of a trait. They obtain these pure lines by breeding plants and animals that are closely related for many generations. They repeat crosses many times and try to obtain many offspring. They keep the experimental organisms in an environment in which heat, light, nutrition, and other factors can be carefully controlled.

Of course, it is not possible to carry out such experiments on people. But geneticists have learned a great deal about human genetics in other ways. One way is by tracing the inheritance of traits. They observe the distribution of a trait in as many generations of a family as possible. Then they put the information in a structured form called a pedigree. Figure 2 is a pedigree for a family with CF.

Study the pedigree of the Laxalt family in Figure 2. The grandparents were not affected; but Mary and Bob, the parents in the next generation, were both carriers. At the moment, there is no proven test to detect a carrier of CF, but in time one may be devised. The fact that the parents in this pedigree were carriers could not become apparent until they had their first affected child, John. The second child, Sarah, did not have the disease. Whether or not Sarah is a carrier cannot be determined. If she is a carrier, the disease could occur in her children only if she married a carrier.

We cannot know exactly which of the grandparents were carriers. But we can reason that either Michael or Emma must have been a carrier. Either Herman or Ann also must have been a carrier. How do we know this?

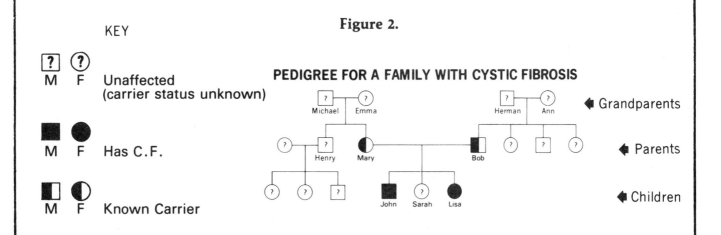

KEY

PEDIGREE FOR A FAMILY WITH CYSTIC FIBROSIS

Unaffected (carrier status unknown)

Has C.F.

Known Carrier

Grandparents

Parents

Children

Figure 2.

"Maybe it'll help if I draw you a picture," Lisa said. This is what she drew:

Figure 3.

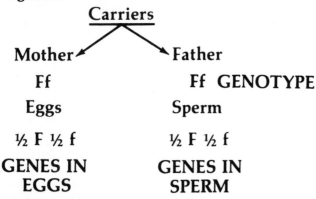

I had to interrupt her again to find out why *both* members of the pair of genes did not end up in the *same* egg or sperm.

"Oh, no, they never do," she said. "The members of the gene pair are on different chromosomes. Each member is on one of two paired chromosomes. An egg or sperm has only 23 chromosomes–one of each of 23 pairs. That way, when the egg and sperm meet, the new cell will have the correct number of chromosomes–46–and the 23 pairs match. If the gene pairs were not separated in the egg and sperm, we would be doubling the number of genes in every cell of our bodies in each generation." That impressed me as a reasonable argument. But it did not explain how these two genes got sorted out from each other to end up in two different cells. So Lisa began to tell me about "meiosis."

Lisa quickly drew a picture of a person,

Figure 4.

BODY

and labeled it "Body." Then, she drew a picture of a heart,

Figure 5.

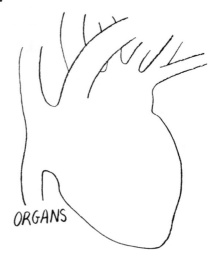

ORGANS

next to which she wrote "Organs."

"The organs all consist of cells," she said. And she drew several kinds.

Figure 6.

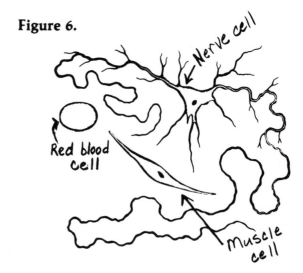

Nerve cell

Red blood cell

Muscle cell

All the cells, except the red blood cells, had a nucleus. In the nucleus of a large cell, she drew many wiggley lines. She called these strands "chromatin."

Figure 7.

Chromatin

Cell Membrane

Nucleus

Cytoplasm

The chromatin in a nondividing cell is all of the material of the chromosomes of the cell in a sort of unravelled state. This makes the chromosomes difficult to see except during cell division. Stuck in her social studies book Lisa had a beautiful photo that the new geneticist at Shodair had given her. It showed her own chromosomes from a dividing cell.

Figure 8. Human chromosomes

"Is that a karyotype?" I asked her, using the only technical term in biology that I thought I understood.

"Of course it isn't," she said. "People don't have karyotypes. They have chromosomes. Chromosomes contain the genes—lined up inside them, or on them, sort of like beads on a necklace. Many thousands of genes are packaged into only 23 pairs of chromosomes. And one member of each pair comes from the mother; the other comes from the father. It's only when you cut out the chromosomes in this picture and line them up in this order that you make a karyotype." She carefully removed a karyotype from between the pages of her Spanish book.

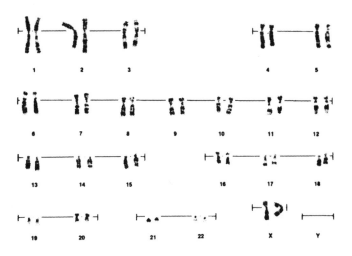

Figure 9. Human karyotype

As I studied the karyotype, she continued, "Now you must imagine that on one of the pairs of chromosomes is a pair of CF genes—one gene on each of the two chromosomes. When most body cells divide, the chromosomes are first doubled in number and then the nucleus divides. Each of the two new nuclei has the same number of chromosomes as the first cell did. This process is called *mitosis*. Through mitosis, the number and kind of chromosomes in most kinds of body cells remain the same. So each of my body cells has a pair of CF genes in it.

"But the process is different when reproductive cells—egg cells and sperm cells—are formed. The process of chromosome duplication and nuclear division is called *meiosis*. It differs from mitosis in several ways. One of the differences is that the cells end up with half as many chromosomes as the original cell had (instead of the same number as with mitosis). Producing the sperm of the egg cell requires two divisions. Let me draw you a diagram. To make the drawing simple, I'll just show one pair of chromosomes instead of all twenty-three pairs. And I will mark a place on each chromosome to stand for the CF gene. (Actually, scientists don't know yet which pair of chromosomes has the CF gene.)"

Figure 10. Lisa's Diagram of Meiosis in Her Eggs

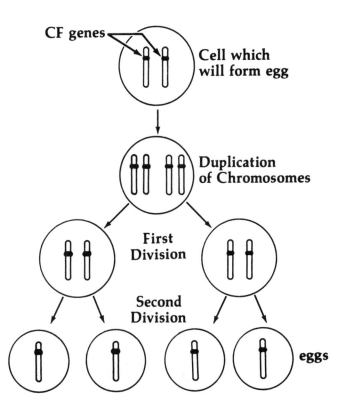

CF genes

Cell which will form egg

Duplication of Chromosomes

First Division

Second Division

eggs

"My mom or dad's cells in meiosis would be diagrammed differently. Because they are carriers, only one of the two chromosomes would have the CF gene." Lisa proceeded to sketch the situation in her mother and father.

Figure 11. Lisa's Diagram of Meiosis in Her Mother and Father

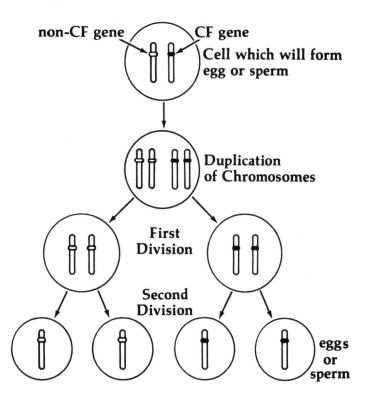

"In the first cell division, the chromosomes line up in pairs. Then they double and separate. When the cell divides, each new cell contains 23 pairs of chromosomes. These new cells then divide, and the chromosome pairs are separated. That's right, only 23 chromosomes, not 46. That's why each egg and each sperm can contain only one gene that may or may not result in CF."

The force of Lisa's argument was convincing. But it took a little more study for me to take it all in and to learn all the new words.

While Lisa was explaining meiosis to me, Sleeper kept nudging me about my leftover chocolate chip cookie, which he swallowed in one gulp without chewing. He also noticed my untouched milk glass, and I quietly emptied it into his dish. Now I have a new friend. Whenever we meet in town, he jumps on me with much tail wagging and playful barking. I have never seen his eyes, but I'm told they are a lovely golden brown.

As I scratched Sleeper's ears, I said to Lisa, "So CF is caused by a recessive gene and not by a dominant gene. Right?" Lisa responded thoughtfully to my question. "Well, Alex, yes and no. It depends on how you look at it. If you are using the word dominant the way we do in ordinary conversation, then you are wrong. But if you mean dominant as the characteristic that is expressed even if only one allele of that type is present, then you are right."

---

11 Meiosis

If we look at Lisa's two diagrams of meiosis, maybe her explanation will be a little easier to understand. Of course the cell which will form her eggs has 23 pairs of chromosomes but she is diagramming only the one pair on which the genes for CF are found. The chromosomes duplicate and then separate. The two new cells each contain one pair of chromosomes. These new cells divide, and the chromosome pairs are separated. So the number has been reduced by one-half. In Lisa's diagram—from two to one; in her cells from 46 to 23.

The same process goes on in her mother's egg-producing cells and her father's sperm-producing cells. The difference is that all of Lisa's eggs contain a chromosome with the CF gene. But only one half of her mother's eggs and her father's sperm contain the CF gene. The other half do not.

---

12 Dominant and recessive characteristics

Lisa's point about dominant and recessive genes is a subtle, but very important distinction. We talk about dominant and recessive genes only as a matter of convenience. Actually, it is the characteristic (phenotype) that is dominant or recessive—that is, expressed or not expressed. Saying "dominant gene" is a quick way of talking about a gene whose effect is expressed (the phenotype) even if only one of that kind of allele is present. "Recessive gene" is a quick way of referring to a gene whose effect is not expressed in the phenotype unless *both* alleles are of the same type.

In ordinary language, we define the word dominant as meaning controlling or overpowering something else. But genes do not work that way. Genes provide the "instructions" for making certain cellular products—usually proteins. A gene "codes" for a particular protein. If a cell contains a so-called "dominant gene," the protein that will be evident in the phenotype is the one coded for

Continued on next page

by that gene. If a "recessive gene" is present along with a dominant gene, the recessive gene will produce a gene product that is different in structure and function from the product of the dominant gene. But the product of the recessive gene will not be evident in the phenotype. If two "recessive genes" are present, the only protein produced will be the one coded for by those genes, and that protein will be expressed in the phenotype. Therefore, the terms dominant and recessive do not refer to one gene dominating another. Rather, they refer to the allele or alleles whose product is expressed in the phenotype.

Lisa should also remind Alex that, while CF is inherited as a recessive characteristic, some genetic disorders are inherited as dominant characteristics.

By this time it had become dark outside and Mary had dinner ready. Bob returned and, looking over our studies, kissed Lisa on the head: "At it again, Missy? That's good; the best way to live with a condition is to understand it." I gladly accepted an invitation for dinner. Mary had prepared delicious broiled fish and fresh fruit.

During dinner I asked Bob the question he must have been asked hundreds of times. "No, we are not related to Paul Laxalt, the U. S. Senator from Nevada, although both families are of Basque descent."

He explained that the ancestors of both families had come to the West as sheepherders. Bob's grandfather had been an independent sheepherder near Dillon, Montana. But after the First World War, he sold his ranch and began the construction firm in Helena. When I asked if the CF had anything to do with Basque ancestry, he grew thoughtful.

"Maybe, but I'm not sure. I know several other Basque families who've had CF children. The best known, of course, is State Senator Etchart of Glasgow. Etchart has been very active in CF volunteer work and was responsible for the passage of a law in Montana that provides direct financial support to families being drained by high medical expenses. The research and library assistant at Shodair did a search of medical literature for me on a possible relationship between Basque and CF, but we came up with nothing. However, that's something I'm going to do some research on—if I ever can get away from the office long enough." The last remark drew several laughs and good-natured remarks from around the table.

13 Genetic disorders in ethnic groups

Some recessive disorders occur more often among certain populations or ethnic groups. Tay-Sachs disease, for example, is more frequent among Jewish populations that trace their ancestry to northeastern Europe. It is assumed that the gene for Tay-Sachs arose by mutation in that population many generations ago.

Religious and cultural traditions have resulted in a tendency for individuals from that population to "marry within the group." This is not unusual in human populations. The result is an increased probability that individuals who are heterozygous for the Tay-Sachs gene will marry. This increases the probability that they will bear a child with Tay-Sachs disease.

Some populations are so restrictive in their matings that the frequency of certain disorders is extremely high. These populations, called isolates, have very few marriages with individuals from outside the group. As a result, many marriages take place between closely related individuals—inbreeding. Closely related persons are much more likely to have the same genes—harmful or not—than unrelated people. When these genes combine in their offspring, the likelihood of a genetic disorder is higher. The Amish, for example, have a very high frequency of a certain type of recessive dwarfism.

The increased probability of genetic disorders resulting from inbreeding probably is one of the reasons for the long-standing cultural taboos against incest. The Bible (Old Testament) cautions that "none of you shall approach to any that is near of kin to him, to uncover their nakedness" (Leviticus 18:6).

There does not seem to be any particular ethnic group in which the frequency of CF is higher than in other groups. However, CF occurs most often among whites, seldom among blacks.

Over dessert Lisa took me on again. "I'm not going to let you get away until you understand why the unaffected brother or sister of a person with CF has a 2/3 chance of being a carrier." I groaned a bit but submitted humbly to my young teacher, who drew another picture (Figure 12).

Then she explained the picture. "You can see that half of the eggs and sperm carry the CF gene (f) and half carry the normal gene (F). This scheme is called a Punnet square. It gives you all the outcomes possible at each conception. There

Figure 12. Punnett Square

SPERM

	½ F	½ f
½ F	¼ FF	¼ Ff
½ f	¼ Ff	¼ ff

EGGS (label on left side)

are only three: **FF**—the affected; **Ff**—the carriers; and **FF**—the normal, noncarrier persons. And they occur in a ratio of 1/4:1/2:1/4, right?"

"Right," I responded. "So how come the 2/3 chance?" Then I thought about it for a moment, and it became clear. One-fourth are affected—they have the CF phenotype. *Three*-fourths are not affected. Theoretically, one of the unaffected three would have the **FF** genotype—no recessive CF gene. The other *two* would have the **f** gene in their genotypes. Thus, we could predict that two out of the three without CF are carriers—a 2/3 chance.

---

14 What are the chances?

The ¼:½:¼ ratio of genotypes is only what we might *expect for each pregnancy* when both parents are CF carriers. Let us suppose that these parents plan to have four children. For each child the chances are the same: ¼ that it will be normal, ½ that it will be a carrier, and ¼ that it will be affected with CF. It does *not* mean that we would expect one of the four children to have no gene for the CF condition, two to be carriers, and one to have CF.

Look back at the pedigree in Figure 2 on page 11. The carrier parents in this pedigree had three children. Two of them had CF. There is a case of a family with eight children, five of whom have CF. Or there could be a family of eight children, none of whom would have CF, even though both parents were carriers. Probability tells us only what we might expect *each time* a child is conceived by parents who are CF carriers. Each child has the same ¼ chance of have CF.

I heaved a great sigh of relief. I had just learned some basic ideas of genetics in a most agreeable and meaningful manner. I thanked Lisa and rose to leave, but she was relentless.

"One last thing, Alex. You should learn a little bit about the Hardy-Weinberg law before you can really understand genetics." Now I was really excited, for I had not expected anything more. Mary poured me another cup of coffee, and I was ready for this last challenge.

---

15 Clearing up a misconception

Lisa knew that there is a common misconception about recessive traits. She wanted Alex to understand the Hardy-Weinberg law so he wouldn't get the same idea. Some people assume that, because a trait is recessive, the genes eventually will disappear from the population.

The fact is that recessive genes will not disappear unless some forces are operating that change the frequency of the recessive gene. For example, pea plants survive and reproduce perfectly well whether they have round seeds or wrinkled seeds. Therefore, the frequency of the recessive gene does not change over time, assuming certain, special conditions, such as no mutation.

In 1908, two scientists, G. H. Hardy, an English mathematician, and W. Weinberg, a German physician, worked out this principle. They showed that the frequencies of genes and the genotype ratios remain constant within a population. This principle holds true *in the absence of* forces, such as nonrandom mating or natural selection, that can alter the frequencies. Hardy, in his 1908 paper, stated that "there is not the slightest foundation for the idea that a dominant character should show a tendency to spread over a whole population, or that a recessive should tend to die out."

Of course, with CF, there are forces at work that change gene frequencies—there is selection against the CF gene. Only a few years ago, few children who were born with CF lived past infancy. Even now, many people with CF may not marry, and many of those who do choose not to have children. Also, most males with CF are sterile. But, there are many more heterozygotes than homozygotes. For this reason, it would take perhaps hundreds of generations to reduce the frequency of the gene very much. So we can expect the frequency of the gene that causes CF to diminish, but not very much.

"I don't think it is necessary to go into all the detailed mathematics of the Hardy-Weinberg law," Lisa said gravely and without the slightest hint of condescension, "but an understanding of what we call 'gene frequencies' in a population is important. Let's use the figure 1/1600 for the frequency of CF among white people. I should use 1/1800, the frequency for all live births in the U.S.," she noted, "but the arithmetic is harder." Now if we have a population of 1600 newborn white children, we can predict the frequency of the genotype in this population. Tell me, what is the frequency of genotype ff?" I thought for a moment and said "1/1600." Lisa laughed and said, "You are a fast learner, Alex" and wrote: ff=1/1600. Then she continued.

"The gene pool is the term geneticists use to describe all the genes that the members of a population may contribute to the next generation. There are just two alleles for CF—the F allele and the f allele. In the gene pool, a certain proportion of the alleles are F and the rest are f. The proportions must add up to 100%, or 1. In this case, 1 means 'all' or 'the whole.'

Using the formula developed by Hardy and Weinberg and the one piece of data we have, ff = 1/1600, we can calculate the frequencies of the genes F and f in the gene pool. Once we know this, it is easy to calculate the frequencies of the other genotypes, Ff and FF, in the population. The key step is to determine the frequency of the recessive gene, f, in our population. We do this by taking the square root of the frequency of homozygous recessives. The square root of 1/1600 is 1/40. This is the frequency of the recessive gene: f=1/40. Earlier I said that the frequencies of the recessive gene (f) and of the dominant gene (F) must add up to 100%, or 1. So knowing this, how can I get the frequency of the dominant F gene?"

I am not great when it comes to math but it seemed almost too simple to be true. I said, "If the frequency of the recessive gene plus the frequency of the dominant gene must equal one, and we know the frequency of f is 1/40, then the frequency of F must equal 1 - 1/40—which is 39/40." Again Lisa laughed with glee because her student seemed to be learning very rapidly.

Lisa continued, "Now in each population there are two gene pools that must be combined into one. Each population has a male gene pool (in the sperm) and a female gene pool (in the eggs). The frequency of the f gene in the sperm and the eggs is 1/40 while the frequency of the F gene is 39/40 in the eggs and the sperm."

"One of the laws of probability states that 'the chance of two independent events occurring at the same time is the *product* of their chances of

occurring separately.' When we combine the gene frequencies of both the male and the female gene pools, we get the proportions of FF, Ff, and ff individuals among all of the offspring.

"As we determined earlier the frequency of the F gene in both the male and female populations is 39/40. The FF genotype is the

---

16 The Hardy-Weinberg law

To better understand the Hardy-Weinberg law, let's look at another trait and determine its gene and carrier frequencies. The ability to taste a chemical called PTC is inherited. To some people the substance tastes bitter. Others cannot taste it.

In one class in an American school, the PTC test showed 30 tasters of PTC and 10 non-tasters. Each student took home a small amount of the PTC solution and tested her or his parents. Their results were as follows:

Figure 13.

Parents	Student Tasters	Student Nontasters
taster x taster	20	2
taster x nontaster	10	5
nontaster x nontaster	0	3

From these data can you determine which of the traits is dominant and which is recessive?

When parents having the dominant phenotypes are crossed, the recessive trait may appear in their offspring. But when both parents are of the recessive phenotype, all their children also should be of the recessive phenotype. In this test, only the nontaster by nontaster matings gave that sort of result. Therefore, the nontaster trait must be recessive. Tasters may be either homozygous dominant (TT) or heterozygous (Tt). Nontasters must be homozygous recessive (tt).

Now let's consider a population in which 64% of the population are tasters and 36% are nontasters. What are the frequencies of the gene? What are the frequencies of the genotypes?

What is the one genotype frequency we already know? With that value, what gene frequency can we determine? Knowing that the frequency of T and the frequency of t must equal 1, what is the frequency of the dominant gene? Now calculate the genotype frequencies of the carrier and the homozygous dominant.

result of chance union of an egg and sperm each carrying an **F** gene. Using the second law of probability this is 39/40 X 39/40 = 1521/1600. So 1521 out of our population of 1600 will have the **FF** genotype. The **Ff** genotype can occur in two ways: **F** sperm can combine with **f** eggs, or **F** eggs can combine with **f** sperm. To calculate the **Ff** genotype we must take 2(39/40 X 1/40). We multiply by 2 because the **Ff** genotype can occur in two ways. That works out to 78/1600 or about 1 out of 20. That means that almost 5% of the white population are carriers of CF," Lisa concluded.

Lisa's calculations surprised me, and I redid the arithmetic several times to see how she had gotten to 5% from 1/1600. I finally had to concede that she was right.

"Now look at the picture of this iceberg," Lisa urged me as she drew another picture.

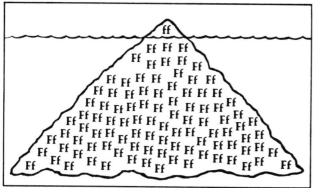

Figure 14.

The picture represented all the **f** genes in the population. As you can see, for every affected person with two **f** genes, there are 78 normal carriers with a single **f** gene. The rarer the recessive condition, the greater is this ratio of carriers to affected persons. In a rare condition occurring once in a million, there are almost 2,000 carriers for every affected person.

At this point, I asked a question that had been in the back of my mind. I asked Lisa, "Can we figure out what the chance would be for two unrelated carriers, like your mom and dad, to meet and marry?"

"That's easy, Alex. We know that the frequency of the heterozygous phenotype (**Ff**) is almost 5% or 1/20. So the chance of two unrelated carriers, like my mom and dad, meeting and marrying is 1/20 X 1/20 = 1/400. Since each pregnancy between two carriers has a 1/4 chance of producing a CF child, the frequency of CF children is 1/400 X 1/4 = 1/1600. This gives the birth frequency of CF kids in the white population."

17 Carriers of CF

It was easy for Lisa to do the mathematics to answer Alex's question. As her father had said earlier, "The best way to live with a condition is to understand it." Lisa can cope with her condition because she has worked hard to understand it.

But how about you? Do you understand it? Let's review what Lisa just explained.

Bob and Mary Laxalt are carriers of CF. Their genotype, **Ff**, will be found in 1 out of every 20 people in their population. What are the chances that two people who are carriers will marry? The probability that two independent events will occur together is the product of their individual chances of occurring separately. Now, with the background you have in probability, answer the following questions.

1.   What is the probability that a woman is a carrier for CF?

2.   What is the probability that a man is a carrier for CF?

3.   What is the probability that two carriers will marry?

4.   What is the probability that these married carriers will have a CF child?

With my new knowledge of the population genetics of CF, I was able to answer the question: "What is the chance that a non-CF sibling (brother or sister) of an affected person will have an affected child if he or she marries a person from the general population?"

2/3 X 1/20 X 1/4 = 2/240, or 0.83%.

And the chance that an affected person will have an affected child is

1 X 1/20 X 1/2 = 1/40, or 2.5%.

I left the Laxalts much wiser than I had arrived. I was impressed with the way they had met a tremendous challenge so successfully.

Sarah **had asked** me to give her a ride to the **basketball game**. On the way we talked.

Sarah turned out to be a worrier. She chewed her fingernails and bit her lip. She was not comfortable talking about being the sister of someone with CF. Did she worry about having affected children in spite of a less than 1% risk?

"Well, yes! Look at my mom and dad. They only had a 1/1600 chance to have an affected child and they had two. My chances are about 13 times greater than theirs!"

What if a test were to be developed to diagnose carriers? What if Sarah then learned that she was a carrier and a man she wanted to marry was also a carrier? She was worried about that, too. Her dad, who keeps a close eye on these developments, had said only yesterday that no test was reliable and that progress in that field seemed slow.

---

18 An increased probability

Something seems wrong here. We just looked at the probability that two white people are carriers and at the probability that two such people will have an affected child. We found the probability to be 1/20 X 1/20 X 1/4 = 1/1600. What is different about the question now being asked?

"What is the chance that a sibling of an affected person will have an affected child?" The math given is 2/3 X 1/20 X 1/4. Where does that 2/3 come from? Look again at Figure 12 on page 6.

Suppose you are the brother or sister of someone with CF, like Sarah in our story. You don't have CF, so your genotype is not **ff**. But it could be **FF** or **Ff**. Of the remaining 3 chances in 4, you have 1 chance of having **FF** and 2 chances of having **Ff**. Thus, your chances of being a carrier (**Ff**) are 2 out of 3 (2/3).

If you have a sibling with CF, the probability that you are a carrier is 2/3. It is not the 1/20 that we would expect in the general population. And your chances of having a CF child would be 2 out of 240 rather than 1 out of 1600 as it is for the general population.

Now, figure out for yourself why the probability of an affected person having an affected child is 1 out of 40.

There are some factors that can change this probability. Most CF males are sterile, and CF females often have difficulty conceiving. Thus, the chance that an affected person actually will have an affected child depends on whether pregnancy is possible. It also will depend on the decisions that individuals with CF make about having children.

But what if in five or ten years a really reliable test were developed so she could determine if a baby she was carrying had the disease?

"Then I would have to decide whether to end my pregnancy or try to care for a child with CF."

Sarah was appalled by the idea of abortion. She pointed out: "Look at my sister—she gets along okay; she gets all A's in school. My baby could turn out like that. I don't think I could have an abortion!"

But has it always been a complete joy to live with her sister? The answer was prompt and vehement: "Absolutely not! I used to be so angry at her because *she* got all the attention. And she never had to help with any of the housework. Because of her we were always broke and never could go anywhere or get nice things. I can't get a car, and whenever she gets pneumonia I get blamed that she caught the infection from me because I had a cold the week before."

Her eyes filled with bitter tears as she tried to light a cigarette. "My parents won't let me smoke at home because of her. My friends are all mad at me because I can't have any parties at my house. They smoke, or she might catch a cold or the flu from them. And my boyfriend thinks I'm some sort of freak being related to someone with a horrible genetic disease..."

We were almost at the high school, so I had to ask Sarah what I thought was the big question: "But aren't you glad, Sarah, that you don't have CF?"

At that, she bowed her head, put out her cigarette, and wiped her tears. She blew her nose and sat quietly for a long time. Then she turned to me and smiled.

"I'm sorry I blew my stack, Alex! I didn't really mean it. You are right, I am pretty lucky! Thanks for the ride." With that she blew me a kiss, jumped out and joined a group of her friends, laughing. The young man who put his arm around her waist did not seem to think of her as a freak.

19 Tests for genetic conditions

Reliable tests do exist for a few genetic conditions—Down syndrome and Tay-Sachs, for example. And it is possible that a similar test will be developed for CF. The tests for genetic conditions involve many steps. A brief explanation of each will give you more insight into the subject of human genetics.

Amniocentesis

This procedure consists of inserting a small needle through the skin of the abdomen into the uterus of a woman in the 16th to 18th week of pregnancy. A tablespoon or two of the liquid, amniotic fluid, surrounding the fetus is withdrawn. Suspended in the amniotic fluid are cells, some living, that have been sloughed off naturally from the fetus. Small quantities of the fluid may be used for biochemical analyses. The remaining fluid is placed in tissue-culture flasks. It is incubated so that the living cells in the fluid will multiply. This usually takes two to four weeks.

Prenatal Diagnosis

The fluid and the cells are examined very carefully to determine if there is any abnormality. Some disorders that can be detected are those caused by chromosomal abnormalities. They are usually due to an abnormal number of chromosomes. The most common of these disorders is Down syndrome. In one form of Down syndrome, the cells of the fetus each have three, rather than the usual two, of chromosome number 21. Some other disorders that are caused by a defect in a single chromosome can also be detected.

Other disorders that can be detected by amniocentesis are diseases caused by biochemical defects, known as inborn errors of metabolism. About 75 of these inborn errors can be diagnosed. Each is quite rare, but collectively these disorders are the source of much human suffering. Tay-Sachs disease is a well-studied inborn error of metabolism.

In addition, disorders classified as "neural tube disorders" now can be detected by testing the amniotic fluid for a substance called alphafetoprotein. Spina bifida is an example of a neural tube disorder.

Genetic Counseling

If the tests show some definite abnormality, the parents will have the help of a genetic counselor in looking at any options available to them. The counselor will give the parents as much information as he or she can about the disorder and what treatment, if any, is available before and after birth. Some parents, after receiving all the available information, will decide that an abortion is the best solution. Others will decide to have the baby and care for it. The genetic counselor also can give the parents some idea of the chances that it could happen again.

THE DOCTOR'S ADVICE COLUMN

Over the last few weeks, I have exchanged letters with a student at Bay Shore High School in Suffolk County, New York. The student, Suzie Hickman, raised many interesting and important questions. I thought I would run the series in my column this month. Thank you, Suzie, for your help and enthusiasm!

JDM

January 3, 1983

Dear Dr. Mason:

I am a tenth grade biology student who is working on a science project on human genetics. Please tell me all you can about human genetics. Thank you.

Yours truly,
Suzie Hickman

January 12, 1983

Dear Ms. Hickman:

Your request for "all" I can tell you about human genetics is an impossible request. Even the experts don't know "all" there is to know. Besides, to do a good science project, you need to identify a very specific topic or problem that you think is interesting and important. And you need to plan your work so you can do a good job in the time you have to complete your work.

Sincerely,
Joseph D. Mason, MD

January 19, 1983

Dear Dr. Mason:

I apologize for my initial request for "all" you can tell me about human genetics. Thank you for the advice that I must concentrate on a specific topic or problem. I hope you still will be able to help me and I hope my request this time will be specific enough. Looking through my biology book I came across the name "Gregor Mendel" and I saw him referred to as the "father of genetics." Could you please tell me something about him and his work?

January 24, 1983

Dear Ms. Hickman:

Being curious about something or questioning some phenomenon in nature often has led to important discoveries in science. Gregor Mendel, a monk living in Austria in the 1800s, wondered why the pea plants in his garden were different from one another. He had planted the same kind of seeds, but the plants had different stem lengths. Some were short and others were long. The peas they produced were different in color and texture. These variations puzzled Mendel. He set out to find what caused them.

Mendel conducted experiments involving crosses of the peas. These experiments were different from those carried out by other scientists of that time. First, Mendel repeated the crosses of different pure varieties many times to be sure of the results. (Pure varieties are those that "breed true"—always producing the same kind of offspring.) An example of this kind of experiment is a cross between tall and short plants. Second, Mendel used mathematics to analyze the data and to arrive at a hypothesis. When Mendel began experimenting, biologists knew very little about chromosomes or cell division. Mendel's conclusions were based only on the results of experiments.

Mendel made hundreds of crosses to study certain traits. One of these was a cross between pea plants whose seeds were always round and plants whose seeds were always wrinkled. When a cross is made between two varieties, the parent generation is called the P_1 generation. The offspring of the P_1 cross are the first filial (FILL-ee-ul), or F_1, generation.

In every case, Mendel found that all the F_1 plants had round seeds. When one form of a trait appeared in the F_1 of a cross of pure varieties, Mendel called this the dominant trait. The trait that did not show was called the recessive trait. The offspring in all of Mendel's crosses were exactly like one of the parents. There were never any in-between types nor any that showed a mixture of the parents' traits.

Mendel let the F_1 plants self-pollinate. In the next generation, the F_2, the dominant trait (round seeds) appeared in 75 percent of the offspring. In 25 percent, the recessive trait (wrinkled seeds) reappeared. This gives a ratio of three dominant traits to one recessive trait in the F_2 generation.

What Mendel explained to the world in 1865 became the foundation for the science we call genetics. All living things are controlled by factors that express themselves during the development and life of the individual. These factors are inherited from parents and transmitted to offspring. These factors distinguish human beings from nonhuman beings. They also characterize certain groups of humans, certain families, or certain individuals.

So there you are, Suzie. I hope I have given you enough background material so that you can pick a specific topic to work with in your science project. If you need any more help, please write.

January 27, 1983

Dear Dr. Mason:

Thank you for introducing me to Gregor Mendel and his garden peas. Now that I have that information, I think I need to know more about how we learned some of the basic facts about genetics in people.

January 30, 1983

Dear Ms. Hickman:

Gathering knowledge about and developing an understanding of the genetics of non-human life has been going on since Mendel's time. Getting similar knowledge and understanding of humans is much more difficult. In the laboratory, geneticists prefer to work with pure lines. They repeat crosses many times and try to obtain many offspring. They keep the experimental organisms in a constant environment. Obviously, it is not possible to carry out such experiments on people. But geneticists have learned a great deal about human genetics by tracing the inheritance of traits. They do this by studying as many generations of a family as possible. They put the information in a structured form called a pedigree. A pedigree can reveal many interesting facts about human genetics. I'll use a pedigree for a family with cystic fibrosis, an inherited condition, as an example.

Cystic fibrosis affects children. It is often fatal by the teen or young adult years. In children with cystic fibrosis, a thick, sticky mucus clogs the lungs and breathing passages, making breathing difficult. Other organs, such as the liver and pancreas also are affected. Cystic fibrosis occurs most often in families of European descent. The disorder is inherited as a recessive trait. Thus, a person may carry the gene, but not actually have the disorder. The

trouble arises when two people who carry the gene marry. They have a 25% chance of having an affected child. Look at this pedigree for cystic fibrosis. Note that the grandparents were not affected but that Cynthia and Joseph, the parents in the next generation, were both carriers.

There is no proven test to detect a carrier of cystic fibrosis. (But scientists may be close to developing one. By the time you read this, they may have developed one.) The fact that the parents were carriers did not emerge until they had their first affected child, Martha. The second child, Eric, also had the disorder.

Whether or not Steve and Patricia are carriers cannot be determined. Even if they are carriers, the disorder will only occur in their children if they marry another carrier. We cannot know exactly which of the grandparents were carriers. But we can reason that either Michael or Emma must have been a carrier. Either Herman or Ann also must have been a carrier. How do we know this?

I think I've given you enough information for you to deal with for a while. As you study this, see if you can figure out how the pedigree for cystic fibrosis follows some of the patterns that Mendel discovered. Keep in touch.

February 2, 1983

Dear Dr. Mason:

Your last letter cleared up a few things. But I still don't see how parents who do not have a certain genetic condition, like

cystic fibrosis, can have children who do have the condition. If you could just address that problem, it would help me a lot.

February 17, 1983

Dear Ms. Hickman:

Let's start with a child with the condition. Let's take Martha from the pedigree I sent in my last letter. Martha inherited cystic fibrosis as a recessive gene. That means that she has two recessive genes for this trait. We know this because, in general, recessive genes express themselves only when two of them combine in the zygote of a potential new child.

You know that Martha had to get one of these recessive genes from her father and one from her mother. Neither parent had cystic fibrosis. If you think back about the effects of different kinds of genes, I think you can figure out why. The other gene in the gene pair in each parent was a non-cystic fibrosis, or "normal," gene. Scientists have not yet determined exactly what the chemical problem is in cystic fibrosis. One possibility is that the "normal" gene in the carrier parent makes enough of some "normal" product to prevent a problem, but this product is missing in the child with CF. In a sense, the "normal" gene of the carrier dominates the effect of the cystic fibrosis gene.

The recessive gene stayed with the parents. It wasn't expressed, but its potential was still there. When Martha's parents produced eggs and sperm, half of them received the dominant, non-cystic fibrosis

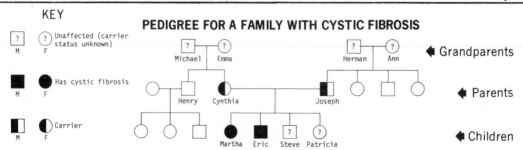

KEY

PEDIGREE FOR A FAMILY WITH CYSTIC FIBROSIS

gene. The other half received the recessive, CF gene. At conception, when Martha was first formed, one of her mother's eggs was fertilized by one of her father's sperm. The egg and the sperm each contained a recessive, cystic fibrosis gene. The two recessive genes resulted in the cystic fibrosis condition in Martha.

Now, I hope you see that other gene combinations could have happened when Martha was conceived. I want you to figure them out. Also, figure out what the result of each particular gene combination would have been.

You might ask now what caused a particular egg to be fertilized by a particular sperm. The answer is that there is no cause. It is all a matter of chance. Because it is entirely due to chance, we can predict gene combinations using a tool of mathematics called probability. We can take this up later, or you can investigate other sources for information about probability.

One final bit of information. The gene combination that Martha inherited resulted in a trait—in this case, cystic fibrosis. Gene combinations cause the appearance of traits, not only cystic fibrosis but also things like eye color, hair color, and the slope of the nose. The appearance of the traits in an individual is referred to as the phenotype. The combination of genes that causes a trait—such as Martha's cystic fibrosis trait, or any other trait, is referred to as the genotype.

Once again, I think that is enough for now. I'll be waiting for your next letter, because I am sure you will have more questions. That always happens in science. As we get answers to some of our questions, we get many more questions to deal with.

February 28, 1983

Dear Dr. Mason:

Your last letter was very informative and has raised many questions—just as you said it would. I still am not sure I understand how traits, like cystic fibrosis, can show up in some of a couple's children and not others. Also, I've run across a few words in my reading—like het— erozygote, and homozygote —that I don't really understand. Please help me with these things.

March 17, 1983

Dear Ms. Hickman:

I think I can help you. I'll describe a situation that may seem very artificial, but it will help you understand how traits are transmitted from parents to offspring.

A certain human characteristic can be expressed in two forms. We will call these forms **A** and **a**. If a mother is pure for trait **A** and the father is pure for trait **a**, how will this trait be transmitted to their children? You will be asked to answer this question later. Traits are controlled by genes, which are located on chromosomes that are in the nuclei of all your body cells.

To simplify my explanation, I will assume that only two genes are responsible for the trait in each parent. So, the mother has two **A** genes and the father has two **a** genes. These people are called homozygotes. The prefix, homo-, means "the same." Thus, homozygotes have two genes that are the same for the trait in question.

During meiosis, the reproductive cells (eggs and sperm) are formed. In our example, the mother produces eggs that have **A** genes and the father produces sperm that have **a** genes. At conception, one of the

eggs carrying the **A** gene will be fertilized by a sperm carrying an **a** gene.

The new child will have inherited an **A** and an **a** gene for this characteristic. An individual with the genotype **Aa** is called a heterozygote. This prefix, hetero-, means "different." This is a person with a pair of genes that are different for the trait in question.

The **A** gene is called dominant, because it shows up in the phenotype of the individual. The **a** gene is recessive. It does *not* show up in the phenotype unless *both* genes in the pair are of the recessive type. Thus, there are three possible genotypes: **AA**, **Aa**, and **aa**. Can you identify these as either homozygous or heterozygous?

Now, I'll give you a tough problem to solve. Suppose each parent had the **Aa** genotype. What could you predict about their children?

April 1, 1983

Dear Dr. Mason:

Over the last few months, I've really gotten this story from you piece by piece. Now I think I have it all put together. I'll just tell you the answer to your problem, but I won't tell you how I got it. All I will tell you is that I got an A on my science project. My topic was probability!

The answer is: Chances are
¼ for **AA** offspring
½ for **Aa** offspring
¼ for **aa** offspring

That's for the genotype. The phenotypes would be a 3:1 chance of a dominant to a recessive.

Aren't you proud of me? Thanks for all your help.

Yours truly,

Suzie Hickman

CONSTRUCTING A PEDIGREE

My name is Steve Thacker. I'd like to tell about an experience I had that taught me some important lessons about genetics. For years my dad, John Thacker, has been telling me stories about his family—his father and mother, his two sisters, and his three brothers. Our family moved from his hometown in Ohio to California when I was only a year old, so I have never really known the people he was talking about. His stories made me very curious about all these relatives of mine that I had never seen.

Last summer, I got a chance to satisfy my curiosity. The Thacker family decided to have a family reunion on the 4th of July in the old hometown of Cos Cob, Ohio. Dad could hardly wait to get back and see his family again for the first time in fifteen years. My mother, Marie, is from the same town, and she was eager to see her own family as well as my dad's. My 12-year-old twin sisters, Laura and Mary Jo, and my 8-year-old brother, Tom, also had heard a lot about the people in Cos Cob. They were delighted at the thought of a trip to Ohio.

We decided to make a real vacation out of our trip back for the reunion. We drove back at a leisurely pace, sight-seeing and camping along the way. We did so much sight-seeing that, on the morning of July 3rd, we realized we were still 700 miles from Cos Cob. And the reunion was to begin the next morning at 10 o'clock! Dad said we would have to drive straight through and get a good night's sleep so we would be ready to meet all our relatives and enjoy the reunion. It was a long 14-hour drive. We got into Cos Cob about 9 o'clock the evening of the 3rd. Everybody

was so tired we decided to get motel rooms and go right to bed.

In spite of all the travel and excitement, I slept pretty well and so did Tom and the twins. In the morning, after we all got cleaned up, we had a late breakfast. Then we set out for Grandpa and Grandma Thacker's house on Pine Street. We got there at exactly 10 o'clock and were amazed to find that we were the last of the Thacker clan to arrive at the reunion. For about 15 minutes there was a lot of hugging and kissing and squealing. I was introduced to all those aunts, uncles, and cousins that I had heard about but never met. But I have to admit that I didn't get all the names and faces staight.

After the turmoil of the initial meetings was over, I was able to step back and take a better look at my relatives. It was obvious that we all are family. My dad's brother and sister were easy to spot because they look so much like him. My grandparents are older copies of their sons and daughters. The third generation—my sisters, my brother, all our cousins, and I—are alike in many ways. At the same time, all of us have our own special traits that make us different. I remembered one of the big lessons I learned in biology last year. The set of chromosomes we inherit, half from our mothers and the other half from our fathers, interacting with our environment is responsible for the similarities and the differences that I was observing.

Then I noticed Grandpa Thacker's hands. I thought my Dad had been joking when he used to say that Grandpa Thacker had two little fingers on each hand. But sure enough, it's

true. I then checked out Aunt Shirley, Uncle Pat, and Uncle Dave. Again Dad was right! They too have extra little fingers. Aunt Shirley's daughter Sue does not have the extra digits. Uncle Pat has three girls and a boy. One of the girls, Maureen, and the boy, Mike, have the extra fingers. Uncle Dave has a boy, Dan, who does not have the extra digits and a girl, Karen, who does. Dad's sister, Betty, and her son, Jim, do not have the sixth finger. His other brother, Gary, and his two daughters, Patty and Barbara, also do not have the sixth finger. Of course, nobody in my immediate family has the variation.

After my initial observation of this variation in our family, I promptly forgot about it and spent the rest of the day meeting, talking, and playing volleyball with my grandparents, my five aunts and uncles, my ten cousins, and, of course, my own immediate family. The big event of the day was a sit-down dinner that evening. We ate one of the best meals I have ever had. Many stories were told, and every member of the family—all 28 of us—was included in the stories at least once. Before we knew it, it was nearly midnight and time for the reunion to end.

We said "good night" and went back to our motel, where we talked among ourselves for another hour or so. We spent two more days in Cos Cob visiting my mother's and father's old friends. We also did some fishing and picnicking out in the country around Cos Cob.

It wasn't until we were back in California that I remembered the variation I had observed in my grandpa, my aunt and two uncles, and three cousins. I

LEARNING FROM PEDIGREES

One key to successful genetic counseling is an accurate family history. A good way of illustrating the history is in the form of a pedigree chart. Different kinds of inherited conditions will show different patterns of heredity in a pedigree chart.

Consider three types of patterns of heredity:

a. a *dominant* condition carried on an autosome (autosomal dominant)

b. a *recessive* condition carried on an autosome (autosomal recessive)

c. a *recessive* condition carried on the X chromosome (X-linked recessive)

Study the pedigrees and indicate:

1. the type of inheritance shown by each

2. your reasoning for your answer

3. the probability ratio in each case

4. a particular genetic disorder that might be illustrated by each case

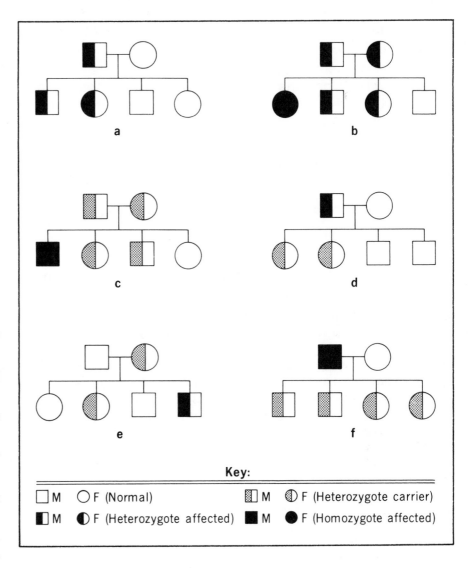

Key:
☐ M ◯ F (Normal)   ▨ M ◐(dotted) F (Heterozygote carrier)
◧ M ◖ F (Heterozygote affected)   ■ M ● F (Homozygote affected)

knew this had to be a genetic trait, but I was curious to find out more about it. In my biology class, I had learned that one of the first things you should do to learn about a trait is to make a family history and trace the transmission of the trait through the family. I remembered that you use a square ☐ to stand for a man, and a circle ◯ to represent a woman. You shade in the squares or circles that represent people who have the trait (in this case an extra little finger). With that little background, I began to construct our family history. After I had constructed the pedigree, I was able to answer a few questions.

1. Is the trait carried on the autosomes or sex chromosomes?

2. Is it a dominant or recessive trait?

3. Are the people with the trait homozygous or heterozygous?

One question the pedigree did not answer for me was, "What is the medical term for the variation of having an extra little finger"? For this answer I had to go to the library. When I did, I learned much more about this variation and many other variations common to humans.

THE PROBABILITY GAME

Careful readers of this magazine have undoubtedly become experts in calculating probabilities and ratios of genotypes and phenotypes. If a ratio of 3:1 sounds familiar to you, you may be in that category. To find out, you can test your skills on a more complicated problem, involving two pairs of genes instead of one. Consider the following situation:

A widow's peak at the hairline is the result of a dominant gene we'll call W. A smooth hairline is the product of two recessive genes that can be labeled w. Similarly, a cleft in the chin results from a dominant gene, C; a smooth chin requires two recessive genes, cc.

Imagine a mother and a father, each of whom has a widow's peak and a cleft in the chin. Both are heterozygous, that is, each has a genotype, WwCc. What are the probabilities of genotypes and phenotypes in their children?

Approach the problem systematically:

Father's genotype—WwCc. What are the possible combinations in the sperm cells? (Hint: There are four.)

Mother's genotype—WwCc. What are the possible combinations of the alleles in the egg cells? (You don't need a hint here.)

What is the chance that any particular sperm or egg contains any particular one of the four possible combinations?

Now, you can proceed in one of two ways. For *five* points, use a Punnet square to determine the possible genotypes of the offspring and the ratio of phenotypes. For *ten* points, do the calculations without a Punnet square. (Remember: The chance that two independent events will occur together is the product of their individual chances of occurring separately.)

What is the expected ratio of phenotypes in the offspring?

*For dedicated players of the
PROBABILITY GAME*

Earn an extra five points each by determining the genotypes and phenotypes that would result from these crosses:

CCww *X* CcWw   CcWw *X* ccww

               ccWW *X* CCww

ccWw *X* ccWw   CcWw *X* CcWW

ESSAYS

A NEW VIEW OF HEALTH: GENETICS AND ENVIRONMENT*

The application to medicine of genetic principles, now called medical genetics, has grown by leaps and bounds over the last 20 years. The number of human abnormalities attributed to the action of a single gene is now more than 2,800.[1] Hundreds of chromosomal defects are known, and it is commonly stated that 20 to 30 million Americans have "genetic diseases." It is often pointed out that up to 30% of the pediatric hospital beds are occupied by children with those same conditions. [2,3] This is the generally held view of things and it represents an important advance in medicine.

But these statements are ambiguous and somewhat misleading. They are ambiguous because "genetic" and "disease" are not precisely defined, and they are misleading because it is implied that the 20 to 30 million people with genetic diseases are radically different in some way from everyone else and that 30% of pediatric patients are a well-defined group.

These problems of definition are a consequence of the categorical system of disease classification used in medicine. Such classification fails to take into account people who are susceptible to particular diseases but do not yet have them, and it makes too sharp a distinction between health and disease. Furthermore, it focuses on each disease as if it were a thing in itself, coming from outside and descending upon a patient. It fails to take account of the patient as an individual.

But things are changing. Today health and disease are being examined not only as biological problems but also as social problems. Economists, sociologists, philosophers, and legislators have become interested and are looking to see that medical services are being fairly distributed and conscientiously provided. Everybody wants something to be done. Some, including the Minister of Health in Canada, say that the surest road to improving health care is outside the field of medicine. What is required, they say, is a change in the ways people live—or in how we use and control the environment.[4] Physicians conventionally think in terms of

treatment and management of the sick; the new voices call for prevention of illness—with emphasis on people staying well.

To my mind, genetics can be very useful in bringing together the conventional treatment mode of medical practice with this new emphasis on prevention. Why? Because genetics shows that the cause of disease lies in the complex relationships between a particular person and his or her unique experiences and conditions of life, rather than in some outside agent.

What are some of the elements in those relationships? First there is the individual's genotype. Then there are developmental properties that are the result of the person's genes and his or her special experiences. In addition, there are temporary states of nutrition, stress, and fatigue, as well as health habits—eating, drinking, exercise, smoking, and the like. These latter are matters of what are called "life-style" and represent a person's own choice. But there are also environmental conditions to which we are exposed unwittingly; these conditions are products of the "styles" of industry, commerce, government, and society.

A New View

So we need a new view of medicine in which genetic differences are seen to be important in thinking about disease in general and in which the individual genotype is taken into account when physicians talk with patients and their families. In this view, genes are seen not as causes of disease, but as the origin of susceptibility or resistance. Disease can then be viewed

*Adapted from an article of the same title by Barton Childs, M.D., *BSCS Journal* 1(1):9-12. Dr. Childs is professor of pediatrics, The Johns Hopkins University School of Medicine.

as the result of a "bad fit" between an individual's genes and his or her experiences.

What, then, are the so-called "genetic diseases"? First of all, nothing can be either "genetic" or "environmental." Genes don't act except in environments, and environments don't act on anything other than molecules, cells, or organisms—that is, the genes and their products. Neither is sufficient to produce a phenotype; both are necessary. To fail to keep this important point in mind is to become bogged down in the argument about whether nature is more important than nurture—or vice versa—with all the social and political traps that lie ready for the unwary traveler who takes that road.

So if we are going to call anything a "genetic" disease, we must talk about a situation in which the gene effect is expressed under any conceivable condition. For example, the development of the nervous system being what it is, it's hard to imagine any circumstance in which an individual lacking the enzyme called hexosaminidase A can escape having Tay-Sachs disease. And there may be some reason to call a disease "environmental" if the environmental agent prevails over all genotypes—that is, all human beings are equally susceptible. Gunshot wounds, the effects of earthquakes, and dog bites might be examples.

These are two opposing, relatively clear positions. But we run into trouble just as soon as we leave them. For one thing, many conditions associated with the effects of genes at a single site on a pair of chromosomes show a wide range of expression. These variations must be due to the condition of the environment, both within and outside the body. Similarly, bacteria or toxic agents, commonly regarded as the agents of environmental disease, also produce a wide range of effects. Some individuals are severely affected while others are totally resistant. Thus, because the expression of disease is the product of many factors, these labels, "genetic" and "environmental," are ambiguous and misleading.

Microbial diseases usually are called environmental simply because viruses and bacteria attack apparently healthy people. Recently, we have learned that there are genes in humans that specify proteins normally found on cell surfaces. One such protein binds the polio virus. Without this protein, the virus cannot get in the cell and cannot cause the disease. Now, it is likely that there are people whose genotype is such that they do not bind the polio virus at all.

Thus, they cannot get polio, even if they come in contact with the virus. Is polio a genetic disease, or is it environmental?

Still, whatever label one prefers, the possibilities for prevention are obvious. People who know something about their genes have some chance of avoiding certain illnesses, whether through reproductive choices or controlling environmental conditions. I am not suggesting that—because not everyone is equally prone to disease—government, commerce, and industry are relieved of their responsibilities to control the release of harmful substances into the environment. I am merely pointing out that people do make choices. And knowledge of our genes may allow us to choose courses of action that will prevent disease.

All of us carry genetic susceptibilities to something, some of us to many disorders, *depending on conditions we face.* It is commonly said that we all have four to eight harmful genes. But that figure is inaccurate and misleading, I think. The true number may be 40, 400, or 4,000. A gene that produces a neutral effect in one environment may cause a harmful effect in another.

Medical geneticists encourage people to learn something about their genetic constitutions. In the past, people were not asked to know anything. They were expected to leave matters to their doctors. Paradoxically, now that doctors know more than ever before and can act in many instances to alleviate illness, people are asking more pointed questions. And they should! Attitudes toward the prevention of disease are based, in part, on how much knowledge a person has. As people learn more, they may take a more active role in working for themselves and with health professionals to promote their own well being.

I am not saying that everyone must be an expert on all things genetic. But everyone does need to know about his or her own family. Everyone needs to be aware of the existence of genes, how they work, how they are transmitted. Each person also needs to be aware of options for decision making should problems arise—such options as early detection, treatment, and management, as well as reproductive and preventive options.

But, at the moment, we know too little about many of the problems that are caused by interactions of genes and environment. We know only a little about the genes that predispose certain individuals to hypertension (high blood pressure), birth defects, "hardening of the arteries," gout, chronic lung disease, varicose veins, and some psychiatric problems. And we know only a little about the special environmental conditions that favor or prevent the development of these disorders. So preventive measures, if any, cannot now be directed to the most susceptible people. For the time being, they must be directed at everyone. But people resist warnings that they should change their habits. And the decision to change is made very difficult by the reluctance of industry and commerce to change advertising that promotes products known to produce harmful results in some people.

Why don't we know more about our genes? One reason is that the genes associated with conditions caused by many factors don't sort themselves out into neat patterns that are easy to identify. A more important reason is the limitations set by our present model of medical research. We look for just "one cause." We are not in the habit of looking for a set of genes with their variable effects under different conditions. Such research is difficult. And we are not used to approaching problems this way. Nevertheless, this is the area in which we find the most challenging problems that confront us today.

Several Missions

In conclusion, there are several missions. One is to support research designed to gain understanding of the complex causes of disease—how people's genes and experiences work to keep them well or make them sick. Another is to prepare people to know about the few rare genes associated with specific diseases that may have entered their families by chance. People should learn about common genes that may predispose anyone to an illness that might be prevented. And the public needs to know enough to be able to act intelligently and effectively in matters of public policy. Important issues include control of potentially harmful materials that can be introduced into the environment, remembering that some may be harmful to only a few "susceptibles," while others may be harmful to all.

Finally, although we must make counts of the number of "genetic" diseases and of the people who have them for public health and other medical purposes, we should keep in mind that such counts create a narrow view. They obscure the true picture of the range of conditions that constitute health and disease. In this light, genetics is not a "specialty area" of interest to only a few. Rather, it is a wide-ranging idea that reveals much about human health and well-being. That is why education in genetics is so important.

References

1. McKusick, V. A. *Mendelian Inheritance in Man,* 5th ed. Johns Hopkins Press, Baltimore, 1978.
2. Childs, B., S. M. Miller, and A. G. Bearn. "Gene Mutation as a Cause of Human Disease." In H. E. Sutton and M. I. Harris, eds., *Mutagenic Effects of Environmental Contaminants.* Academic Press, New York, 1972, pp. 3-14.
3. Scriver, C. R., J. L. Neal, R. Saginur, and A. Clow. "The Frequency of Genetic Disease and Congenital Malformation Among Patients in a Pediatric Hospital." *Canadian Medical Association Journal,* 108:1111-1115, 1973.
4. Lalonde, Marc. *A New Perspective on the Health of Canadians.* Information Canada, Ottawa, Catalogue Number H31-1374.

THINKING ABOUT ETHICAL QUESTIONS

Making decisions about right and wrong is often very difficult. First, one must identify what *can* be done. Usually, more than one choice is available. If one choice is obviously superior to the other alternatives, then the decision can be made with relative ease and confidence. But many times two or more choices seem defensible and, worse yet, both may seem good solutions to our problems. A genuine dilemma arises when one can identify and understand logically acceptable sets of reasons that seem to justify opposite courses of action.

A respected philosopher, Gerald Dworkin, has written about this problem. He points out that there is no "theory of morality" that corresponds to theories in the physical and life sciences. For example, the theory of evolution in biology (a) explains some observable facts, (b) predicts the outcomes of experiments, and (c) allows scientists to ask new questions that can be researched. Furthermore, hypotheses derived from the theory can be tested by experimentation. Hypotheses can be accepted or rejected based on the experimental results. Moral questions cannot be approached in this way. No experiment can be conducted to show that one idea is more legitimate than another.

But the lack of a testable theory of ethics does not mean that moral questions cannot be answered or that one point of view is necessarily just as good as another. Dworkin explains there are three broad categories of moral considerations: goals, rights, and duties. Applying these categories to the analysis of ethical problems does not guarantee easy answers. But Dworkin's definitions and examples do give us a way to think through difficult ethical questions. His approach does so by helping us to identify what counts as clear-headed reasoning and what does not.

Goals, rights, and *duties* may be in conflict in many situations. Confusion can arise when we fail to distinguish one from another. If we look at the arguments that people give to justify one course of action over another, we often find all three. Usually, however, one of them—a goal, a right, or a duty—will be offered as the most important or most compelling reason. Even specialists in the field of ethics disagree about which is the most important in any given situation. So we should not be surprised when we find ourselves torn between competing positions when a difficult decision must be made.

Let us first examine what we mean by goals, rights, and duties. Then, we can go on to look at ways in which these ideas can be applied to the analysis of ethical problems.

1. *Goals.* One can judge the morality of an act by looking at what it intends to accomplish. We can ask ourselves about the objectives or outcomes. We can focus on consequences. In this pattern of thought, then, a "good" outcome may be judged morally correct regardless of how the goal was achieved. This may be termed the "any means to an end" idea.

Consider some examples. Suppose we could agree that a father caring for his children is a morally desirable goal, and that a father should take any and all necessary steps to assure that his children survive. We might then conclude that stealing food from a neighbor to feed his starving children would be a morally justified choice. We might be tempted to qualify this judgment with statements like "if there were no other way," but in offering such exceptions we would be calling upon other moral ideas such as the duty to be honest.

Another example may help further define moral arguments that rely on goals. A physician may view his or her primary mission as the preservation of life. Life, by this view, is to be sustained as long as possible by any means possible. In this goal-oriented view, then, a physician might refuse to disconnect a respirator on a comatose patient whose vital signs were being maintained only by the machine. The physician might take such action against the wishes of the patient's family or even against the previously expressed wishes of the patient. In the physician's view, then, going against the rights of the patient would be justified by the *goal* of preservation of life.

2. *Rights.* Moral arguments that involve the notion of rights are familiar to us in many areas besides genetics, health, or medicine. One is said to have a *right* if one is entitled to a certain kind of treatment, no matter what the consequences. The founders of our country spoke of the inalienable rights of life, liberty, and the pursuit of happiness. They claimed that one could expect these things regardless of the situation or the outcomes—just by virtue of being an individual human being. Thus, we have derived as part of our political heritage the belief that each

person has a right of free speech, a right to vote, or a right to own property.

It is not hard to think of situations in genetics and medicine where one might use arguments about rights to support a particular course of action. For example, consider the matter of informed consent. Informed consent—the full disclosure of all relevant information so a patient can accept or refuse some treatment—rests on the belief that a person has a right to know all there is to know and to make up his or her own mind freely. In this view, no treatment can be given unless the person understands the procedure and chooses to undergo it.

This right to know and choose is widely acknowledged among physicians, and informed consent is routinely practiced. Imagine, however, a physician who feels that some treatment will save a patient's life. But the physician knows also that this patient will refuse if all the possible consequences of the treatment are spelled out. How much information should the doctor share? Would the physician be justified in violating the patient's *rights* because the *goal* is the saving of a life?

You can readily see how goals and rights can come into conflict. What situations can you imagine in which the rights of different individuals are in conflict? How are rights gained or lost? Can rights be limited by authority or by mutual agreement?

3. *Duties.* The duty or obligation to act in a certain way is often cited in ethical argument. We typically think of having a duty to tell the truth, keep a promise, or help a friend. Usually, duties are justified by suggesting that the act will achieve some worthy goal,

or that the act is required because of someone's right. Thus, duties may be derived from goals or rights and may be in conflict with either goals or rights or even other duties.

A defending lawyer's relationship with the accused lawbreaker involves duties that are derived from goals and rights. It is the *right* of the accused to have legal representation, regardless of innocence or guilt. It is the attorney's *duty* to represent the accused, also without regard to guilt. Further, it is the lawyer's *duty* to seek the goal of acquittal, without consideration of the consequences for either the defendant or for society.

The logic of duties can become very complicated. Suppose a dying man asks a physician not to take any extraordinary steps to prolong his life. Does the doctor have a *duty* to comply with the man's wishes because of the patient's *right* to die? Or does the physician have a *duty* to ignore the man's wishes because of the *goal* of the preservation of life?

Obviously, ethical dilemmas usually involve all three elements: goals, rights, and duties. Seldom is it possible to combine all three into a single, satisfying solution. Why, then, are they so important? The answer lies in the usefulness of these notions in helping us *understand* situations involving difficult choices. Goals, rights, and duties won't make our choices for us. But identifying the competing goals, rights, and duties that seem to be operating in a particular situation will help us see more clearly the choices that are available. It may even sharpen the focus enough to allow us to predict benefits and losses with greater precision. Also, goals, rights, and duties are the lan-

guage of justification, of defending the responsibleness of one's choices.

We can analyze case studies (see "Case Studies in Genetics," page 16) using goals, rights, and duties as tools for working through a practical problem. Consider the following case:

Leonard Steinman is a 23-year-old college student of Jewish descent. In a large university-sponsored screening program, he is identified as a carrier of Tay-Sachs disease. During counseling, he reveals that he is engaged to marry a Jewish woman in three months. He tells the counselor that he has a 20-year-old sister and a 16-year-old brother. He refuses to reveal his carrier status to his fiancée, his parents, or his brother or sister. He also forbids the counselor to tell them.

What should the counselor do? The counselor has a number of alternatives including persuasion, referral of Leonard to another counselor, waiting for Leonard to change his mind, and others. But, for the sake of argument, let's just consider the most extreme and opposite choices: to tell or not to tell. Going against Leonard's wishes can be justified on several grounds—such as the *rights* of the others to know about their own health status, the *goal* of health promotion for all these individuals and, thus, the counselor's *duty* to pursue that goal. On the other extreme is the counselor's *duty* to maintain confidentiality and respect Leonard's wishes. This *duty* may be seen as derived from Leonard's *right* to privacy or his *right* to determine how he will interact with other family members. In keeping silence, the counselor would see the *goal* of respect for persons, in this case Leonard, as of a higher value than the *goal* of promoting health in the possible future offspring that Leonard or other members of his family might have.

To expand this type of analysis further, consider what kinds of ethical arguments might arise if Leonard's fiancee called and asked the counselor about the results of Leonard's screening. Should the counselor divulge the results to her? Suppose the situation were even more complicated. What if the fiancee indicated that she herself is a carrier? What should the counselor do then? Why?

By now, it should be apparent that the identification of goals, rights, and duties doesn't solve the problem. But it does make the choices involved clearer. And it can break one big decision down into several smaller ones. Sometimes, the smaller ones can be resolved one at a time, making the situation more manageable. For example, in the case of Leonard Steinman, we can identify at least three sets of "rights" that may be in conflict. Leonard has rights. His fiancee has rights. And the child they may have someday will have rights, too. One can imagine landmark court cases in which decisions might go against or in favor of any one of these three. Depending upon the number and nature of such cases, society might eventually come to accept the view that one of these three has rights that predominate over those of the other two. Once the question of rights had some history of debate and decision, a trend might emerge that would make the decision "to tell or not to tell" a bit easier in the future.

Nevertheless, we are not likely to see some theory of morality arising that will settle these questions once and for all, at least not in the near future. Students of ethics are still some way from a single unifying theory that will serve philosophers as the theory of relativity serves astrophysicists. As Dworkin has noted: "In many ways it is easier to agree on the nature of distant galaxies than it is to agree about the proper way to treat one's neighbors."

Reference

Dworkin, Gerald. "Analyzing Ethical Problems," from *Hard Choices*, A Magazine on the Ethics of Sickness and Health. Office of Radio and Television Learning, Boston, Massachusetts.

CASE STUDIES IN GENETICS

There are many human problems associated with new knowledge and technologies in genetics. By far, the majority of these problems are ethical in nature. The term *ethics* describes systems of moral behavior—what individuals, or groups, may believe to be right or wrong conduct. Philosophers who specialize in ethics try to examine the different arguments that are used to justify one course of action over another. In simplest terms, these arguments relate to issues of *goals, rights,* and *duties* as outlined in "Thinking about Ethical Questions" on page 30.

One of the tools for analyzing ethical problems is the "case study." A case study is a story of a real, or possibly real, situation. Case studies in ethics are stories in which one can readily see some conflict between two or more positions or two or more courses of action.

The case studies that follow present such situations. The questions that follow each case study are intended to help interested readers think through the alternative courses of action and the arguments that would support each course. There are, however, no right answers. Each situation requires analysis of personal and professional codes of conduct. It is not expected, however, that any agreement can, or even should, be reached. Each case should be discussed in terms of what different individuals might consider as the relevant *goals, rights,* or *duties*.

Case Study 1: Marilyn Parks, 23, is referred to a genetic counselor. She has given birth to a second child with physical defects and mental retardation. A physician has diagnosed both children as victims of fetal alcohol syndrome—a set of developmental defects caused by the mother drinking too much alcohol during pregnancy. Marilyn tells the counselor that she does not plan to have any more children.

The counselor learns from the physician that Marilyn is psychologically fragile and has been severely depressed since the birth of the second child. In addition, the physician relates that Marilyn's home environment is not supportive. Her husband has threatened to leave her because he thinks she is not a good mother.

1. Should the counselor tell Marilyn what caused the defects in her previous children? Why or why not?

2. Suppose that, instead of planning no more children, Marilyn revealed that she was three months pregnant with her third child. What should the counselor do? Why?

Case Study 2: Pat Jackson is a young black man. He has been screened for the sickle-cell gene and has been found to be a carrier. He has no health problems and no symptoms of the disorder. He applies for health insurance. He does not know where this particular company stands on policies for those with sickle-cell trait. The application asks, "Do you have any genetic or inherited disorders?"

1. How should Pat answer the question? Why?

2. What are the possible consequences of the action you recommend?

Case Study 3: There is a screening program for carriers of sickle-cell disease being advertised widely in your community. You know that the disease can be severe, even fatal in some homozygotes, while relatively mild and treatable in others. A local newspaper accuses the screening program of being just another attempt at discrimination—a racist attempt to discourage reproduction among black people. What would you want to know before you could decide whether there is any truth to the accusations the paper is making? (NOTE: This case does *not* ask you to decide whether the paper is correct. Instead, you are being asked to *reserve* judgment and identify what a person should try to find out *before* making up his or her mind.)

The following letters to the editor are reprinted by permission from *The New England Journal of Medicine*, Vol. 303, No. 15, Oct. 9, 1980, and Vol. 304, No. 3, Jan. 15, 1981

LEVODOPA PROVOCATIVE TEST FOR HUNTINGTON'S DISEASE

To the Editor: I appreciated reading the letter by Klawans et al. in the May 8 issue of the *Journal* regarding eight years of follow-up on the levodopa provocative test in persons at risk for Huntington's disease. I was greatly disappointed, however, that these investigators did not state unambiguously that they do not recommend this test as a routine clinical procedure. They did mention in their last sentence that no new patients are being enrolled in the provocation protocol, but this statement may not be strong enough to discourage clinicians from using this test.

Readers should be aware of at least three major problems with use of this test in subjects at risk. First of all, a positive result produces the phenotypic expression of the disease, i.e., chorea. Subjects are therefore aware of the test results. Many are not psychologically capable of handling this information, and a positive result could lead to disastrous consequences, such as suicide.

Secondly, the levodopa provocative test, like all other proposal tests to detect presymptomatic Huntington's disease, has not yet been validated. I encourage the efforts of Dr. Klawans and his colleagues to validate the test in their 30 subjects, but clinicians should be aware that it will take time to validate the test completely. The eight-year follow-up has indicated that there are false-negative results, and I am aware of other reports of false-negative results from physicians through word of mouth. It is still too early to know whether there will be false-positive results with this test. So far, five of the 10 subjects with positive responses have not yet had evidence of Huntington's disease. More time is needed to assess all subjects fully.

Thirdly, the test can be considered invasive. In giving

levodopa, one is altering the neurotransmitters in the striatum. It is conceivable that this alteration could induce onset of the symptoms of the illness sooner than it would otherwise have occurred. Invasive tests have their potential risks, and these risks must be given due consideration before any study is carried out. Many clinicians may not be fully aware of the potential risks of the levodopa provocative test.

I welcome the development of a useful test for presymptomatic subjects at risk for Huntington's disease, in the hope that someday there will be the means to prevent progression of the illness or to detect the affected subject in utero. The ideal test would be one in which the subject is not aware of the results (at least at present, when preventing the progression of this disease is impossible) and one that has no false-negative or false-positive results and can be done with little or no risk. Although I do not believe that the levodopa provocative test should be used, I look forward to continued follow-up reports by Dr. Klawans and his colleagues on the patients already studied.

Stanley Fahn, MD
College of Physicians
and Surgeons
of Columbia University
New York, NY 10032

ETHICS OF PROVOCATIVE TEST FOR HUNTINGTON'S DISEASE

To the Editor In a letter in the October 9 issue, Dr. Stanley Fahn wrote that the levodopa provocative test for Huntington's disease (HD) should not be used. I agree with his conclusion on the bases of validity and safety, but I strongly disagree with his opinion that the results of any presymptomatic test for HD should be withheld from all the subjects involved.

The assumption implicit in Dr. Fahn's reasoning is that it is better for persons to live with the knowledge that they have a 50% chance of having HD than to live with the certain knowledge that it will develop. This assumption is not valid. There are many people who would find the unpleasant truth easier to bear than the Damoclean uncertainty.

There is understandable reluctance on the part of the medical profession to tell a patient that he or she is destined to acquire an incurable disease. The argument seems to be that since nothing can be done, such news deprives the patient of hope and thus increases the risk of severe depression and suicide.

There are two flaws in this reasoning. The first is that because HD is more treatable at present than ever before, because there has been a recent explosion of interest in research on HD, because of the existence of such organizations as the Committee to Combat Huntington's Disease, and because many patients with HD live happy, useful lives for many years after the onset of symptoms, there is more reason than ever before for families with HD to have hope.

Secondly, although extremely early diagnosis serves no medical purpose, it can give a person time to prepare emotionally, financially, and in other ways, so that when the symptoms appear they are not as devastating to the patient and family as they might otherwise be. Giving the patient time to cope, prepare, and plan while still healthy may actually reduce the possibility of suicide. Of course, appropriate psychologic screening and counseling should be made available.

Many personally important decisions involving marriage, bearing and rearing children, insurance, financial planning, career choices, and life style must be made by every adult. A person who is considering changing careers at the age of 35 might not be willing to take the financial risk involved in such a move if HD were a few years ahead. Someone who will have HD may choose not to have children or may decide to have or adopt children as soon as possible to maximize the number of healthy years with them. A decision between a career in medicine and a career in the family business could be heavily influenced by the outcome of a predictive test for HD, if one existed.

Decisions of this sort are agonizing for persons at risk; if the information that would help them make the right decisions were available, it should not be categorically withheld from them.

The ethical issues involved in this situation should be discussed and, if possible, resolved before research produces a safe and reliable test. Of course, not all persons at risk should be given such a test. Each case must be governed by the sensitivity and careful judgment of the physician in charge. Let us not adopt a policy by which neither the patient nor the physician has any choice about the disclosure of such important information.

These opinions are my own; the Committee to Combat Huntington's Disease has no official policy on this issue.

Madeleine Bates, PhD
Committee to Combat
Huntington's Disease
Boston, MA 02118

IN THE NEWS

ROBERT VANDENBERG WINS SPECIAL OLYMPICS

Jefferson High School in Spanishburg, West Virginia, has had special education classes for almost five years. One of the special education students is Robert Vandenberg. Robert, age 16, recently took part in the Special Olympics games. He won two first prize medals—one in long jump and one in swimming.

Robert was thrilled. He wore his heavy medals on a ribbon around his neck when we went to his home for an interview. Robert explained that, because his mom and dad had to work, his uncle Joe had taken him on the train to Roanoke, Virginia. Joe had rented a car in Roanoke. They stayed in a motel near the sports arena with almost 200 other young people from the region who were there to compete in many different events. The motel had a gym and a swimming pool, so Bob was able to practice. To keep in shape, he and his uncle jogged twice a day. After the Olympics were over and Bob had collected his medals, Joe took him to the zoo, several movies, and a hockey game.

During our interview, we noticed that Bob's speech was sometimes slurred and was difficult to understand when he became excited. We also noticed some other unusual aspects of his appearance and behavior. So we decided to interview Bob's parents to find out more about him.

Harold and Margaret Vandenberg were happy to talk to us—mostly, they said, because so many people misunderstand Bob and his condition. Bob is not stupid, but his view of life and the way he expresses himself are certainly less mature than one might expect in a 16-year-old boy. Bob has a jolly personality—an enjoyment of life that is gratifying to his family and friends. The fact that he is so active in sports evokes admiration from other students in his school. But not everyone is kind. Especially when he was younger, Bob was the brunt of many cruel jokes and chides.

Bob is busy at home. While his mom and dad both work in offices, he does most of the housework, including laundry and cleaning. He cuts grass, rakes leaves, and shovels snow. He takes care of the family's two beautiful Irish setters. He washes the car cheerfully, but he is very unhappy about being denied the chance for driver's education.

Bob also does most of the grocery shopping. Harold or Margaret orders meat by phone and Bob picks it up. Since Bob cannot read very well, Harold has made a small ring-bound notebook of photographs of grocery items. To make up the grocery list, Harold puts into the notebook pictures of the items needed that week. To fill the order, Bob simply turns to the pictures in the book. Bob cannot make change, but all the checkout clerks know him, and he always brings home the correct amount.

In his vocational training classes, Bob has learned machining, assembling, and packing skills. After graduation, he will be able to work full time, under supervised conditions. He is looking forward to his first job.

Bob often goes to a nearby town on the bus with some of his friends. When he goes on these trips, he wears a bracelet that gives his name, address, phone number and the statement "I have Down syndrome."

What is Down syndrome? The Vandenbergs explained that Down syndrome (DS) is named after John Langdon Down, a British physician, who gave one of the first descriptions of it.

Down noted that the condition was common in institutions for the mentally retarded. Indeed, DS is the most common form of severe mental retardation in the population: One-third of people who are mentally retarded have DS. The proportion would be higher, but the death rate of DS infants is high. DS infants often die as a result of serious heart defects. Only about half of DS children survive to adult life.

What kind of a condition is DS? It is a genetic syndrome—specifically a malformation syndrome. That means that the affected person has several malformations—more than would be expected based on the frequency of these malformations in the population. Mostly, the malformations are minor ones, but they help doctors diagnose the condition. Some of these minor malformations occur in individuals in the general population as normal developmental variants.

The physical appearance of people with DS is a result of several subtle developmental changes. People with DS usually are shorter than others of the same age. They usually are heavier and their muscles are not as firm. Their posture may not be good, and they frequently have flat feet. The facial features of a person with DS may include a sloping fold of the eyelid; small, low-set ears; low nasal bridge; a broad neck; and an open mouth and protruding tongue.

People with DS tend to be gentle and happy. We noticed these characteristics when we spoke with Bob. The I. Q. range goes from 20 to 60 with a median of 40 to 50. Those at the upper level of the I. Q. range can sometimes be educated to read and write. A few can learn to get along in the community. The vast majority are unable to function on their own in society. Some are profoundly retarded and need institutional or nursing home care.

At one time, many DS children were automatically admitted to institutions for the mentally retarded shortly after birth. Today, the exact opposite is true. Most parents try to educate the child to attain maximum skill and knowledge. That is why more people with DS now are seen in streets, schools, and stores. They are living much happier and more productive lives than ever before. Bob's pride in his Olympics medals, his freedom of movement, his ability to perform useful work, and his anticipation of future semi-independent work and living conditions have given him hope and optimism. He has achieved a level of dignity and self-respect that, until recently, was rarely possible for retarded people.

Women 35 and older have a greater risk of having a child with DS than do younger mothers. And the risk increases with each additional year of maternal age. But ¾ of the children who are born with DS have mothers under the age of 35. Why, then, do we say the risk is greater? The answer lies in the fact that women 35 and older have a *disproportionately* large number of children with DS. Of *all* children born, fewer than 10% are born to women 35 and older. But about 20% of the children with DS are born to older mothers. For women under 35, the risk of having a child with DS is approximately .9/1000 (0.09%). For women 35 and older, the risk is approximately 7/1000 (0.7%). So the risk is almost eight times greater than would be expected on the basis of random chance in the population.

Readers who have already tried "Countdown on Chromosomes," page 22, may have a good idea of the genetic causes of the kind of DS that Robert has. DS is caused by extra chromosomal material, usually an entire extra chromosome 21. This is called trisomy 21. Robert has 47 chromosomes instead of the usual 46.

Another, more rare cause of DS, is when most of an extra chromosome 21 is attached to another chromosome—such as 14 or 22. These people with DS have the normal 46 chromosomes, but on closer inspection, the extra 21 chromosome can be seen attached to 14 or 22, giving the characteristic number for DS of 47.

How does the extra chromosome get into the fertilized egg? It does so through a process of meiotic nondisjunction. Nondisjunction may occur in the first or second meiotic division. Nondisjunction means that during cell division, a pair of chromosomes does not separate. Instead both chromosomes enter a single cell. This results in one egg or sperm that has only 22 chromosomes. Such reproductive cells usually die. Another cell has 24 chromosomes. It contains two members of the pair. During fertilization of such a cell, a third chromosome of the same kind is added. Trisomy results.

Nondisjunction is quite common in humans. Possibly, almost half of all human embryos are chromosomally abnormal. All human chromosomes, except 1 and 17, have been seen in a trisomic state. The most common occurrence is trisomy of chromosome 16. Most humans with trisomies die. Fewer than half of the humans with trisomy 21, a rare case of trisomy 13, or trisomy 18 survive. About 60% of all spontaneously aborted human embryos and fetuses have a chromosomal abnormality. About 6% of stillborn infants have a chromosomal defect. Of liveborn infants, only 0.6% show the effects of trisomy.

The situation at birth is as follows:

Total infants examined	54,749	
Total abnormal	326	(0.6%)

Type of abnormality	Number	Percentage of total
Sex chromosomal	120	0.22%
Autosomal trisomy	74	0.14%
Structural defects in chromosomes	132	0.24%
TOTAL	326	0.6%

These data make more sense if we review what karyotypes show. The twenty-third pair of chromosomes are the *sex chromosomes*. They occur in two forms, called X and Y. The sex chromosomes determine the sex of an individual. An individual with two X chromosomes is female. And an individual with one X and one Y is a male. The other 22 pairs of chromosomes are called *autosomes*. Autosomes are all the chromosomes *except* sex chromosomes. Thus, trisomy 21 is an autosomal condition. Autosomal defects usually are very serious. They are almost always associated with severe or profound mental retardation and a high death rate. Only about half of DS children survive to adult life.

Theoretically, all of the more obvious chromosomal defects can be detected before birth using a technique called amniocentesis. (See "Prenatal Diagnosis," page 68.) But, right now, it is neither possible nor desirable to perform amniocentesis on every pregnant woman. Genetic counselors usually recommend amniocentesis for women over 35 or for those with a history of a genetic disorder in their families.

STUDYING HUMAN CHROMOSOMES

Not many years ago, the correct number of human chromosomes was unknown. Simple ways of studying chromosomes inside cells had not been invented. Chromosomes could only be studied by slicing cells *very* thinly and trying to count the pieces of chromosome material in each section. Doing so was like trying to assemble a very difficult puzzle, and often incorrect answers were obtained. Fortunately, new methods have been devised that give us reliable results. Chromosome studies are carried out now by growing cells in a test tube in a broth of special chemicals and nutrients. The cells are then broken open and examined under a microscope.

The first step is to obtain cells that will grow. Many different kinds of cells can be used, but white blood cells and skin cells are the most commonly used types because they are simple to obtain and easy to grow.

After a few white blood cells or a small bit of skin has been obtained, the tissue is placed in the special nutrient mixture. Different types of cells have slightly different nutritional needs. Thus, great care must be taken to select the right materials in the correct amounts. Furthermore, the fluid must be kept at just the right temperature and have enough oxygen. Steps must be taken to keep bacteria and other microorganisms out or they too will grow. The cells take from several days to several weeks to begin growing. Sometimes chemicals are added to stimulate growth and cell division.

Once the cells have begun to grow and divide, other chemicals (such as colcemid) are added to prevent normal division of the cells. Cell division is usually stopped when the chromosomes are tightly condensed and lined up in the center of the cell.

After the cells have reached this stage, other chemicals are added to cause the cells to swell with fluid. The nuclear membrane bursts. The chromosomes from each cell nucleus fall in a small cluster. The chromosomes are then stained so they can be seen easily under a microscope. Specially trained laboratory technicians look carefully at the chromosomes of many different cells. They take pictures through the microscope of "well-spread" clusters where all the different chromosomes can be seen. After the picture is developed the chromosomes are cut out and sorted according to their size, shape, and banding pattern for further investigation.

Sometimes several different types of staining chemicals will have to be used in order to learn more about tiny details of chromosome structure. This process is tedious and time consuming, with the result that chromosome studies are often rather expensive—$300 to $500 at present in most laboratories. Imagine how difficult and expensive it can be to study an entire family! Nevertheless, in special situations, such investigations can give extremely valuable information about the health of individuals and their reproductive risks.

COUNTDOWN ON CHROMOSOMES

Understanding human genetics requires some study of chromosomes. Technicians in hospitals and genetic service centers can use special techniques to take pictures of the chromosomes in a dividing white blood cell. (Red blood cells cannot be used because they do not have nuclei.) The picture looks like Figure 1. The chromosomes can then be cut out of the picture and arranged in a standard sequence. This standard sequence, like Figure 2, is called a karyotype. Note that there are twenty-three pairs of chromosomes in this karyotype. Twenty-two of the pairs are called autosomes and are numbered from 1 to 22. The twenty-third pair is the sex chromosomes. These chromosomes are usually either two X chromosomes in a normal female or an X chromosome and a Y chromosome in a normal male. What is the sex of the person whose chromosomes are shown in Figure 2?

Look now at Figures 3 and 4. What can you tell about the chromosomes of these individuals? Probably not much without making a karyotype. Interested readers can follow the procedure on page 39 to make karyotypes and answer the question.

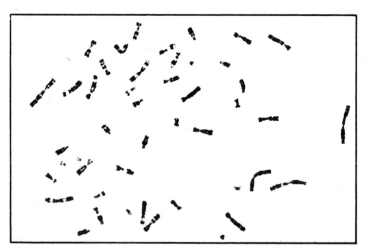

Figure 1.

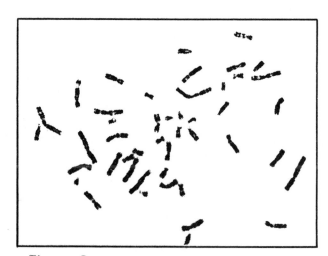

Figure 3.

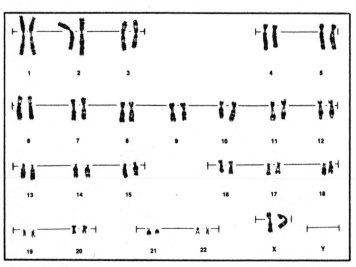

Figure 2.

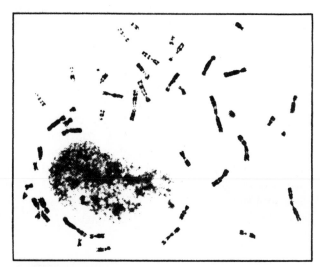

Figure 4.

Materials Needed

Copy of Figure 3
Copy of Figure 4
Scissors
Pencil
Paper
Tape or Glue

Procedure

1. Work first with the copy of Figure 3; then repeat this procedure for Figure 4.
2. Circle each chromosome with a pencil.
3. Cut out the individual chromosomes.
4. Using Figure 2 as a key, mark a blank sheet of paper with the appropriate spaces for the pairs of chromosomes. Use numbers as in Figure 2.
5. Arrange the cut-out chromosomes in pairs. (Hint: Use size, shape, and the patterns of light and dark bands as clues for matching up the chromosomes and determining their proper numbers.)
6. Use glue or tape to affix each chromosome in its place on the karyotype.

Interpreting the Karyotypes

1. What is the sex of the individual whose chromosomes appear in Figure 3? in Figure 4?
2. Compare the two karyotypes you have made. What specific difference can you find?
3. How important is this difference? If you don't already know, you should read "Robert Vandenberg Wins Special Olympics," page 35.

SICKLE-CELL TRAIT IS NOT SICKLE-CELL ANEMIA

A few years ago, our editorial office received a number of reports that some companies were denying insurance to certain individuals. These people did not have sickle-cell anemia but, instead, they had sickle-cell trait. It was obvious at that time that there was a lot of confusion about the difference between sickle-cell anemia and sickle-cell trait. Thus, we published a number of articles to explain the situation and clear up some of the confusion.

It appears now that our efforts—as well as those of other magazines, newspapers, television and radio stations, teachers, and volunteer groups—have helped alleviate the problem. We do not receive as many reports of misunderstanding or outright discrimination as we used to. Nevertheless, we know that the problem is not completely solved. Some people are still confused about what sickle-cell anemia is and how it is inherited.

One of the reporters in our education division recently submitted a story that seemed timely and important enough to include in our IN THE NEWS section. We hope our readers will learn as much from the story of Emmet Richardson as we did.

Emmet Richardson went to a neighborhood health fair. The fair was being sponsored by the local television station and the medical society. Emmet was impressed with the many screenings, demonstrations, and exhibits related to health promotion and disease prevention. He had his blood pressure taken at one booth and his lung capacity determined at another. His hearing was excellent, but he was not able to see the tiny letters near the bottom of the eye chart. Emmet already knew he needed glasses. Next, he stopped at a booth marked "hemoglobinopathies" (HE muh glow bun AH puh thies). He watched as others ahead of him had their fingers poked and several drops of blood placed on a card. Emmet read the brochures. He watched and listened to the automatic slide presentation.

The narrator talked mostly about sickle-cell anemia. Emmet knew something about sickle cell. Michael Patterson, a member of Emmet's church, had the disorder and suffered fatigue and periodic pains in his joints.

Emmet learned that sickle-cell anemia is an inherited disorder of red blood cells. The disorder causes the red blood cells to become distorted into forms resembling sickles (Figure 1) when the oxygen level in the blood is low. Because the cells

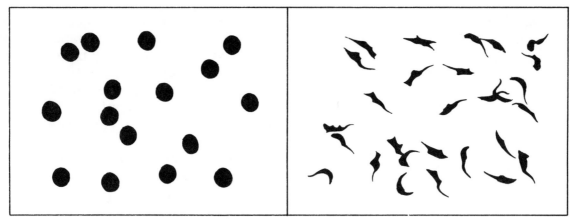

Figure 1. Normal cells and sickled cells

that become sickled cannot flow easily through the tiny capillaries, they create a "traffic jam." This decreases the blood supply to the vital organs such as the heart, spleen, kidneys, and brain, and these organs may be damaged.

Although the symptoms of sickle-cell anemia are quite variable, there are some general clinical features. In infants, jaundice (yellowing of skin and other tissues due to the breakdown products of red blood cells), anemia, pain and a predisposition to infection may be observed. In later years, due to the "traffic jam" in the capillaries, the disease may cause leg ulcers, anemia, kidney failure, stroke, and heart failure.

Emmet realized why Michael was short of breath, tired, and could not participate in the YMCA basketball league. Emmet also learned that not all patients with sickle-cell anemia have the clinical symptoms. Some people may be completely free of serious illness, while others have only a few symptoms. The severity of sickle-cell anemia and the symptoms differ for various age groups. While some people with sickle-cell anemia do not have any problems, others die at an early age.

The narrator of the slide show used a pedigree chart to explain how sickle-cell anemia is inherited (Figure 2). Emmet saw that, in the first generation, each parent has one gene for normal and one gene for sickle hemoglobin. The sickle-cell gene is recessive. Sickle-cell anemia occurs only when a person has two recessive genes. A person with one normal gene and one sickle gene has sickle-cell *trait*. Both parents shown in the pedigree have sickle-cell trait. People with sickle-cell trait do not have the disorder. Their life expectancy is the same as that of people with normal hemoglobin. Only occasionally have any symptoms been associated with sickle-cell trait.

Emmet examined the pedigree chart carefully. The pedigree shows a couple with five children. The first two inherited normal hemoglobin genes from both parents. The third and fourth are carriers; they have sickle-cell trait like their parents. The fifth child received the sickle hemoglobin gene from both parents. She has sickle-cell anemia. When both parents have the trait, the probability of inheriting two sickle hemoglobin genes is 25% (Figure 3). The 25% chance does not mean that 25% of the children in one family will automatically have sickle-cell anemia. Probabilities are based on large numbers of families with carrier parents.

Emmet saw that no one was in line. He decided to find out if he was a carrier. The technician

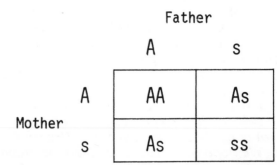

Figure 3. When both parents have the trait, the probability of sickle-cell anemia in the offspring is 25%.

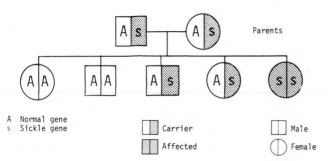

Figure 2. Inheritance of sickle-cell anemia

asked Emmet to fill out a form and to have one of his parents sign at the bottom. Emmet knew that his parents would not be home from work for another half hour. He decided to stay and ask more questions about sickle-cell anemia.

Emmet noticed that the drops of blood on the cards were drying. He asked the technician where the cards were going and what would happen to them. The technician told him that the cards would be taken to the University Hospital. There, other technicians would use a process called electrophoresis to separate the proteins in blood. Electrophoresis is the movement of charged particles in an electrical field.

Because the hemoglobin that causes sickle-cell anemia has a different charge than normal hemoglobin, the two forms will separate in an electrical field. A person with sickle-cell trait has both kinds. Such a person can, therefore, be identified through electrophoresis. Emmet was surprised to learn that there are more than 180 other known variant forms of hemoglobin. Each form is caused by a different gene mutation.

Emmet looked at his watch. It was about time for his parents to be home. He thanked the technician and left the health fair with the consent form. Later, Emmet returned with his parents and two younger sisters. They all had decided to be screened for sickle-cell trait. The technician assured them that the results of the tests would be confidential and that they would be notified in a week.

The results of the preliminary lab test using electrophoresis showed that Emmet, his father, and one of his sisters were carriers. Additional laboratory tests confirmed these results. A genetic counselor prepared a pedigree chart for the Richardson family (Figure 4).

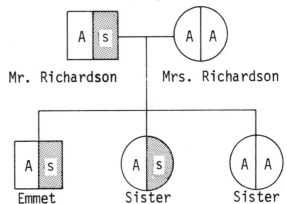

Figure 4. The Richardson family's pedigree chart

Emmet figured out that, if his parents decided to have more children, none of them would have sickle-cell anemia. But, there would be a 50% chance of a child having sickle-cell trait. His other sister does not have the trait. She will only pass normal hemoglobin genes to her children.

Emmet thought about his trait. Although he knew that sickle-cell trait is not a disorder, he wondered about the children he might want to have someday.

HIGH SCHOOLS IN BLOOD DONOR CONTEST

Last week, students and faculties of the George Washington and Thomas Jefferson high schools, arch rivals on the athletic field, became arch rivals at the blood bank. For several weeks, the student councils of both schools campaigned vigorously to recruit blood donors from among students and staff. The campaign became so intense that one of the local merchants announced that she would donate a trophy to the school with the greatest number of donors.

When the last drop of blood had been drawn from the last donor, John Drexler, President of the George Washington Student Council, accepted the trophy on behalf of his school. However, in this contest there were no losers. The two schools collected a total of 400 pints of blood from student and staff donors. A continual supply of fresh blood is extremely important. The members of these two schools can be very proud of their efforts.

In an interview with John after he had accepted the trophy, we found that he has always been interested in the study of blood.

When John typed his own blood during a biology laboratory, he was surprised to learn that he was the only AB type in his class. He also learned that about 6% of the people in the U.S. have Type AB, 44% have Type O, 37% have Type A, and 13% have Type B.

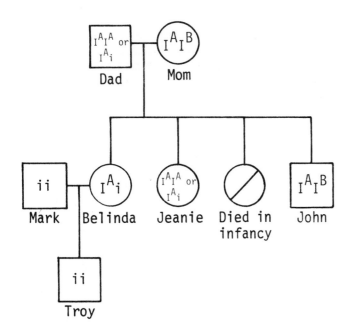

Pedigree chart:

- Dad (I^AI^A or I^Ai) — Mom (I^AI^B)
- Children: Mark (ii) — Belinda (I^Ai), Jeanie (I^AI^A or I^Ai), Died in infancy, John (I^AI^B)
- Mark & Belinda's child: Troy (ii)

BLOOD TYPE	GENOTYPE	FREQUENCY IN J.S. POPULATION
A	I^AI^A or I^Ai	37%
B	I^BI^B or I^Bi	13%
AB	I^AI^B	6%
O	ii	44%

Gene I^A and I^B are said to be *codominant*. This means that *both* are expressed in the phenotype. Since John and his mother both have Type AB blood, John was able to determine their genotypes easily. But he could not determine Belinda's and his dad's genotype until Troy, his nephew, was born. Can you guess why? (*Hint:* The **i** gene is not expressed unless it occurs in the homozygous state—that is, two **i** genes.) Since Troy did not inherit any antigens from Mark and Belinda, his genotype was **ii**.

Can you now determine the genotype of John's dad and sister, Jeanie? Can you determine your own genotype?

John also found that his mother is Type AB and his father is Type A. John drew a pedigree chart to see how the genes were distributed.

JOHN DREXLER INVESTIGATES BLOOD TYPES

John Drexler is President of the Student Council at George Washington High School. He is also a member of the track team. With his height advantage, he is a better-than-average high jumper. During a recent sports physical, John's doctor typed John's blood. Several days later, John received the lab report. When he examined the report, John noticed that his blood type was AB. The test also showed that he was Rh negative. He had hoped that he would be positive like his father and sister, Jeanie. His mother and sister, Belinda, were Rh negative. His first reaction to the report was one of disappointment.

John looked over his pedigree chart. He noticed again, but with greater awareness, the death of his third sister at infancy. He thought for a moment that her death might have been caused by the negative blood. He even worried that, if he got injured in sports, the negative blood might kill him.

But John wasn't the type to jump to hasty conclusions. He decided the question was important enough for him to spend some time in the library. The librarian helped him find a book that was not too technical but provided the facts he wanted. John took notes:

April 3
Rh factor

1. The letters Rh come from the first two letters of *Rhesus monkey*. Rhesus monkey was used for experiment. Rh antigens were discovered in the Rhesus monkey.

2. About 85% of human population have some Rh antigens. These people are called Rh positive.

3. 15% of the human population do not have the antigens and are classified as Rh negative. * This is me!

4. Rh antigens are inherited:
   RhRh is Rh positive homozygous
   Rhrh is Rh positive heterozygous
   rhrh is Rh negative homozygous

5. The Rh blood group system is very complicated, but all we need to know is shown in number 4 above.

6. If RhRh and rhrh have children, all of them will be Rhrh — a Rh positive

7. If Rhrh and Rhrh have children, there is a 25% chance of an Rh negative child. * ME!

Father

	Rh	rh
Rh	Rh Rh	Rh rh
rh	Rh rh	rh rh

(Mother labels the rows)

8. If Rhrh and rhrh have children, there is a 50% chance of an Rh negative child. ← ME AGAIN!

Father

	rh	rh
Rh	Rh rh	Rh rh
rh	rh rh	rh rh

(Mother labels the rows)

9. If father is Rh positive and mother is Rh negative, the first Rh positive child is okay. The mother usually does not have any antibodies produced to react with the baby's Rh positive antigens.

10. However, as the first child is delivered, there may be some mixing of blood between mom and child. This mixing of blood occurs when the placenta is separating from the uterus.

11. The baby's blood, carrying Rh antigens, can enter the mother. If it does, she will react to the foreign antigens by developing antibodies. But the baby is already delivered, the antibodies will not affect the child.

12. If the couple has a second child with Rh positive blood, there is a chance that the mother's antibodies may pass through the placenta into the fetus and destroy the red blood cells that carry the Rh antigens. The cells will clump together. The condition is called erythroblastosis fetalis.

13. The mother is said to be "sensitized" when the first Rh child leaves the antigens and the mother begins producing antibodies.

14. If the first child is Rh positive but the second child is Rh negative, the latter is not affected because the child has no antigens to react with the mother's antibodies.

15. If the mother is injected with anti-Rh-positive gamma globulin (RHOGAM) within 72 hours after the first Rh positive baby is born, it will eliminate foreign Rh positive cells that may have entered the mother's bloodstream.

16. The mother will not be sensitized and she will be able to have a second child with Rh positive blood. She will need an injection after each Rh positive child.

John was excited when he got home. He explained to his sister, Jeanie, how they had inherited their Rh blood types. That evening, John mentioned to his parents that there was a possibility that the third sister might have died from *erythroblastosis fetalis*. He concluded that Belinda was not affected because she was Rh negative. Jeanie was the first Rh positive child. But since his mother was not given Rhogam following Jeanie's delivery, she became sensitized. The third daughter was affected by the mother's antibodies. John's mother confirmed that she did not receive Rhogam and that her third daughter had died in infancy due to *erythroblastosis fetalis*.

John was happy to learn later that his sister Belinda received Rhogam after Troy was born. He was able to figure out the Rh genotype for Troy but only the phenotype for Mark. And he had learned that negative blood is *not* bad.

ZOO ANIMALS SHIPPED ACROSS COUNTRY TO MATE

Our news office receives many reports of zoo animals being sent to other zoos to mate. We wondered why all this bother and expense. Why not just breed the animals at home, in their own zoo? To find the answer, we contacted Dr. Mary Ann Hopkins, Curator, San Diego Zoo. She told us that the animals are mated at other zoos to avoid harmful or lethal characteristics. Every organism carries some lethal genes. If the lethal gene is recessive and is paired with a normal, dominant gene, the lethal gene causes no harm to the individual. But harm may result if, by the normal processes of meiosis and fertilization, two recessive lethal genes come together in the fertilized egg that will develop into an offspring.

Dr. Hopkins suggested that interested readers follow the procedure given below to demonstrate why the danger is very real:

ZOO ANIMAL PEDIGREE

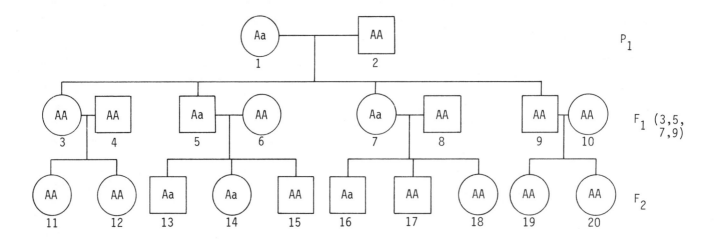

1. Work with a partner. It makes the organization and paperwork easier.

2. Imagine a species of zoo animal that is rare—perhaps an endangered species. Then study this pedigree for one "family" of that species living in a zoo. On the chart, **A** stands for a normal, dominant gene. The **a** stands for a recessive, lethal gene that is very rare in the general population. Individual members of this "family" are identified by numbers.

3. For the various matings listed below, determine the probability that an offspring will be affected. Which matings could result in an affected offspring?

   a. The parents: Female 1 X Male 2

   b. First generation (F_1) matings of unrelated individuals as shown in the pedigree: Female 3 X Male 4; Female 6 X Male 5; Female 7 X Male 8; Female 10 X Male 9.

   c. First generation (F_1) matings of siblings: Females 3 and 7 X Males 5 and 9.

   d. All possible first generation matings: Females 3, 6, 7, and 10 X Males 4, 5, 8, and 9.

   e. Second generation (F_2) matings between first cousins and/or siblings: Females 11, 12, 14, 18, 19, 20 X Males 13, 15, 16, and 17.

4. Identify—in each of the matings that has a possibility of an affected offspring—the relationship between the parents.

5. The frequency of **a** in this population is very low. Based on this fact and your data, give your best answer to the question "Why are zoo animals shipped across the country to mate?"

6. (Optional) Try some other kinds of matings—for example, parents with offspring, siblings only in the F_2, first cousins only in the F_2, and so on. Do the patterns you found in the other kinds of matings persist?

7. Most states have laws prohibiting the marriage of brothers to sisters and first cousins to each other. Most cultures have unwritten laws, "taboos," against marriage between close relatives. What are the practical implications of such laws and taboos? How do you think they might have arisen?

THE MYSTERY OF THE KILLER BEES

August 27, 1983. At his palatial Chelsea home, Lord Myron Thistleroot was opening his mail at tea time. He found a curious envelope with no return address. Lord Thistleroot tore open one end of the envelope, and out flew four bees. He panicked. He was allergic to bees—a bee sting might be fatal. as he fought off two bees buzzing in front of him, one bee stung him behind his left ear.

Thistleroot immediately reacted to the sting and went into shock. Three guests who had joined his lordship for tea quickly administered first aid. Lord Thistleroot was taken to a nearby hospital in an ambulance.

Scotland Yard arrived soon after. They had elicited the help of the famous Sir Lock Romes in solving the mystery of the killer bees. Sir Lock quickly examined the room and directed several questions to each guest. He decided that one of them was the person who wanted Lord Thistleroot incapacitated.

Sir Lock asked the three guests for several drops of their blood. He quickly typed their blood and found that all three were Type A. Then, Sir Lock took the envelope that had contained the bees and scraped the flap. He removed some of the glue that had been moistened with the saliva of the guilty party. He mixed a serum with the glue. The result was positive. The person who put the bees into the envelope was a secretor with blood Type A. Another test showed that some H substance also was present in the glue from the envelope.

Next, Sir Lock asked the three guests for one more drop of blood. He added a different serum to the blood. The results were

Guest 1	Guest 2	Guest 3
AA	AO	AO
secretor	secretor	nonsecretor

Do you know who put the bees into the envelope? Read "Are You a Secretor?" Then you will be able to solve the mystery of the killer bees.

ARE YOU A SECRETOR?

ABO antigens occur on red blood cells. They also occur in many other tissues. The interesting part is that many people have ABO antigens in their secretions. The ability to secrete antigens in the saliva is inherited as a simple Mendelian trait. Secretion depends on a single dominant gene, **Se**. Secretors can be **SeSe** or **Sese**. Nonsecretors are homozygous for the recessive gene, **sese**. About 78% of the U. S. population are secretors, and 22% are nonsecretors.

If saliva secretions contain antigens, then the blood type of the secretor can be determined. In addition to AB antigens, H substance also can be found in secretions. H substance is a product from which the A and B antigens are produced. A person who is Type O will have no A or B antigens but will have H substance. A Type-A person who is genotypically AA will not have as much H substance as a person who is genotypically AO.

Geneticists have found solutions that will react with H substance. Therefore, in determining the genotype of a person with blood Type A, the anti-H serum can be added to the blood. If the person is genotypically AA, the reaction will be negative. If the person is genotypically AO, there is still some H substance not used and thus the cells will react positively with the anti-H serum.

THE "ICE DIAMOND" HEIST

September 12, 1983. Immediately after his brilliant solution of the "Mystery of the Killer Bees," Sir Lock Romes once again makes news with his brilliant solution of the "Ice Diamond" heist. On September 3, the safe in the Raleigh Mansion in New Portsmouth was blasted open. Sir Lock was able to deduce the true thief from fingerprints found on a jewel case. The thief had carelessly tossed the case into a bush outside the Mansion.

Scotland Yard was holding two suspects. The first, Lady Margaret Mitchum, denied having been near the Raleigh Mansion, despite the fact that her monogrammed scarf was found near the blasted safe. Duke Dan of Dorchester also was being held. He had been a guest in the Mansion the evening of the theft and had mysteriously disappeared just before the blast.

Sir Lock solved the case without looking at the fingerprints of either suspect. He was able to charge Lady Margaret with the crime using nothing more than the fingerprints from the jewel case.

How did Sir Lock accomplish this amazing feat? Interested readers can follow these steps and learn how the mystery was solved.

Materials Needed

hand lens or magnifying glass
low-power microscope (optional)
white paper
stamp pad
graph paper (2 pieces)
ruler (optional)

Procedure

Using the magnifying glass, examine the ridges on your fingertips. At first, they may look confusing. But if you look carefully, the ridges will fall into three main types: arches, loops, and whorls.

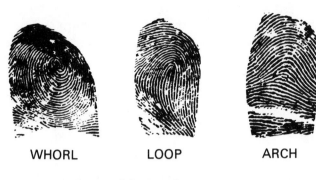

WHORL   LOOP   ARCH

Figure 1. Types of fingerprints

The classification is based on the number of triradii present.

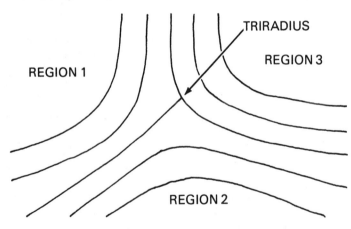

Figure 2. A triradius is the junction of three regions, each containing ridges and its own pattern. (Source: Sarah B. Holt, *Quantative Genetics of Fingerprints*)

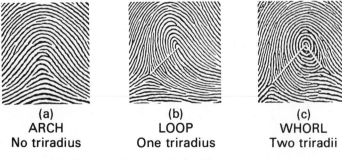

(a)
ARCH
No triradius

(b)
LOOP
One triradius

(c)
WHORL
Two triradii

Figure 3. Fingerprints and triradii

In Figure 3b, a line points from the center to a triradius. *You will be counting the ridges along this line.* Figure 3a has no triradii. Figure 3b has one triradius, and Figure 3c has two triradii.

1. Look at Figure 3b. How many ridges are there along the line between the triradius and the center of the loop? Do not include the triradius in your count. Also, do not count the final ridge as it forms the center.
2. There are two triradii in Figure 3c. What is the ridge count for the left (7 o'clock) line? What is the ridge count for the shorter line at 5 o'clock?

Make neat prints of all your fingers on a piece of white paper. Rolling each finger will assure you a clean and complete print. Wash your hands after making the prints. Place the prints in an orderly sequence.

3. Are your prints arched, looped, or whorled?
4. How many triradii do you see?
5. Do all ten fingers have the same classification?

Don't be surprised if your fingers show different patterns. If you have the arch pattern, there is no triradius and the ridge count is 0.

Cut the row of fingerprints into a strip. Avoid smearing the prints. Use a microscope or a strong magnifying glass to study the patterns. Draw an imaginary line from the center to the triradius. Count the ridges for each finger and record them in a table such as the one below. (For a whorl pattern with two triradii, use the larger of the two ridge counts.)

	LEFT			
1	2	3	4	5
	RIGHT			
1	2	3	4	5

46

6. Is the ridge count the same for all ten fingers?
7. What is the total for all ten fingers?

On the chalkboard, tally everyone's total ridge counts. Make two lists: one for males and one for females.

8. What is the average ridge count for the males?
9. What is the average ridge count for the females?
10. Is there a difference between the two counts?

List several ideas that might explain the similarity or difference in the data between the sexes.

Rearrange the ridge counts for the males from low to high. Round each count to the nearest 10. Plot the number of males who have each ridge count on a piece of graph paper. Repeat this procedure for the female data.

11. How do the two graphs compare?
12. How, then, did Sir Lock Romes solve the "Ice Diamond" heist?

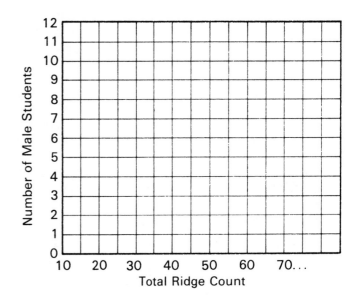

Figure 4. Example of graph for male ridge count total

REPRODUCTIVE TECHNOLOGY: TODAY AND TOMORROW

July 25, 1978, Oldham General Hospital in England. Louise Brown, normal and healthy, weighing 2.6 kilograms (5 pounds, 12 ounces) was delivered to her proud parents. What is unusual about Louise? She is the first "test tube" baby. She was conceived outside her mother's body and then transferred to her mother's uterus. The process is called *"in vitro"* fertilization. *"In vitro"* is Latin, meaning "in glass"—thus, fertilization in glass—rather than *"in vivo"*—"in the living body."

Informed sources at the scene are quick to point out that the phrase "test tube" baby is really *not* correct. The baby does not grow and develop in a test tube. Only fertilization and some early cell divisions occur outside the mother's body. Prenatal growth and development occur in the uterus of the mother, just as they do in any pregnancy.

How Is In Vitro Fertilization Performed?

In vitro fertilization is still an experimental procedure. It is not available as routine medical treatment, because a great deal of research needs to be done. The procedure begins with a carefully kept record of the woman's menstrual cycle. Just before the time she would normally ovulate— release an egg from the ovary—one or more eggs are surgically removed from her ovaries.

The egg or eggs are then put in a laboratory solution that is similar to body fluid. Sperm from the male are placed in this same solution. The eggs and sperm are incubated until fertilization occurs. The fertilized egg or eggs are then transferred to another solution. Each embryo is allowed to develop to the 8-to-16 cell stage. An embryo is then transferred to the uterus. If it implants in the uterine wall and develops, the woman will then give birth.

Another procedure is to deep-freeze the embryo at the 8-to-16 cell stage and wait until after the female's next menstrual cycle. At the appropriate time, probably 2 to 3 days after ovulation, the embryo is thawed and transferred to the woman's uterus for further development.

Who Might the Procedure Help?

Nearly 12% of couples in the U.S. are infertile. About 1/3 of these are infertile because the female is sterile. *In vitro* fertilization and embryo transfer can help *only* those females who are sterile because their Fallopian tubes are blocked. About 40% of sterile women have ovarian or uterine problems that *in vitro* fertilization cannot solve.

Several surgical procedures are available for repairing blocked Fallopian tubes, but these work for fewer than 50% of the women who have them.

Considering these statistics, it was estimated that perhaps 500,000 women in the U. S. would have no way of having their own children except by *in vitro* fertilization and embryo transfer.

A clinic in Norfolk, Virginia was opened in January, 1980. This is a privately funded program at General Hospital set up by the Eastern Virginia Medical School. It provides *in vitro* fertilization and embryo transfer services and carefully researches these techniques. Of the many women who desire these medical services, only a few will be accepted because of limited facilities. However, other clinics have been organized and are now in operation.

Why Is In Vitro Fertilization Controversial?

In the U. S., the public debate about the ethical implications of *in vitro* fertilization began long before the birth of Louise Brown. James Watson, a biologist, started the debate. Watson was concerned that research advances in human *in vitro* fertilization and the cloning of frogs would lead to attempts to clone, or "copy," human beings. A public debate ensued. In 1973, the Department of Health, Education, and Welfare (HEW) drafted a policy stating that, "All proposals for research involving human *in vitro* fertilization must be reviewed by the Ethical Review Board." The policy, in effect, called a halt to all HEW-supported research on human *in vitro* fertilization in the U. S.

In 1978, when Louise Brown was born in England, the debate exploded once again. Women who desperately wanted children but had blocked Fallopian tubes argued for development of this technology in the U. S. Others were concerned about the safety of the procedure, the ethics of experimenting with human embryos, and the possible future technologies that might develop.

Much of the controversy about *in vitro* fertilization centers around the debate over abortion. Louise Brown was the first success of many trials. At least 200 transfers in various women were attempted without success. Should the lost embryos be considered abortions? Is the situation the same as making a decision to terminate a pregnancy?

Some people feel that the fertilized egg is a human being, in the moral sense, because it is biologically alive and because there is continuous development to birth and adulthood. Opponents of abortion, *in vitro* fertilization, and other reproductive technologies often feel that it is morally wrong to interfere with the natural process of human reproduction under most, if not all, circumstances.

Others believe that the embryo is not a human being in any morally relevant sense because it is incapable of sustaining its own life outside the mother's uterus. They also argue that the potential quality of life for a diseased or unwanted child is low. Harm, they say, can be avoided by preventing the birth of such a child. On the issue of rights, they believe that the rights of adults, particularly the pregnant woman, make matters of abortion or *in vitro* fertilization private, rather than public, decisions.

They also point out that the natural reproductive process includes heavy mortality. Available data show that about 16% of the eggs that come in contact with sperm are never fertilized or never undergo the first cell division. Another 15% are lost prior to implantation, and 22% are lost before a woman misses her first menstrual period. Spontaneous abortions occur in 12% of the cases. Thus, only about 35% of the eggs that come in contact with sperm—under natural conditions in the human female—actually develop into live babies.

Future Possibilities

Another major question that has been asked is, "What are the potential long-term consequences of *in vitro* fertilization procedures?" Will this lead to future problems? Again, there are those who feel dangers are great and research and clinical procedures should be stopped now. Others feel that the benefits outweigh future risks. Some of the future possibilities are as follows:

Cloning. A clone, in the simplest sense, is a group of cells produced asexually from a single cell. Therefore, *all the progeny are genetically identical* to each other and to the single parent cell from which they arose. They may or may not be organized into a specific organism. In a sense, therefore, an identical twin could be considered a clone.

Scientists have been using "clones" experimentally for years. Microbiologists, for example, make a dilute suspension of bacteria and plate them out on a culture medium so that they settle as single cells. Then, by asexual fission, colonies *which are true clones* grow from the single cells. Often a selective culture medium is used that permits only those cells with certain specific characteristics to grow. This is the procedure by which the special "phenylalanine dependent" bacteria used in PKU screening were produced. (See "The Screening of Benjamin Miller," page 87.)

Today, clones of bacteria containing a tiny fragment of human DNA are being put to work to produce large quantities of otherwise very scarce human gene products, such as insulin and growth hormone, which will be made available for the treatment of human diseases. It is quite reasonable to anticipate many more useful applications of cloning in science and medicine.

In the opinion of most experts, the cloning of a human being is science fiction and should remain so. To do it, one would have to take a cell from some tissue, like skin or liver, and somehow induce it to grow into a replica of the entire person. An alternative approach would be that used successfully in frogs. A nucleus is removed from a cell of an adult frog and transplanted to an embryonic cell of another frog after the nucleus of the embryonic cell has been removed.

The problem with either procedure in higher animals relates to differentiation. Although every nucleus of every body cell contains the full set of chromosomes and genes, only a tiny proportion of the gene set is functioning in any given cell. We have no idea about how to "turn on" all the genes so that the progeny of our single "parent cell" would develop all the appropriate organs and tissues. Perhaps a more important issue is "Why bother?" The technical problems are staggering, to say nothing of the ethical issues. And the scientific information one might obtain can be derived from much more feasible studies on simple cell cultures.

Sex Selection. A variety of techniques that are already available could be used to allow parents to preselect the sex of their offspring. "Prenatal Diagnosis," page 68, describes fetal sex determination by amniocentesis and chromosomal analysis. In the future, it may be possible to isolate fetal cells from the mother's blood or from the cervix. However, if the fetus is of the "undesired" sex, the only alternative is abortion of a presumably normal fetus. Many people find that morally unacceptable.

In the future, it may also be possible to separate the sperm with a Y chromosome from those with an X. The X chromosome is larger than the Y. Therefore, the X-bearing sperm cells are *slightly heavier* than those with a Y. When spun at high speeds in a centrifuge, the heavier sperm tend to settle to the bottom of the test tube. If the two kinds of sperm are separated and only one kind is used to impregnate the woman, then the sex of the offspring could be determined before birth.

What do you suppose would happen to the sex distribution of the population here in North America if many or all parents preselected the sex of their children? Do you know of any cultures where children of one sex are more highly valued than the other? What would happen in such a culture?

Try this simple number exercise. Assume that in a group of 100 couples, half can choose the sex of their first offspring and each selects a male. The other half of the 100 couples takes their chances. After each couple has had one child, what has happened to the *sex ratio* of the population? What do you suppose would be the consequences of a society where males significantly outnumber females? Do you think that research into methods of sex selection should be stopped by law? See if you can find another example of scientific research being questioned or stopped for social or moral reasons.

Repair of Genetic Defects. This is a fascinating branch of medicine that has been practiced for much longer than most people realize. The catch-phrase is "genetic engineering." The thought seems to frighten some people, but it really should not. Consider, for example, the large number of individuals who wear glasses. Many of them have a genetically determined visual problem. But we manipulate the environment and circumvent the defect. Even before the invention of glasses, surgeons repaired birth defects, most of which were and are genetically determined. Today, the surgical repair of such abnormalities as cleft lip and palate has reached a level of excellence that was undreamed of even a decade ago.

Other avenues are being explored today. Biochemical geneticists are trying to find ways to replace missing enzymes in persons with inherited metabolic diseases. This effort is complicated by the need to get the enzymes to the right target organ (often the brain) without triggering the body's immune defense systems. Someday, new techniques of gene splicing and cloning may allow us to isolate a specific human gene, attach the gene to some harmless virus, and use that virus to carry and insert the gene into the genetic makeup of the cells of a person who inherited an abnormality of that gene.

Some aspects of the three items listed above are technically impossible today. Some people argue that some or all of these would improve the human condition if they were developed. Others view some or all of them as dangerous. Discussion of these and other issues is sure to continue in the coming decades. Points of view may become polarized and debates may be heated. Whatever happens, we can be sure that scientists and citizens alike will be called on to make some very important and difficult choices.

HUMAN VARIABILITY

The next time you attend a concert, assembly, or sports event, notice the variability of the people in the crowd. People vary in many ways—the size, shape, and arrangement of body parts; shades of skin; hair styles; behavioral characteristics; and many more. No two people are exactly alike, even if they resemble each other closely. It is very easy to observe a remarkable degree of variability among people.

But we must also recognize that there are limits. Only a few people cannot see or hear. Those lacking an arm or a leg are in the minority. And none of your classmates weighs 10 kilograms or 1,000 kilograms. And none is a mermaid or a centaur!

What accounts for the wide range of human variability? How do we explain its limits? One way of explaining both variability and constraint is through the idea of natural selection. Variations that improved the chances of survival and reproduction in the human species tended to be maintained in the population. Such variations were adaptive in that they enhanced (or, at least, did not reduce) the ability of humans to deal with their environment. It appears that extreme divergence from the "usual," "average," or "normal" must have been nonadaptive—actually decreasing the chances of survival and reproduction. Thus, evolution theory helps us understand both the variations and the commonalities we see in people today.

The Long and Short of It

One need not go to a stadium

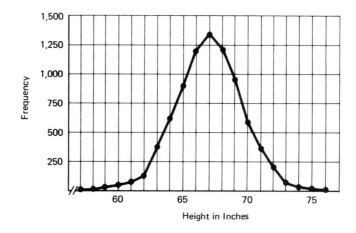

Figure 1. Frequency of heights of 8,585 adult men born in Great Britain during the nineteenth century*

or a concert hall to observe human variability. Did you know that any time thirty people are in a room together, the chances are very good that two of them will have the same birthday? It is also true that those thirty people will be able to notice both variation and constraints on some of their characteristics. One very obvious and easily measurable characteristic is height. Try the following exercise.

Measure the height of everyone in the group. Make a frequency distribution of the measurements, using intervals of perhaps 5 or 10 centimeters. Which interval occurs most frequently? Which occurs least frequently?

Now look at the frequency distribution of the heights of a very large group of people as shown in Figure 1. What is the shape of this distribution? How does this shape compare with the shape of the graph you made?

*Figures 1 and 4 from K. D. Hopkins and G. V. Glass, *Basic Statistics for the Behavioral Sciences,* Prentice Hall, Englewood Cliffs, N. J., 1978.

What is the average height of the individuals whose heights are represented in Figure 1? What is the average in your data?

Now you should be able to answer the following questions:

1. What factors explain the shape of the distributions in Figure 1 and in the graph you prepared?
2. What accounts for the variability expressed in these distributions?
3. What constrains this variability? In other words, what prevents people from being very, very tall or very, very short?

Causes of Variation

What accounts for human height, whether great or small? To begin with, the genetic blueprint sets the limits beyond which it is impossible to go. The genes are like a building plan. The plan tells the builder what materials to use and just how to use them. If the builder does just exactly what is called for, then the only limitation is the plan itself. But it's unlikely that everything will go just right. The builder may misread the blueprint. Some of the construction workers may make slight changes. Or the contractors may be unable to obtain the requisite materials and may resort to substitutes. So the building may diverge from the plan. It may even be imperfect or defective in some way. But it will always resemble what it was supposed to be—what the blueprint intended.

What caused the building to be constructed? The plan? The builder? The construction workers? The materials? The obvious answer is that a blueprint without a builder and materials is just a plan. And a builder who has workers and materials but no plan has nothing to construct. All the elements are necessary. None can do the job without the others.

In human development, the genes are the blueprint. The cellular machinery acts as the builder and the construction crew. The environment supplies the materials. Genes without materials are only a plan. Materials without genes are only chemicals. So it is idle to argue whether genes are more important than environmental conditions, or vice versa.

What are the genes that determine human height? They are many and various. They include those genes that govern the chemical processes in the cells of all the organs that contribute to the growth and development, especially of the skeleton—the spine, the skull, and the arms and legs. So height is a *polygenic* quality. Polygenic literally means "many genes." Many genes are involved in the determination of height.

These genes require a wide range of nutritional materials: minerals (especially calcium), phosphorus, sulfur, nitrogen-containing amino acids, and many vitamins. And the growth process needs, in addition, freedom from infection, adequate rest, exercise, and other favorable conditions. So human height is a multifactorial process. Multifactorial means "many factors." Many environmental factors influence growth.

If we all had exactly the same genes, and if we all had exactly the same nutrition and life experiences, we would all measure the same. But in height, as in other characteristics, there is great genetic variation among people. It should also be evident that there are substantial differences in nutrition, in freedom from infection, and in other aspects of life that bear on growth and development.

So, in summary, the height each of us achieves must be a product of the action of the genes we inherit from our parents, working in the conditions under which we live. It is a familial property; children will, on the average, achieve heights similar to those of their parents. And when we consider all the combinations that are possible when different genes work under different environmental conditions, it is no wonder that human heights vary so much.

It is worth noting that we don't have separate and discrete classes of tall people and short people. If we had such classes, a distribution of heights might look like Figure 2, but in fact we have already seen that the actual distribution looks like Figures 3 and 4. What do you think accounts for the differences in the distributions when Figure 2 is compared with the others?

The Limits of Normal

It might amuse you to ask yourself just where in the distribution tallness ends and shortness begins. How tall is "too tall"? How short is "too short"? How can one determine what is "normal" or "abnormal"? Suppose you were asked to choose two points in the distribution marking the limits of medium height. Which points would you choose? How might you explain or defend your choices?

Now look again at the distribution of heights in Figure 1 and ask yourself why so many people are represented by the measurements in the middle and so few by those at the ends. It must be that most of the genes available to human beings contribute to middle heights, while those contributing to the two ends are less frequent, and those for the extremes are rare. And the contribution from the conditions of

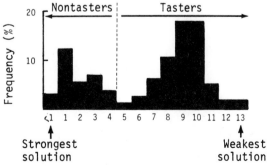

Figure 2. Distribution of the ability to taste phenylthiocarbamide (PTC)

51

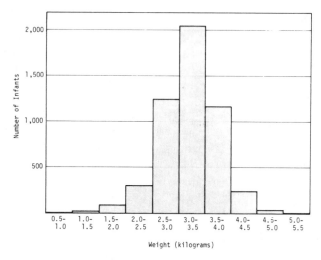

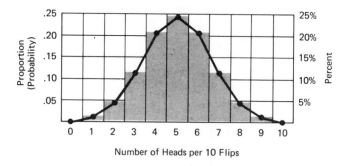

Figure 3. Birth weights of infants (surviving, normal, male and female combined)

Figure 4. Distribution of the number of heads in ten flips of a fair coin

Data from Leigh Van Valen and Gilbert W. Mellin, 1967, "Selection in Natural Populations: 7. New York Babies (Fetal Life Study)," *Ann. Hum. Genet.* 31:109-27.

life are likely to be distributed in the same way. Thus, the very tall and the very short stand out by virtue of their infrequency as well as their height. This rarity may itself add to the difficulty of living in a society organized by and for people of more average height. After all, doorways, beds, stairs, automobiles, and clothing are seldom created with people of extreme height in mind. But we must remember that tallness and shortness are not separate qualities, but only infrequent parts of a *continuous distribution* of measurements.

The Height of Individuals

So far we have suggested that variations in height among human beings are due to both genetic and environmental forces. So height is both a polygenic and a multifactorial property. But how can we answer the more specific question of what accounts for an individual person's height?

The answer is that for those near the middle of the curve—those that all would agree are normal in height—we cannot single out any particular gene and say that this one contributed so much or detracted by so much. Nor can we do any more for any environmental conditions, except possibly chronic infections or episodes of nutritional deprivation.

But the farther the height diverges from the average, the more likely we are to be able to point to some gene, some chromosomal abnormality, or some event as responsible for excessive or retarded growth. There are many defects of cartilage and bone that interfere with growth and cause short stature. Some are due to single genes including, for example, certain deficiencies of thyroid, adrenal, and pituitary hormones. Some chromosomal abnormalities are associated with slowed growth as well. At the opposite pole, unusually tall stature is characteristic of Marfan's syndrome and acromegaly (both single gene disorders) and of the XXY and XYY chromosomal constitutions.

As we have seen, infections and nutritional want can interfere with growth either because the deficiency of some vitamin or nutrient has been so complete as to stop growth no matter what the genotype, or because the deficiency has interfered with the growth of some genetically vulnerable people, while sparing others. As for excessive growth, no agent of the environment has been observed to produce it.

Many of the genes associated with alterations in growth produce other adverse phenotypic effects. It is easy to identify in families and, therefore, easy to establish modes of inheritance. But there are other, multifactorial causes of growth alteration for which neither the genes nor the environmental events or agents can be precisely described. So, the greater the divergence in height from the average, the more likely we are to be able to detect the genes and the environmental events responsible. But some cases, even at the extreme ends of the distribution, continue to defy our current knowledge. Nevertheless, we can be sure that genetic vulnerability is involved.

Summary

We've been dealing with some subtle but important principles in this section. They can be stated in the form of several propositions:

1. Neither genes nor environmental events are sufficient to produce any phenotype. Both are necessary.

2. A human being's height is determined by the way the genes he or she inherits work in the environment experienced during the period of growth.

3. Measurements of stature are continuously distributed so that it is not possible to decide just where medium height ends and "short" or "tall" stature begins.

4. Similarly, it is impossible to point to any points in the distribution beyond which stature is "abnormal." One aspect of such a designation is how tall or short people fit into society and what people think of them.

5. Extreme tallness and shortness are the exceptions rather than the rule, doubtless because of the relative infrequencies of the genes and environmental factors involved.

6. It is possible to describe the genes and environmental events involved only for the most divergent and most nonadaptive cases. This is a property not of the genes themselves, but of the limitations of the knowledge currently at our disposal.

DOES EVERYBODY NEED MILK?

Actually, most people in the world don't need milk, except as babies. They get sick if they drink it. Milk has a sugar in it called lactose. Most adults can't use this sugar, because they have very little of the intestinal enzyme, lactase. All human babies, like most baby mammals, make large quantities of this enzyme in the small intestine. Their bodies release the enzyme into the intestine. The enzyme breaks the chemical bond in lactose that binds glucose and galactose. The cells of the small intestine can absorb these two simple sugars, and the body can use them as energy.

If lactase is produced in very small quantities, as in most adult humans, the milk sugar, lactose, never gets used. It isn't broken down and absorbed by the cells of the intestinal wall. That doesn't seem as if it would be much of a problem. We might guess that only a little energy would be wasted, because cow's milk and human milk are only about 5% lactose, anyway. The body should be able to use all the other parts of milk, such as the

protein and fat.

However, lactose that isn't absorbed by the small intestine is used by bacteria that normally live in the intestine. When the bacteria use lactose as food, they release gas and other waste products. As a result, the person doesn't feel well. He or she has diarrhea, intestinal pains, and gas. Because of this reaction, most adult humans in the world don't drink milk or eat ice cream. If they use milk, it is in the form

of yogurt, cheese, or other sour milk products. Bacterial action in souring breaks down the lactose; thus the enzyme is not required for digesting sour milk products.

So, why do so many people in the U. S. drink milk? If people in the U. S. were "normal" human beings, we wouldn't see many ice cream stands. Supermarkets wouldn't sell so much milk. However, many people in this country continue to produce the enzyme, lactase, as adults. We still don't have a complete answer to why this happens. We do know that there is a geographic pattern that indicates who will be able to drink milk without getting sick.

As you can see, most people in Europe can drink milk. In addition, people in a few isolated locations in Africa and Asia also can drink milk. Apparently, the reason most people in the U. S. can drink milk throughout their lives is that they are of European descent. They are both genetically and culturally quite similar to people in Europe.

There are at least two possible explanations for why most people in the U. S. continue to

53

make lactase throughout their lives.

1. This trait may be an example of geographic genetic variability. There may be a genetic basis for this difference among populations living in different areas of the world. We know that there are other genetic differences among people in different locations. Ethnic groups are known to vary in their blood types. For example, Blood Type B is much more common in India than in England or the U. S.

2. Continued lactase production may have no genetic basis at all. It may be a matter of continual exposure to milk. If babies drink cow's milk or goat's milk after being weaned from their mother's milk, the enzyme, lactase, may just continue being produced. If this were true, we would see the ability to drink milk mostly in those areas where milk is available throughout a person's life.

These two explanations have been studied by testing individuals' tolerance to milk and by looking at family histories of this characteristic. Even if children keep drinking milk after weaning, many lose the ability to produce lactase in large quantities. As adults, these individuals cannot drink milk without getting sick.

In another study, in Finland, the ability to drink milk throughout life followed certain patterns in families. If neither parent could drink milk, none of the children produced large quantities of lactase as adults. If both parents could drink milk, almost all the children were able to do so as adults.

Occasionally, however, one of the children was not able to drink milk. If one parent could drink milk and the other could not, most of the children could drink it. But quite frequently,

one of the children would not be able to do so. This indicated that production of large quantities of lactase throughout life is genetically based and is inherited as a dominant trait.

This is a slightly different type of genetic trait, however. People who have the trait and those who don't have it produce lactase throughout their lives. But those with the trait produce it in much larger quantities. In these people, lactose never builds up to quantities large enough to cause the symptoms. Even people without the trait have the gene coding for lactase, but they don't have whatever genetic material is needed to regulate the production.

But why do people from some regions of the world produce large quantities of lactase throughout their lives? Why do these people have the regulatory gene that allows them to do so?

The fact that most other mammals do not produce quantities of lactase throughout their lives (the house cat is a notable exception) suggests that this regulatory gene occurred through mutation sometime in early human evolutionary

history. In some populations, the mutation must have helped individuals survive and reproduce. The mutant gene would have become more common in these populations, as it passed from parents to children. In areas where the gene provided the individual little or no help in survival and reproduction, it would not have become common.

Milk is a very nutritious food. If it is available when other foods are scarce, milk could mean the difference between survival and starvation. If this is the evolutionary advantage of lactase production, we would expect this trait only where domestic animals, such as cows or goats, have been kept for many, many generations. Tribes in Nigeria provide a test of this hypothesis. The Fulani tribe (see map) has kept herds of cattle throughout its history. Tribes to the south of the Fulani live where the tsetse fly also lives. Cattle can't live where tsetse flies are common. These southern tribes are not herders.

People of the Fulani tribe do

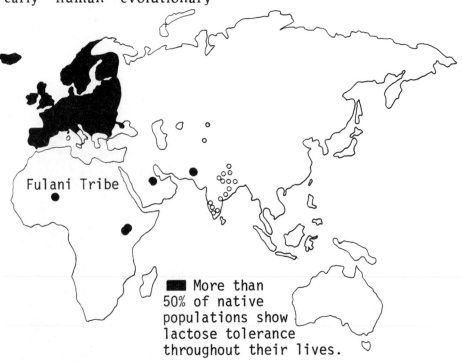

Fulani Tribe

■ More than 50% of native populations show lactose tolerance throughout their lives.

have the gene for continual lactase production. They can drink milk. Most people in the southern tribes do not have this gene. It appears that, in this example, where milk has been available for a long time, the gene is common. Where milk has not been available, the gene occurs only occasionally.

Do other data support the hypothesis that the ability to produce lactase as adults evolved primarily because milk drinkers had a more nutritious diet than nonmilk drinkers? If this were the case, we would expect that areas where milking of domestic animals is common would also be areas where the gene controlling continued lactase production by adults also would be common. On the one hand, where the gene is common, milk is available. However, even where the gene is uncommon (where most adults cannot digest milk), milking of domestic animals may occur. People in Northern Asia have milked domestic animals throughout history. But the gene regulating lactase production is not common. In these areas, the milk is used by "souring" it first. Thus, availability of milk is not always associated with the ability to use it as fresh milk.

Because of these problems with the first hypothesis, a second was proposed. In 1973, two scientists suggested that the sugar, lactose, can increase calcium absorption. Therefore, it is important in the process of making and repairing bones. Vitamin D does the same thing, but sunlight is required for the body to produce Vitamin D. Therefore, in areas where people are exposed to less sunlight, lactose may help prevent the bone disease, rickets. Northern Europe is such an area. It is also the area where most people can make large quantities of lactase. According to this hypothesis, the adaptive advantage is the prevention of rickets, and the ability to drink milk is coincidental.

This hypothesis has not yet been studied, and it also has problems. Why don't *all* North European people have the regulatory gene for lactase production if it's important in areas where exposure to sunlight is low?

We still don't know the answer to our question: Why is the regulatory gene for lactase production common in some human populations and rare in others?" Further research may provide some answer, too, but it probably will suggest further questions.

CHEMICALS AND MUTATION

More and more, substances in our environment are reported to be "mutagenic" or "carcinogenic." What do these words mean? How are we to make decisions about what we should eat and drink? Should new chemicals be tested before they are sold to the public? Who should test them? Who should regulate them?

Mutagens are physical or chemical agents known to cause mutations. Mutations are changes in single genes or in chromosome structure. The first strongly mutagenic chemical identified was mustard gas. During World War II, this gas was being manufactured secretly as a potential weapon. Some of the people who worked with mustard gas in England were exposed to it accidentally. They reacted in much the same way that individuals react to X rays. Tests on fruit flies showed that mustard gas was highly mutagenic. (In 1927, an American geneticist, Hermann Muller, had shown that X rays could cause mutations in fruit flies.)

Carcinogens are physical or chemical agents known to cause cancer. All carcinogens have been found to be mutagens, also. Why do we see this relationship between mutagens and carcinogens?

TYPE	CLASSIFICATION	RADIATION	SOURCES
Electromagnetic radiation	Nonmutagenic	Visible light	Sun, lamps
		Microwave and infrared radiation	Microwave oven, sun
		Radio and television	Broadcast media
	Mutagenic	*X rays	Dental and medical X-ray machines
		*Gamma rays (short wavelength)	Natural radioactivity
		Ultraviolet	Sun
Subatomic particles	Mutagenic	*Protons (hydrogen nuclei) *Neutrons	No significant radiation from any general sources
		*Electrons	Radioactivity Interaction of cosmic rays
		*Alpha-particles	Radioactivity

*Ionizing radiation

Cancer is a group of poorly understood diseases, but we do know that all cancers involve a group of cells dividing faster than cells normally divide. In fact, cancer is more common in tissues where cell division goes on throughout life, like skin and intestinal tissue. If a mutation occurs that increases the rate of cell division, cancerous growths can result. This is the hypothesis suggested by John Cairns for why chemicals that can cause mutations often also are found to be carcinogenic.

Can we tell in advance which chemicals are mutagenic? Can we pass laws to keep these chemicals out of our air, water, and food. Actually, this is more difficult than we might think, and the attempt to do this is expensive. The Environmental Protection Agency estimates that it takes a team of researchers, 300 mice, two to three years, and $300,000 to determine if a single new chemical *might* cause cancer in humans.

Testing new chemicals does help us make good predictions about whether or not these chemicals would be mutagenic in humans. However, even extensive testing cannot absolutely assure the safety of a new chemical. There are two main reasons for this.

First, it is difficult to predict how a chemical will be metabolized. Chemicals interact with the internal environment of the human body. It is probably a rare case when an ingested chemical passes through the digestive tract unchanged. If the organisms in the digestive tract or the cells lining the digestive tract absorb the chemical, it may be converted into some other, more dangerous or less dangerous, product. The human body provides a somewhat different environment, with different metabolic pathways, than do other organisms. For this reason, tests of potentially dangerous chemicals using bacteria or even mice may or may not show the same effect as would be seen in humans. Even if a culture of human body cells is used to test a chemical, there is no assurance that the results will be absolutely accurate. Processes in the human intestine might convert the chemical to some more or less dangerous substance before it ever got into a body cell. To be absolutely sure that a chemical is not mutagenic, all the chemical pathways by which that chemical could interact with the human body would have to be understood. But human beings are amazingly variable. A chemical might be mutagenic for some people but not others, just as lactose in milk is a problem for some people but not for others.

A second problem exists. Chemicals that seem perfectly harmless alone can be mutagenic in combination with other substances. Ideally, we need to know not only how a particular chemical works alone but also how it works in combination with other chemicals with which it might be found.

Even if we could predict the harmfulness of a new chemical accurately, it still might be diffi-cult to make decisions about what to do about new chemicals in the environment. A new pesticide may do more "good" than "harm," even if it has some dangerous effects. About 45,000 chemicals and several thousand pesticides are now in commercial use. Thousands of new chemicals are introduced each year. How should we regulate these? Should the producer have to show that the chemical is safe? Should chemicals already on the market be removed if they are found to be mutagenic?

Caffeine is an example. Caffeine is associated with higher mutation rates in fruit flies. It interferes with the normal repair processes that go on in the cell. Most breaks and gaps occurring during DNA replication are repaired by special enzyme systems. Caffeine interferes with this repair process.

Caffeine alone may be only a minor problem to most nonpregnant adults. But in combination with a mutagen that directly affects DNA, it can greatly increase mutation rates. The caffeine alone is of little danger, because few breaks and gaps appear in normal DNA replication. And the mutagen alone may be of only minor danger, because the damage it causes is repaired by the enzyme repair systems. Both together, however, can be very dangerous. The mutagen damages the DNA, and the caffeine inhibits normal repair. But how many people do you know who would stop drinking coffee even if they knew there was a 5% higher risk of their getting some form of cancer 20 years from now?

The serious threat posed by radiation to living tissues became apparent shortly after the discovery of radioactivity toward the end of the last century. Although the damage to body tissues became clear rather quickly, the effect of radioactivity on reproductive cells was not demonstrated until 1927. Following the explosion of the atomic bomb during World War II, extensive research was begun to study the effects of radiation on living things.

There are some natural and artificial sources of radiation. The natural sources of radiation include the sun, unstable elements in soil and rocks, and cosmic rays. Dental and medical X rays are the chief source of artificial radiation today. Although scientists do not know how radiation or chemical carcinogens induce cancer in normal cells, it is widely believed that the mutagenic ability of these agents is primarily responsible.

Radiation may be classified into two major categories, electromagnetic radiation and subatomic particles. The mutagenicity of electromagnetic radiation is determined by the amount of energy carried by each particle or photon. Speed and mass, as well as the electric charge, determine the mutagenicity of subatomic particles.

It is generally believed that point mutations and chromosome breaks are caused by highly energized photons or subatomic paticles striking an electron in an atom of DNA and bouncing it out of orbit. The ionized atom then reacts chemically to form a different DNA base. Mutations may also be induced indirectly by the reaction of DNA with ionized chemicals in close proximity to the DNA.

Since mutations may affect the rate of cell division, the carcinogenic potential of radiation has become a major concern. Although radiation from natural sources is unavoidable, preventive measures may reduce the levels of radiation from artificial sources. Medical and dental X rays are the major source of artificial radiation. The use of a lead shield as a simple precaution against radiation of the gonads significantly reduces the risk to reproductive cells. The avoidance of unnecessary or excessive use of X rays for medical or dental purposes also reduces the level of exposure and possible mutations.

Doctors are also concerned about exposing the developing embryo to X rays. Since most women don't realize they are pregnant until a few weeks after conception, radiologists (physicians who are specialists in X ray diagnosis) have adopted the "ten day rule." Except for emergency situations, X-ray studies on any woman in the child-bearing age group (13-50) should be carried out during the first ten days of the menstrual cycle (counting from the first day of menstrual bleeding), a time when she is unlikely to be pregnant. Protection of the fetus, however, is a *shared* responsibility between the parents and the health care system. Hospitals are busy places and a physician's life is often hectic. Any woman scheduled for an X ray who thinks there is *any* chance she might be pregnant should mention it to the doctor. On the other hand, it is important to recognize that X-ray techniques are important diagnostic procedures, and that recent data have indicated that the human fetus is remarkably resistant to damage from X rays.

We cannot accurately evaluate the immediate danger of low intensity chronic doses of radiation or low levels of chemical mutagens. We also have limited ability to predict the long-term effects. Although it is difficult to establish minimal thresholds for radiation, the evidence suggests that the risk of mutation is proportional to the dose. Thus, any level of exposure carries with it the risk of mutation. For these reasons, some people have suggested a vast reduction in new chemical production and a halt to the construction of nuclear facilities. What do you think?

IS MUTATION RATE HIGHER IN MALES THAN IN FEMALES?

Melissa Brian, age 11, couldn't wait until Jeremy came home from work. Her brother, who was 18, would finish high school in a couple of months. Then he planned to move to Omaha to work for their uncle who owned a hardware store there.

Melissa wasn't very happy about his leaving. Jeremy always got home about 4:30 every evening and her mother didn't get home till almost 6:00. It was nice to have company until Mom came home.

Ah, here he was. "Hello, Shrimp! How was school today?"

"I'm not a shrimp!" she retorted and thought to herself: Maybe it won't be so bad when he's gone. At least he won't be calling me names.

"Well, what did you learn in school today?"

Melissa was about to say, "Oh, nothing," as she usually did when he asked that question. But then she thought of a way to get back at him and replied, "Males have a higher mutation rate than females."

Jeremy looked at her quizzically, "Where did you get that idea?"

Melissa paused and looked embarrassed. She really hadn't learned it in class. She had been dawdling in the halls on her way to lunch, trying to catch a glimpse of their neighbor, Albert, who was in eighth grade. She had waited for quite a while outside the science room. And she had overheard some of Ms. Hanson's lecture. And now she wasn't sure she even remembered what she had heard.

"Well, where did you learn that?" asked Jeremy again.

"I heard Ms. Hanson say so," she said and told her brother how she heard it. "Anyway, I'm sure glad I'm not a boy!"

Jeremy looked at her, still puzzled, and said,

"What's so bad about being a boy?"

"I just told you," Melissa replied. "They're more likely to be weirdos."

"Oh, now I get it," said Jeremy. "You think a high mutation rate is like being a weirdo. Do you know what a mutation is?"

"Sure," said Melissa. "It's some weird monster with one eye or two heads or something."

Jeremy laughed. "Listen, shrimp, you've got this notion of mutation all mixed up. Do you want to know what a mutation *really* is?"

"Sure," replied Melissa.

"It's a change of the DNA. If you're talking about mutation rate, you're usually talking about a change in the DNA in a reproductive cell," replied Jeremy.

Melissa didn't answer. Jeremy realized she hadn't understood a word he had said. "Okay shrimp, do you know what DNA is?"

"No," Melissa replied.

"Do you know what a gene is?"

"No,... oh, wait, it's some creature who lives in bottles and gives people all their wishes."

Jeremy almost laughed, but he didn't when he saw that Melissa was serious and really wanted to understand. Instead he said, "No, that's a genie. Let's start somewhere else. Do you know what a cell is?"

"Sure," Melissa replied. "Cells are little things with black spots in 'em. They cause diseases like the flu, right?"

"Well, sort of," replied Jeremy. "Did you also know that your body is made up of cells, just like everybody else's body?"

Melissa looked surprised and replied, "Is that *really* true? We learned that in science class, and I even got all the questions right on the quiz. But I never really believed it. It didn't make sense to me. I figured that I felt fine, so how could I be full of those little things with black spots? Besides, I don't have black spots. I just figured it was one of those things we had to learn that doesn't make sense."

Jeremy looked a bit upset. How could Melissa have gotten so confused? Why hadn't she asked the teachers to explain when things didn't make sense to her? And worst of all, how was he to set her straight? If she didn't even believe her body was made up of cells, how could he ever explain to her what a mutation was? He finally said, "Well, Sis, this isn't going to be easy, but if you want to spend the evening talking about it, maybe we can get somewhere. What do you think?"

Melissa thought about it a minute. She really didn't care whether she understood mutations or not. But she was embarrassed to have failed so miserably in insulting her brother. Besides, he said he'd spend the whole evening talking with her about it. She really did like it when he did things with her. Finally she said, "Okay, lets talk about it. I really would like to know what a mutation is."

"Okay, we'll start the lesson after supper," said Jeremy. That will give me time to figure out how to explain this, Jeremy thought to himself.

After dinner, Jeremy and Melissa went into the front room with Jeremy's textbook in advanced biology.

"Okay," said Jeremy. "Now I've thought about it, and I think we have more than one lesson here. It will probably take two or three nights to get it all in. Okay?"

"All right," Melissa replied. "I'll try."

Jeremy spent the first evening explaining that cells are not just little creatures that make people sick. He told her that her whole body was made of different types of cells.

He spent the second evening talking about the "black spots" in cells. He explained some of the parts of the cell and talked about the nucleus with the chromosomes. He explained what DNA was and tried hard to help Melissa develop an idea of what a gene is. The pictures of cells and chromosomes and DNA in his biology text were a big help. But he had to remind her continually that all those things were going on in her own body. Many chemical reactions were going on in each cell of her body to keep her alive. And those processes were controlled by genes (not genies). Melissa was really becoming interested. After doing the dishes on the third night, they got back to mutations.

"Well, tonight's the night, isn't it?" asked Melissa.

"Sure is," replied Jeremy. "We finally get back to mutations. Now that you believe in cells and know something about how cells work and what genes do, mutations will be easy."

"Good."

"Now, you know that cells divide to make two cells that are identical copies of the first. That's important, because the genetic material regulates the chemical processes that go on in cells. If the new cells didn't have the same genetic material as the old one, some of the important chemical processes that keep you alive might not happen. Remember, we talked about each gene being like a recipe card with specific directions for how to make something."

"Yes, and you said a gene *acted* like a recipe card but it didn't look like one, right?" answered Melissa.

"You got it! And remember how we talked about a whole group of recipes that make up a big meal, some for hors d'oeuvres, one for salad, one for salad dressing, and so on?"

"Yes."

"Now let's say we have a 46-meal menu plan, with one box of recipes for each meal. And let's say an identical group of recipe boxes is made for each new cell. So, each new cell will be able to cook the same 46 meals, so to speak. Now what would happen if the 46 boxes of recipes weren't duplicated quite the same for each new cell?" asked Jeremy.

"Well, I suppose it would depend on what sort of change was made in the 46 boxes of recipes," replied Melissa. "If they forgot a whole recipe box, the menu would miss a meal. If they lost one recipe in a meal, they would be smaller. If they just changed one line of a recipe, it might not make much difference. For example, if I put two cups of chocolate chips in the batter instead of one, the cookies might be even better."

"What if you put the wrong amount of baking soda in them?"

"They wouldn't be very good, and no one would eat them."

"Okay, we are finally there, Melissa. Those same sorts of changes can occur in DNA when new cells are made. The new cells may not be quite the same as the old one. A change in the genetic material is a mutation. There are two major types of mutations. The first type affects chromosomes. One or more chromosomes may be added—like adding an additional copy of one or more of the recipe boxes. One or more chromosomes may be deleted—like subtracting a box of recipes. Pieces of chromosomes might get lost or mixed up—like the recipes in one box might get mixed up with those from another, so the dessert intended for one meal might go with another. The second type of mutation is gene mutation. That is like changing part of a single recipe. For example, substituting one molecule for another on the DNA chain may be like substituting salt for baking soda in chocolate chip cookies. Do you understand what a mutation is now, Melissa?"

"I think so, Jeremy. It's not some scary creature at all. It's just a change in the genetic material. There are mutations that affect chromosomes and there are those that affect genes. And if 46 boxes of recipes are copied each time a new cell is made, I would guess there are lots of mutations. I know, when I try to copy something exactly, I often make a mistake, at least in spelling or something."

"That's what is so amazing, Melissa. The cell seems to be able to make a perfect copy of its genetic material for each new cell. Once in a while there is a mistake but not very often."

"How often," Melissa asked.

"Before I answer that, you have to think about one other thing. You have two major kinds of cells

in your body. Most of them are somatic cells—regular body cells—like blood, muscle, and nerve cells. The other kind of cells are reproductive cells—they give rise to eggs in females and sperm cells in males. Now, if you have a genetic change in one of your somatic cells—a cell in the skin of your little finger, for example—that won't affect your children. But a mutation in your reproductive cells will.

"When people on television or in newspapers talk about mutation rates, or how often mutations occur, they are usually interested in this second kind. They want to know how often an offspring has genetic material different from its parents—that is, how often a fertilized egg has a mutation in it."

"Is that what Ms. Hanson was talking about the other day?" Melissa asked.

"I think so," Jeremy replied.

"Okay, now, can you tell me how often the mutations that can affect offspring actually happen?"

"Geneticists estimated mutation rates for both chromosomal and gene mutations. Chromosomal mutations may be quite common. In fact, it has been estimated that about half the human eggs have some chromosomal mutation. Most of these eggs don't get fertilized or, if they do get fertilized, the embryos do not develop long enough for the woman to realize she's pregnant. However, about 0.6% of live births show some chromosomal mutation. Some of these cause health problems for the person with the mutation. Some have little effect. You know Henry Parkin's little boy? He has Down syndrome. This disorder is due to an extra 21st chromosome."

"Oh, so that's due to a mutation?"

"Yes it is. The other sort of mutation, a gene mutation, is somewhat less common. Human geneticists have estimated that for most genes, less than one person in every million has a recognizable mutation. Some genes show higher mutation rates. For ample, a gene mutation that results in neurofibromatosis occurs in from 50 to 100 individuals out of every million.

"Do I have a gene mutation?" asked Melissa.

"Probably," replied Jeremy. "In fact, if you are just asking how many misprints or copying mistakes occur in everybody's DNA, geneticists do not have a very good estimate, but there may be as many as 35. But many of these probably don't have any effect. Just like when you are hand-copying a recipe from the newspaper for Mom, you may write 'suga,' but she knows you mean 'sugar,' and the recipe is followed as if you hadn't made a mistake."

Melissa interrupted, "But mom caught me the

other day when I wrote '1 tbsp. salt' instead of '1 tsp. salt.' If she hadn't noticed, we would have been putting in three times as much salt as it called for. That pudding wouldn't have tasted very good."

"Yes, that's the sort of error that may lead to a noticeable problem for the person with the mutation."

"Well, I think I have a lot better idea of what mutations are. And I realize they aren't some monster. In fact, some mutations must improve the chemical processes that go on in the body."

Jeremy answered, "You're right, Sis. I think you really do understand. But, here again, think about a very carefully worked out recipe for cookies. Usually, any random error made in copying the recipe would not improve it. If it didn't make the cookies worse, it would at least make the recipe harder to read. Only very rarely will a random error in copying result in a better product. So you're right, some gene mutations must improve the chemical processes that go on in the body, but most do not."

"Now, why did Ms. Hanson say males have higher mutation rates than females?" Melissa asked.

"I wondered about that myself, Sis. In fact, I just figured you had remembered it wrong, because it didn't say anything like that in my advanced biology text. I finally asked Mr. Tsumura if that made any sense to him. He wasn't sure what Ms. Hanson had in mind. But he did tell me there was some evidence for higher gene mutation rates in males than in females.

"Also, the number of gene mutations increases with the age of the father. One explanation has to do with the formation of eggs and sperm. The male continues to produce those cells that give rise to sperm from puberty throughout his life. On the other hand, the female produces, *before birth*, all the cells that will later divide and form eggs. Because of this difference, the sperm of a 28-year-old man are estimated to be the result of about 380 cell divisions. The eggs of a 28-year-old female are estimated to be the result of only 24 divisions. Every time a cell divides, the genetic material must be replicated. Errors—mutations—can occur in this replication process. The more times replication occurs, the more mutations are expected to occur. As males age, more cell divisions occur in the production of sperm. This may explain why the gene mutation rate for hemophilia and other specific genes increases with the age of the father.

"At any rate, you probably did remember correctly what Ms. Hanson said. The mutation rate in males does appear to be higher than the rate for females. That is, if you're talking about gene mutation rate. On the other hand, Mr. Tsumura said there is some evidence, though not conclusive, that the chromosomal mutation rate is higher in females than in males. Now I understand why they think Queen Victoria inherited the gene for hemophilia from her father. He didn't have the disease, but he was 52 when she was conceived. Geneticists think the mutation occurred in a testicular cell and was passed on through the sperm to Queen Victoria."

"You're a good teacher, Jeremy," replied Melissa. "I think you've set me straight about this notion of mutation. But now I'm tired. It's past my bedtime. Good night."

Jeremy replied, "Good night, Shrimp! Sweet dreams!" and winked at her. She headed up the stairs. And Jeremy thought to himself how much he would miss her after he moved to Omaha.

THE FIRST ENVIRONMENT: IS IT SAFE?

The first nine months of human life are spent in a sophisticated environment that carries out life functions including breathing, digestion, secretion, elimination, and filtration (Figure 1). This system functions from the time of implantation of the fertilized egg in the uterus up to the time of birth. The development of the fertilized egg is under genetic control. Genes also program the changes that occur in the mother's body during pregnancy.

Pregnancy

When sperm from a male are deposited in the vagina of a female, they quickly swim from the vagina, through the uterus, into the Fallopian tubes where fertilization occurs. During fertilization, the nucleus of a sperm penetrates the egg and fuses with its nucleus. If the egg is not fertilized, it disintegrates.

The fertilized egg, the zygote, begins dividing shortly after fertilization. One cell divides into two, then four, then eight, and so on, until a ball composed of 16 cells is formed. This ball, called the morula, enters the uterine cavity (Figure 2) after three days. By the fourth day, the morula changes into a hollow ball called a blastocyst, which is filled with fluid. One area of the blastocyst, the blastoderm, appears as a clump of cells on one side of the mass; it will later develop into the embryo. The remaining cells will develop into membranes that

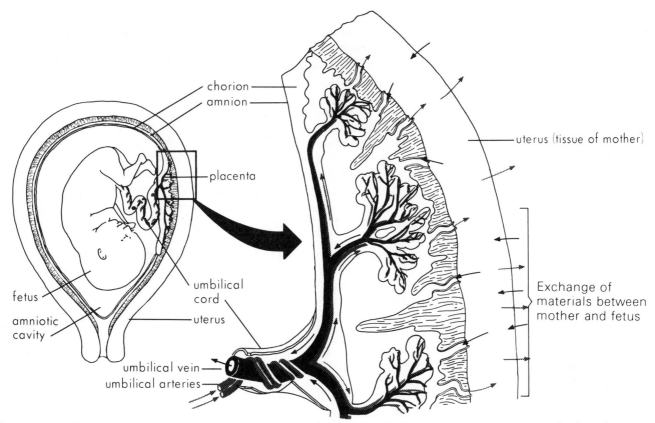

chorion
amnion
uterus (tissue of mother)
placenta
fetus
amniotic cavity
umbilical cord
uterus
Exchange of materials between mother and fetus
umbilical vein
umbilical arteries

Figure 1.   The developing fetus receives nourishment and eliminates waste through the placenta.

protect, nourish, and support the embryo. These membranes are the allantois, chorion, and amnion (Figure 2).

The chorion is the outermost embryonic membrane. Following attachment of the embryo to the inner uterine wall, fingerlike projections from the chorion grow into the thick uterine lining. Blood-filled cavities gradually develop around these projections. The tissues of the uterine wall and the chorion form the placenta. In the placenta, fetal and maternal blood flow close together but usually do not mix. Cell membranes separate the mother's blood from the fetal blood. The amnion lies within the chorion and completely surrounds the developing embryo. It is filled with amniotic fluid that bathes the embryo and protects it from shock. It also prevents adhesion of the embryonic body. It

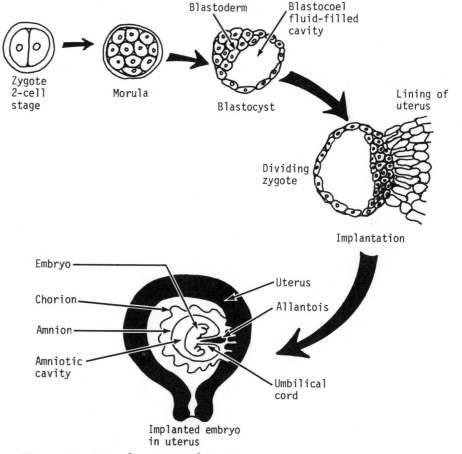

Blastoderm
Blastocoel fluid-filled cavity
Zygote 2-cell stage
Morula
Blastocyst
Lining of uterus
Dividing zygote
Implantation
Embryo
Chorion
Amnion
Amniotic cavity
Uterus
Allantois
Umbilical cord
Implanted embryo in uterus

Figure 2.   Development of zygote

61

facilitates movement and normal symmetrical development.

After about two days in the uterus, the blastocyst begins to imbed itself in the spongy uterine lining. This process, which is called implantation, continues through the second week of development.

During the third week, neural folds become visible along the back of the embryo. These folds gradually fuse along their entire length to form the neural tube, which later develops into the brain and spinal cord. Somites, small cellular blocks, form on each side of the embryo. They eventually form dermal, skeletal, and muscular tissues.

The third week is also marked by the development of a simple cardiovascular system that links the embryo with the placenta. The placenta provides oxygen and removes waste carbon dioxide. The placenta does a great deal more.

---

1. It separates the baby's and the mother's circulatory systems. Any material that passes between the mother and the baby is "screened" by the placenta.

2. The placenta produces hormones and controls the complex processes of fetal development.

3. It controls immunological processes so that the fetus is not rejected by the mother as "foreign protein."

4. The placenta provides the baby with antibodies from the mother. These antibodies, called immunoglobins, protect babies against disease until their own immune systems begin to function.

By the fourth week, the neural tube becomes closed over most of its length; arm and leg buds are visible; and eye bumps are apparent. Most of the major organ systems have started to develop by the seventh week. The legs and arms, with well-formed toes and fingers, are clearly visible. If the embryo is exposed to viruses, chemicals, or ionizing radiation during this time, major morphological abnormalities may result.

Development after the twelfth week involves mainly growth and formation of tissues and organs. There is also a greater degree of differentiation. The embryo is referred to as a fetus from this stage of development until the time of birth.

As the fetus continues to grow and differentiate, the placenta continues to supply it with oxygen and to remove waste carbon dioxide. One might think that, with a fantastic organ like the placenta, the fetus would be perfectly safe from anything that the mother eats, drinks, or encounters. Actually, the first environment is incredibly safe and only occasionally does the placenta fail to screen out teratogenic agents. Teratogens interfere with development and cause birth defects (Figure 3). Perhaps the most famous teratogen is thalidomide. This is the tranquilizer that caused birth defects in England and other European countries in the 1960s.

One of the more common birth defects caused by chemicals is fetal alcohol syndrome or FAS. FAS was first detected in children whose mothers were heavy drinkers. These children were born with abnormalities of the head and face, heart defects, mental deficiency, and joint and limb prob-

lems. The children are slow to learn and grow. Not all children of alcoholic women exhibit all of the characteristics of FAS, but all suffer some ill effects. Scientists are also studying the possible genetic effect of an alcoholic father.

According to recent research, fetal alcohol effects, or FAE, may result from a pregnant woman's moderate drinking in the same way fetal alcohol syndrome can be caused by heavy drinking. Fetal alcohol effects cover a range of physical and mental problems in the newborn rather than the full FAS. The effects of "social" drinking are unknown. Most doctors feel that an occasional drink is probably harmless but that frequent moderate drinking should be avoided.

Many other substances can cause birth defects. The greatest risk of injury to the unborn child from exposure to drugs occurs during the first three months of pregnancy. The critical period of major organ development in the embryo occurs from the fourth through the eighth weeks. Drugs acting adversely on the embryo during this period may cause permanent birth defects. For this reason, the use of any drug during early pregnancy must be considered hazardous (Figure 3).

Fortunately, there are preventive measures that can be taken to make the fetal environment safe. Women should be vaccinated against rubella *before* pregnancy. Do you know why? Mothers should avoid alcoholic beverages and "over-the-counter" drugs. Cigarettes, which are associated with low birth weight in infants, are to be avoided also. Only those medicines prescribed by a doc-

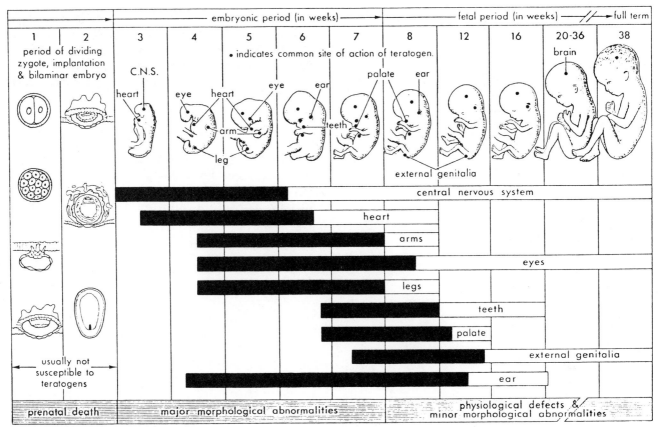

(Source: Keith L. Moore, *The Developing Human*, W. B. Saunders, 1973.
Figure 3.

tor should be used. And women who may be pregnant should let their doctors know before medical X rays are taken.

One last note. The embryo and developing fetus can be affected by substances that are missing from the mother's body as well as by those that are there. Normal fetal growth and development depend on the health of the mother. Good nutrition is especially important. Without adequate amounts of protein, fat, carbohydrates, vitamins, minerals, and water each day, the fetus may not grow properly. Eating the right foods is always important, especially during pregnancy. With a little care and planning, every pregnant woman can make wise decisions to ensure that the first environment is both safe and healthy.

DIFFERENT BUT EQUAL: SEX DETERMINATION AND SEX DIFFERENTIATION IN HUMANS

"Biologically different, but equal before the law." This phrase has only recently begun to receive any acceptance in public opinion—much less in legislatures and courts—in this country and some others. In many societies today, as in the past, men and women are not seen as equal. A long history of social, cultural, and religious thought has relegated women to an inferior status in many parts of the world. There are many reasons for the inequality, some of them related to the poor knowledge of reproduction that primitive societies had. Long ago, people thought that procreation came about through some magic that only women possessed. Males were thought to be unnecessary and uninvolved. Later on, the opposite view emerged—that women were merely vessels for bearing a man's child. In the early nineteenth century, it was believed that the male played the most important role in reproduction. A perfectly formed, minute human being was thought to be inside every sperm cell (Figure 1).

The picture is different today, if not culturally, at least in what the biological sciences can tell us. The discovery of the mammalian ovum (egg) by

Figure 1

von Baer in 1827 led to the recognition of the equally important roles of both sexes in reproduction. The modern insight that some individual women can equal or exceed the physical strength of most men—and that women are potentially superior to men in such sports as long-distance running—has challenged the traditional view. In addition, on the average, women live longer, have slightly higher I. Q.'s, and have lower rates of accident and illness.

Sex Determination and Sex Differentiation

Humans, like all mammals, have two different sexes. Females have two X chromosomes. Males have one X and one Y. Sex is determined in a Mendelian pattern of inheritance. Mating of XX and XY yields offspring in a ratio of 1/2 XX to 1/2 XY. (The behavior of the chromosomes during meiosis is responsible for this ratio. Can you explain how?)

Sex determination refers to all of those processes that begin in the parents with meiosis and formation of reproductive cells. It proceeds to fertilization, development of the embryo—including the initial formation of ovaries or testes. The ovaries and testes are called gonads. Gonads produce the reproductive cells—either eggs or sperm. The end of sex determination is the formation of the organs that produce reproductive cells.

All events after the formation of gonads are called sex differentiation. This includes the completion of gonadal development, the differentiation of internal and external genitalia, and the descent of the testes in males. Sex differentiation also includes puberty and adult sexual function leading to the production of reproductive cells, fertilization, pregnancy, delivery, and breast-feeding.

After birth, individuals assume gender identities and gender roles. This means that they assume certain behavior and activities that the society considers appropriate for males and females.

Sex Determination

The Y Chromosome. In simplest terms, sex determination can be viewed as the result of "maleness" in the presence of a Y chromosome and "femaleness" in its absence. The power of male sex determination in the Y is so strong that, even in the presence of four X chromosomes (in rare 49, XXXXY individuals), clear and unambiguous male sex determination results. The Y is one of the smallest chromosomes. It contains only about 1% of the genetic material in the sperm cell.

The Y chromosome is very different from the X, but is like it in two important ways:

1. At meiosis, the Y chromosome pairs—or synapses—with the X. But the pairing is not the same as the pairing of the autosomes. The X and Y chromosomes pair end to end. This pairing is responsible for rather frequent cases of nondisjunction leading to conception of XYY and XXY, individuals.

2. The Y in males must act like the second X in females, providing additional, necessary genetic information. Evidence for this fact comes from observations of individuals who have only one X chromosome. In humans, the 45, X chromosome constitution is lethal before birth 98% to 99% of the time. The few individuals who are born with this condition, which is called Turner syndrome, usually are short. They also have major and minor malformations of the kidney, heart, and other organs. They are sterile. They fail to develop secondary sexual characteristics (breasts and pubic hair). Thus, without the second X chromosome, sexual development is abnormal. The Y, like the X, must provide genetic information that is essential to normal sexual development.

The length of the Y chromosome varies. Much of it may be missing without any apparent harmful effect on development. Through the examination of many branches of a family, inheritance of a small Y has been traced over several hundred years.

Reproductive Cells. One of the most important events in the early development of the embryo is the separation of two types of cells—the beginning reproductive cells and the rest of the body (somatic) cells. Human reproductive cells arise outside the embryonic gonad and migrate into it. The migrating cells look like large, pale amebas. They travel with pseudopods to the embryonic gonadal tissue. These migrating cells are thought to be necessary for the differentiation of male or female reproductive organs and external genitalia.

The H-Y Antigen. Whether male or female gonads develop is determined by the somatic cells. The somatic cells cause male development by producing a Y chromosomal protein called the H-Y (*Human Y*) antigen. Production of the H-Y antigen is thought to be controlled by a gene on the Y chromosome. Absence of H-Y antigen and presence of two X chromosomes (in 46 XX individuals) leads to the development of ovaries. If a Y chromosome is added (as in 47 XXY individuals) testes develop.

Sex Differentiation

In 1947, Dr. Alfred Jost of Paris reported the results of experiments he had performed on rabbit embryos. The experiments were difficult to perform, but the results revolutionized our thinking about sex differentiation in mammals. Jost found that if he removed the gonads from male and female embryos *before* development of internal and external genitalia had begun, *all* surviving fetuses were born with female internal and external genitalia. How is this explained?

Early in development, male and female embryos have identical internal and external genitalia. It is impossible to tell them apart. At this time, both sexes have *both* sets of internal genitalia. But as development progresses, males and females develop differently. Testes are required for the development of normal male external genitalia. In the absence of testes, the external genitalia of a normal female develop. Thus, a substance secreted by the testes is required to induce the development of normal male external genitalia. Female external genitalia are the "natural, uninduced" state of nature.

Gender Identity and Gender Role.

The view one has of one's sex is called gender identity. It makes one say with conviction, "I am a boy," or "I am a girl." The way in which one acts out this conviction is called gender role. This refers to all aspects of one's behavior. It is not restricted to sexual activities but includes everything one does consciously and unconsciously to indicate one's gender.

It is generally accepted that gender identity is primarily culturally acquired—that is, taught by parents. Parents act on a clear-cut conviction of their child's sex and what they believe to be the appropriate way for the child to behave, play, dress, and interact with other children. By age two years, gender identity is considered to be firmly fixed. Because gender identity is learned, under rare circumstances (so-called XY females and XX males), it may be contrary to one's genetic sex. Though generally fixed by a very early age, gender identity and gender role may sometimes change in later life.

On the other hand, some evidence suggests that there may be a greater genetic influence on gender identity than we used to think. For example, there can be an inherited defect of metabolism in the fetal adrenal gland that causes excess production of male sex hormones. Members of either sex can be affected. The condition is usually diagnosed and treated at or shortly before birth. The sex hormone levels promptly drop to normal. However, follow-up studies of a group of affected females have shown that, on the average, they tended to exhibit more male-associated behavior than a control group of females, even though they had always been identified clearly as girls. They were described as "tomboys," participated more frequently in the so-called, "male games," and were more career-oriented than family-oriented.

Of course, studies of this type can never answer the often-asked question, "Which is more important—genetics or environment?" The fact of the matter is that both are important and that both contribute to the development of individuals—whether tall or short, heavy or thin, female or male. Consider, for example, the fact

		MALE	FEMALE
		Testes	Ovaries
Internal Genitalia		Epididymis Vas deferens Seminal vesicles Ejaculatory duct Prostate gland Prostatic urethra	Fallopian tubes Uterus Upper part of vagina
External Genitalia		Penis Penile urethra Scrotum	Lower vagina Clitoris Labia minora Labia majora

that males tend to score higher than females on tests of reading maps and solving puzzles. Females tend to score higher than males on tests of verbal communication skills. Do physical and chemical characteristics play a part in this trend? What about cultural experiences, parental encouragement, and early childhood learning? And what about variation from one individual to the next?

From the biological sciences, one can learn a great deal about sex chromosomes, gonads, genitalia, and sex hormones. From the social sciences, one can derive knowledge of the effects of learning and other cultural influences on one's behavior and eventual role in society. But the question of equality under the law is not a biological question. No amount of scientific data can decide for us whether we should provide equality of opportunity in education, work, and other areas of life to women and men alike. These decisions must be made by individuals, groups, nations, and all people in terms of their values and beliefs about right and wrong.

INTELLIGENCE, I.Q., AND GENETICS

Whatever intelligence is, it is valued highly in our culture. Therefore, information about who is of high or low intelligence affects how people are treated in our society. What is intelligence? Here is one example:

Some people walk into a situation in which others are floundering, appraise it, and select an effective course of action. If they do such a thing only once, we may say they are lucky. If they can do it only in certain situations, we may say they have a special knack or talent. But what if they do it many times, in many situations for which their prior knowledge is no greater than yours or mine? If this happens, we say they are intelligent.

This seems to be the core, commonsense meaning of the term, intelligence. We may paraphrase it as "general problem-solving ability," if we recognize that the "problem" comprises a very wide range of situations, and that we infer abilities only from words or deeds. Others consider intelligence to be the ability to *learn* problem-solving skills.

There is no reliable test for such all-around problem-solving ability, if such an ability exists. Most people are good at solving certain kinds of problems and not very good at solving others. Whatever people think of as intelligence, it is a complex combination of abilities.

What Is I. Q.?

I. Q. is not the same as intelligence. It is an attempt to measure intelligence, but there is no good way to do that. I. Q., or intelligence quotient, is a standardized score on certain tests. The tests—and there are several available—include many items designed to measure a person's ability to recognize and solve certain spatial, verbal, and mathematical problems.

We know there is cultural bias in the I. Q. tests. A test developed with one cultural group should not be used for another. For example, the tests in the United States, all of which were developed for English-speaking whites, should not be used without modification for other groups, such as Spanish-speaking Americans.

To get an I. Q. number, a standardized score is used to allow easy comparison between scores. A person with an I. Q. score of 100, got the median number of correct answers. This means that about 50% of the population on which the test was developed got higher scores, and about 50% got lower scores. A person with an I. Q. score of 115 scored higher than about 84% of the population on which the test was developed.

What influences a person's performance on an I. Q. test? We know that the score is partly a matter of the experiences a person has had. Is it also influenced by the genetic make-up of that person? We know that you don't inherit your I. Q. score in the same way you inherit your blood type. We know there is no single gene or pair of genes that controls whether you get a score of 95 or 105 on an I. Q. test. Of course, genes are involved in very basic ways, for they control body development, including the brain, from a fertilized egg to full maturity. They also are involved in maintaining all the chemical processes that keep you alive.

Why does it matter whether the score on an I. Q. test is determined more by genes or more by environment? In the best of all possible worlds, it would not matter at all. People would have unlimited educational opportunities, and everyone would learn to the best of his or her abilities. However, in our less-than-perfect world, the answer can influence how individuals and groups of people are treated. It also can influence policy decisions made by governments or schools. Answers to questions of how best to spend the education budget rest on judgments about whether certain programs will "do any good."

In 1969, Arthur Jensen shocked a civil-rights-conscious America when he argued that average differences in I. Q. between blacks and whites in the United States are mostly due to inborn factors. Jensen's supporters maintained that special education programs like Head Start are, therefore, useless. In 1972, William Shockley suggested that people with I. Q. scores below 100 be encouraged to become sterilized so as to not pass on the genes responsible for the low I. Q. scores. As you might imagine, both men have been strongly criticized both for their methods of investigation and for their conclusions.

Genes and I. Q.

What is the evidence that genes have anything to do with I. Q. scores? Because I. Q. does not show simple dominant or recessive patterns, we know it is not controlled by one pair of genes.

Complex characteristics, like height, weight, or the ability to take an I. Q. test are heavily influenced by the environment, as well as by many genes. A method to estimate the amount of influence genes have on these kinds of traits, a measure called heritability, has been developed. Heritability is the percentage of the variation in a population that is *not* due to environmental factors. If all the variation in I. Q. in a population were due to genetic factors, then the heritability would be 1.0 or 100%. If all the variability in a population were due to environmental factors, the heritability would be 0.0 or 0%.

Research on twins has provided one way of estimating the heritability of I. Q. test-taking skills. Identical twins, (monozygotic twins) are identical genetically. Their I. Q. scores are also more similar than are the scores for individuals who are less closely related. Heritability measures calculated from twin studies vary, but may be as high as 0.8. This means that only 20% of the variation is assigned to environmental factors.

A study in 1964 found that when identical twins were raised in different families the average difference in I. Q. scores was eight points. When identical twins were raised in the same family, the average difference was six points. This suggests that the difference in environments has some effect, although perhaps slight.

New studies have been done that estimate

heritability from data on extended families, including identical twins and their children. Here, heritability of I. Q. scores has been estimated to be about 50%, indicating equal influence of genetic and environmental factors.

Problems of Determining Heritability

There are two major problems with trying to estimate genetic influence with measures of heritability using identical twins. First, it is difficult to separate genetic from environmental factors. Identical twins have almost identical environments if they grow up together. Even when they are separated and live in different homes, their environments probably are quite similar. Adoption agencies often try to place children with foster or adoptive parents who meet certain predetermined standards of age, income, educational background, and so on. This may account for some of the similarity among the I. Q. scores of identical twins. The extended-family technique suffers the same problem, because identical twins are likely to provide their children with similar environments. This makes it difficult to separate completely all of the genetic and environmental factors.

A second problem is that heritability measures cannot be applied to any population that is different from the one used to get the heritability estimates. If heritability of I. Q. scores is estimated to be 50% in a population of white U. S. citizens with better than average incomes, this heritability estimate cannot be applied to any other population of humans, such as Oriental Americans, white U.S. citizens with a lower-than-average income, or the entire human population.

To understand this second problem better, consider height as an example. Suppose we wanted to estimate the heritability of height from a population of well-fed U. S. citizens. The heritability estimate would be high, because the environment would be similar for all individuals. Suppose, however, we included both well-fed and undernourished people in our sample population. In this sample, the measure of heritability would be much lower, because environmental differences would be included.

In the same way, if heritability of I. Q. were measured for a population in which all individuals have very similar environments, the estimate of heritability would be higher than if the sample included people living in a wide range of enviroments. This may explain why samples that include only white individuals with above-average incomes show high heritability, and studies using samples that include individuals from lower-income families show lower estimates of heritability of I. Q.

It also follows that differences in average I. Q. between populations cannot be attributed to genetic differences between the two populations. Blacks in the United States, on the average, score somewhat lower on I. Q. tests than do whites. But if the tests had been developed for blacks, whites probably would score lower. In summary, there is no evidence that any ethnic group is, on the average, any more intelligent than another ethnic group.

What does the available evidence suggest about genetic variability of intelligence in the normal range? In their textbook on human genetics, published in 1979, Vogel and Motulsky reply: "The answer is short: very little." They point out that some experts have reviewed the evidence and have suggested that genetic variability does not affect I. Q. performance at all. Other authors interpret the evidence as indicating that heritability may actually be as high as the 0.8 value reported earlier. Vogel and Motulsky conclude: "Most scientists, if asked for an educated guess, will probably settle on values somewhere in-between, more because they dislike extreme points of view than because of a strong conviction in favor of any positive evidence."[1]

[1]Vogel, F. and A. G. Motulsky. 1979. *Human Genetics: Problems and Approaches.* New York, Springer-Verlag. p. 491-92.

PRENATAL DIAGNOSIS

Genetic counseling began centuries before it entered the practice of medicine. Jewish scholars, although having no idea about the existence of chromosomes or genes, recognized the pattern of inheritance of hemophilia. They wrote that if a male infant bled severely after circumcision, later sons born to that mother should not be circumcised. They even noted that male cousins on the mother's side might also be "bleeders" and should not be circumcised. This is an example of genetic counseling from Old Testament times.

In spite of this early "genetic medicine," physicians paid little attention to genetics, primarily because they were unaware of how the complex interactions between genes and environment determine health. Archibald Garrod proposed, in 1909, that alkaptonuria is an inborn error of metabolism. He suggested an enzyme deficiency as the cause and speculated that the deficiency is inherited as an autosomal recessive. But Garrod was ahead of his time for, throughout the first half of the twentieth century, "genetic diseases" continued to be viewed as rare, untreatable curiosities. Then, beginning with Watson and Crick in 1953, research began to reveal relationships between disease and chromosomal or molecular differences in people. Much of this research involved disorders that are evident at birth or even before birth.

In 1956 Tijo and Levan devised a technique for looking at human chromosomes in white blood cells. Three years later, a French physician, Jerome Lejeune, reported an extra chromosome 21 in patients with Down syndrome.

These and other findings set the stage for the development of ways of detecting disorders before birth. The first instance of prenatal diagnosis was reported by Nadler and Gerbie in 1968. A genetic disorder had been detected while the fetus was still in its mother's uterus and the pregnancy was less than halfway along. The procedure that was used to make the diagnosis was called "amniocentesis," from the Greek *amnion*—"the fetal membrane"—and *kentesis*—"a puncture" (Figure 1). Several other techniques have been developed to expand the scope of prenatal diagnosis.

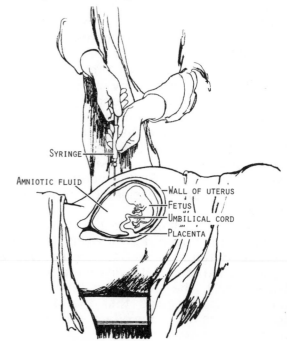

Figure 1. Amniocentesis

Prenatal diagnosis has given a number of families some options that often turn out to involve some difficult moral choices. Nevertheless, without the now widespread availability of prenatal diagnosis in most developed countries of the world, many couples at high risk for a genetically determined disorder would decide *not* to have children at all. Consider, for example, a couple whose first child is diagnosed at one year of age as having Tay-Sachs disease, a progressive, degenerative disease of the brain that inevitably leads to death—usually before the child's fourth birthday. It is inherited as an autosomal recessive trait. Before the availability of amniocentesis for prenatal diagnosis of Tay-Sachs, few if any parents chose to take the chance of having additional children with such a horrible and as yet untreatable disease. Today, with the knowledge that the fetus with Tay-Sachs can be detected prenatally, many parents make the opposite choice, taking comfort in the knowledge that 75% of the time the fetus and subsequent child will *not* have Tay-Sachs. When an affected fetus is diagnosed, couples may decide to terminate the pregnancy.

The Procedures

Amniocentesis. This procedure involves withdrawing from the uterus a small amount of the fluid that surrounds the fetus. Amniocentesis usually is done between the 14th and 16th weeks of pregnancy (16 to 18 weeks after the last menstrual period). The obstetrician inserts a needle through the woman's skin and uterine wall into the amniotic sac. The patient is under local anesthetic. The procedure does not usually require hospitalization. The small amount of fluid that is withdrawn during the procedure is replaced naturally in about four hours. The fluid withdrawn from the amniotic sac contains living cells from the fetus. These cells can be grown in cell culture. (See "Studying Human Chromosomes," page 37.) The culturing and subsequent tests can take up to four or five weeks. The cultured fetal cells are used to determine the fetal karyotype or to look for certain biochemical abnormalities. In some cases, the amniotic fluid itself is used for the prenatal diagnosis.

Ultrasonography. Before the obstetrician begins amniocentesis, the patient's abdomen is scanned with ultrasound. High frequency vibrations are translated into an image of the fetus and the surrounding structures in much the same way as sonar equipment is used on ships to identify submerged objects. The ultra-sound image appears on a television screen and the viewers, including the parents, can actually see the fetus "swimming" in the amniotic fluid. The image allows the physician to obtain an accurate estimate of the fetal age by determining its size. The picture also shows the location of the placenta and the fetus so the doctor can avoid injuring them during the amniocentesis. Twins can be identified easily. Most of the time, the sex of the fetus also becomes obvious.

Ultrasound technology is advancing rapidly. The pictures are now clear enough to allow a physician to identify several fetal abnormalities, including enlarged (cystic) or absent kidneys, hydrocephalus ("water on the brain"), certain forms of dwarfism, spina bifida, and even some cases of congenital heart disease (defects in the structure of the heart that are present at birth). This technique may also permit detection of severe hereditary diseases of the muscles, brain, and spinal cord where fetal movement may be diminished or absent.

X rays. X rays have limited use in prenatal diagnosis. Because the fetal skeleton is only slightly mineralized between 16 and 20 weeks of a pregnancy, it is difficult to see very much. In addition, X rays are a potential hazard to the fetus. However, new X ray technology, such as computerized axial tomography (CAT or CTT scanning), may soon be adapted for prenatal diagnosis.

Fetoscopy. Fetoscopes using fiber optics are now being used on a research basis in several major medical genetics centers. Insertion of the fetoscope into the uterus allows the doctor to see and actually examine the fetus. The "field" one can see with the fetoscope includes, for example, most of the hand of a 16- to 18-week fetus. In addition, a fine needle can be passed down the fetoscope; under direct visualization, a sample of pure fetal blood can be obtained from a blood vessel on the surface of the placenta. Although the total diameter of the apparatus, is only 3.2 mm, fetoscopy as presently done can lead to the loss of 5% to 10% of the pregnancies as a result of the procedure itself. Obviously, then, its use must be restricted to very high risk situations, such as confirmation of the presence of spina bifida (when other tests give inconclusive results) or the prenatal diagnosis of severe hemophilia (for which a sample of fetal blood is required).

Chromosomal Analysis. The chromosomes of cultured cells can be examined for abnormalities in number or structure. Although fetuses with Down syndrome (trisomy 21) represent the most frequently encountered chromosomal problem, there are several other chromosomal abnormalities, rearrangements, and deletions that lead to severe mental and physical defects and to early death of the infant. Chromosomal analysis also reveals the sex of the fetus, which is important when the mother is a known carrier of an X-linked disorder, such as hemophilia or Duchenne muscular dystrophy. Each male fetus, in either case, has a 50% chance of being affected. For hemophilia, it is now possible to detect the affected male fetus by measuring anti-hemophilic factor activity in fetal blood obtained by fetoscopy. In the case of X-linked muscular dystrophy, no specific test is available.

Biochemical Analysis. About 40 "inborn errors of metabolism" have been diagnosed prenatally through biochemical analysis of cultured cells or, in some cases, the fluid itself. Another 35 may be detectable, but definitive diagnoses have not yet been made. Disorders such as Tay-Sachs disease and galactosemia are diagnosable through biochemical analysis. Recently, progress has been made with restriction enzymes—enzymes that separate the DNA molecule at specific sites. This technology has permitted prenatal diagnosis of sickle-cell anemia and thalassemia from amniotic cells. Before that technique was available, the diagnosis required the risky withdrawal of fetal blood. Still another analysis can detect high levels of alphafetoprotein (AFP) in the amniotic fluid. When the neural tube of the fetus—which becomes the central nervous system—fails to close properly, AFP is released into the amniotic fluid. Thus, increased amounts of AFP can indicate the presence of defects of the neural tube, such as spina bifida.

Who Should Have Prenatal Diagnosis?

The procedures described above have been developed so that couples identified as at an increased risk of having children with severe genetic disorders can consider taking steps to reduce that risk. Almost always, the chance of having a perfectly normal child is far higher than the risk of the problem. Thus, in most cases, the test results are normal, and the parents are reassured. When a "positive" test indicates that a fetal abnormality is likely, all possible options are presented and discussed with the couple. Some decide to use the remaining months of the pregnancy to prepare themselves emotionally to deal with the problem their baby will almost certainly have.

With increasing frequency, the information obtained through prenatal testing is used to ensure the best possible obstetric and pediatric care for the infant and the mother. Suppose, for example, that a woman in a small town is found to be carrying a fetus with severe spina bifida, and she and her husband decide to continue with the pregnancy. When the pregnancy is near term, the family doctor would transfer the mother to a large medical center where a team of experts would be assembled to manage the situation. An obstetrician would deliver the baby by Caesarian section in order to reduce the chance of damaging the sac and any parts of the baby's spinal cord that might be in it. A neurosurgeon and a pediatrician would be in the delivery room as well to supervise the immediate care of the baby and to decide if emergency surgery is needed.

In some as yet rare instances, it is possible atually to treat the fetus before birth. For example, special diets for the mother designed to provide the best possible chemical environment for certain enzyme deficient fetuses are being studied. In addition, some surgical interventions prior to birth have been successful in a small number of cases.

Many couples, certainly after much thought and perhaps discussion with their physicians, geneticists, relatives, and others, decide that the fetal defect is sufficiently serious to justify an abortion. It is important to keep the following statistics in mind. Of every 100 women who undergo a prenatal diagnostic procedure, serious physical or mental defects are found in only three or four fetuses (Table 1). It is also

Table 1. Breakdown of situations in which amniocentesis is done (based on 15,000 procedures performed in 1978 in the U.S.)

Situation	Number of Amniocenteses	Expected Abnormal Fetuses	
		Number	Percent
Chromosomal Abnormality:			
Maternal age 35 years or older	8,100	203	2.5
Previous offspring	2,250	27	1.2
Parental translocation*	300	30	10.0
Family history: chromosomal abnormality	900	14	1.5
Other	900	14	1.5
Neural Tube Defect:			
Previous offspring	1,200	36	3.0
Maternal relative	300	3	1.0
X-Linked Disorders:			
(No specific diagnosis possible, fetal sex only)	300	150**	50.0**
Metabolic Disorders: (Specific diagnosis possible)	750	188	25.0
Total	15,000	665	4.4

*In some individuals, segments of two chromosomes may have been exchanged. This has no effect on the individual since all genetic information is still included. The individual's offspring, however, may be affected if some of its genetic information is either missing or duplicated.
**Male fetuses with 50% maximum probability of being affected

important to emphasize that negative test results do not guarantee that the baby is "normal." The vast majority of birth defects, even today, are *not* detectable by any of the available procedures.

You might think that every pregnant woman would benefit from going through some, if not all, of the prenatal diagnostic techniques. In fact, this is not the case. Generally, the decision to proceed with amniocentesis is made only after careful evaluation of the situation by a genetic counselor or other qualified individual or team. The questionnaire in Figure 2 is an example of the kinds of preliminary questions that might be asked by a genetic counselor to assist in that determination.

Currently, about 15,000 amniocenteses are done annually in the United States. Of those, 85% are done for chromosomal analysis. Of that group, about 75% are done for reasons of advanced maternal age. Table 1 explains that

Table 2. Frequency of Down syndrome infants among births, by maternal age

MATERNAL AGE	FREQUENCY
20	1/2000
30	1/885
35	1/365
38	1/176
40	1/109
43	1/53
45	1/32
48	1/16

*From E. G. Hook and A. Lindsjo, Down Syndrome in Live Births by Single Year Maternal Age Interval in a Swedish Study: Comparison with Results from a New York State Study, *American Journal of Human Genetics* 30:19, 1978.

statistic. The remaining 15% are done for detection of neural tube defects, X-linked disorders, and metabolic disorders. Based on the data presented in Table 1 and on an estimate of 3.5 million live births per year in the United States, what percentage of women in the United States are receiving amniocentesis?

The risk of harm to the fetus or the mother imposed by amniocentesis, although small, needs to be considered carefully by each couple. The main concern is that the procedure itself might cause abortion; this occurs about once out of every 200 to 250 amniocenteses. Table 2 shows why geneticists have selected maternal age 35 to 38 as the cut-off area for late maternal age as an indication for amniocentesis. It would be *unethical* to do amniocentesis when the risk of the procedure is greater than the risk of the problem one is trying to prevent.

The diagnostic accuracy of the prenatal diagnostic procedures is high but variable. For chromosomal analysis, precision is close to 100%; rarely, a bit of the mother's tissue may get picked up by the needle and maternal cells grow instead of fetal. The combination of amniotic fluid alphafetoprotein and ultrasound detects 90% to 95% of the *open* neural-tube defects. But about 10% to 15% are not detected because the bulge is covered by skin and the fetal protein does not leak out. The accuracy of ultrasound in detecting other birth defects has not yet been determined. Again, we note that negative tests do not mean that the baby will be "normal." Every couple that has a child faces a 3% to 4% risk of a fairly serious to serious birth defect that cannot be detected prenatally.

Table 3 shows the educational levels of 100

PRENATAL DIAGNOSIS SCREENING QUESTIONS

1. Will you be age 35 or older when the baby is due? ___Yes ___No
   Age when due _____

2. Have you or the baby's father or anyone in either of your families ever had
   a. Down syndrome or mongolism? ___Yes ___No
   b. Spina bifida or meningomyelocele (open spine)? ___Yes ___No
   c. Hemophilia? ___Yes ___No
   d. Muscular dystrophy? ___Yes ___No

3. Have you or the baby's father had a child born dead or alive with a birth defect not listed in Question 2 above? ___Yes ___No
   If Yes, describe_____

4. Do you or the baby's father have any close relatives who are mentally retarded? ___Yes ___No
   If Yes, list cause, if known_____

5. Do you or the baby's father or close relative in either of your families have any inherited genetic or chromosomal disease or disorder not listed above? ___Yes ___No
   If Yes, describe_____

6. Have you, or the spouse of this baby's father in a previous marriage, had three or more spontaneous pregnancy losses? ___Yes ___No

7. Do you or the baby's father have any close relatives descended from Jewish people who lived in Eastern Europe (Ashkenazic Jews)? ___Yes ___No
   If Yes, have either you or the baby's father been screened for Tay-Sachs disease? ___Yes ___No
   If Yes, indicate results and who screened_____

8. If patient or her spouse is Black:
   Have you or the baby's father, or any close relative been screened for sickle cell trait found to be positive? ___Yes ___No

I have discussed with my doctor the above questions which are answered "Yes" and understand that I am at increased risk for _____ and that it is usually possible to diagnose an affected fetus by testing amniotic fluid at about 16 weeks of pregnancy and I DO NOT want the test.

_____   _____
(Patient signature)   (Date)

Figure 2.

Table 3. Comparison of amount of education in amniocentesis sample of population and in 1970 census sample, 30 to 44 years of age

Census Sample		Years of School Completed	Amniocentesis Sample	
Male	Female		Male	Female
37%	35%	less than 12	4%	8%
34%	45%	12 (high school)	28%	36%
4%	5%	13	6%	8%
6%	4%	14	12%	5%
2%	2%	15	2%	2%
8%	5%	16	16%	19%
9%	4%	more than 17	32%	22%

individuals who sought amniocentesis. Figure 3 shows the ages of 320 mothers and 295 fathers who received genetic counseling at the University of California San Francisco Medical School during 1979. What do these data indicate about the patterns of use of amniocentesis?

AGE OF MOTHER	COUNT 0 100 200	AGE OF FATHER	COUNT 0 100 200
Less than 20	— 37	Less than 20	— 11
20-29	——————————198	20-29	——————————179
30-34	— 53	30-39	— 84
35-39	— 26	40-49	— 13
40 or more	· 6	50 or more	— 9

Figure 3. Age groupings of 320 mothers and 295 fathers seen in the Genetic Counseling Clinic, University of California San Francisco Medical School

As with many new biomedical techniques, the implications of amniocentesis have been far-reaching and controversial. Much of the moral controversy concerns abortion. Women found to be carrying a fetus affected by a chromosomal, biochemical, or neural-tube disorder can elect to terminate the pregnancy. The Supreme Court of the United States—*Roe v. Wade, Doe v. Bolton,* 1973—determined that a pregnant woman may legally elect abortion during the first and second trimesters of pregnancy. Much of the controversy surrounding abortion—at least as it relates to genetics—results from conflict between new technologies and traditional values. The procedures of prenatal diagnosis, because they allow decisions about reproduction, family life, and the quality of life, are particularly controversial in that regard.

Moral Controversies

Consider the following issues related to prenatal diagnosis:

1. Do biology teachers have a responsibility to teach their students about issues in human genetics that may affect the students' future decisions regarding marriage and having children?

2. Are the present criteria for eligibility for prenatal diagnosis reasonable?

3. When, if ever, ought prenatal diagnostic testing *not* be performed—even if the woman meets the standard eligibility criteria?

4. Is the patient's physician *morally required* to inform a patient of the availability of prenatal diagnostic procedures? Should a physician be *legally required* to provide such information?

5. What ought the physician do if he or she is *morally opposed* to abortion or to the possible use of the information gained from prenatal tests that might lead to a consideration of abortion?

6. Ought abortion to be performed if, as a result of prenatal diagnosis in the second trimester of pregnancy (12 to 24 weeks of gestation), it is found that the fetus will become a severely mentally or physically defective individual?

7. Since prenatal testing for genetic disorders also reveals the sex of the fetus (and as in most cases the fetus is known to be unaffected), is a decision on the part of the parents to abort the fetus *on the basis of its sex alone* morally acceptable?

8. Should the patient's physician withhold information about the sex of the fetus from the parents in cases where the results of the prenatal diagnostic tests are negative?

9. Should laws be written and enforced to *compel* prenatal diagnosis for all pregnant women who are at "high risk" for having a child with a serious physical or mental defect that is detectable prenatally?

10. Should a couple have the option of aborting a pregnancy when prenatal diagnosis—carried out because of an assumed high risk of a serious disorder—reveals instead a completely different, less serious condition?

11. Should a couple abort a pregnancy when twins are present and *one* of the pair is found to have Down syndrome or some other serious disorder?

GENETIC SCREENING: PREVENTION WITH PROBLEMS

Soliloquy on Screening*

(With Apologies to William Shakespeare)

> To screen or not to screen
> That is the question!
> Whether it is nobler to proceed
> With a test for mutant genes
> Only after the minds of all have been prepared
> By proper education
> Or to begin to test, anon, because
> It is the thing to do.
> One should not ask
> To test
> Without informed consent!

> Alas, in time
> Ignorance and confusion
> In the minds of parents and screenees
> May cause pain, suffering and stigmatization
> To those innocents who ask not
> For the genes they are heir to.
> And, may at some distant day
> Defame those who screen.
> For whether one should test a pound of flesh,
> A single cell or a drop of blood
> It is that person tested who must
> Live with and adjust to
> The label "carrier"
> And therein lies the rub!

Robert F. Murray, Jr., M.D.
Howard University
Washington, DC

The year is 1984. Linda, a newborn baby, is a few hours old. Samples of her blood, urine, skin, and placental tissue are going into the hospital's computer system. Three red lights flicker on the screen. She is a carrier of three gene defects. This fact is placed on her Universal Health Card. The card will be deposited in Washington, D. C. Linda's card has all the genetic information known about her. Each newborn baby has a similar card.

Twenty-one years later Linda and her boyfriend, Mark, apply for a marriage license. At this time, a computer compares Mark's and Linda's health cards. It turns out that Mark and Linda both carry a recessive gene for the same serious defect. Any child they may have has a one-in-four chance of being mentally retarded.

Is this story a prediction of the future or just a fantasy? When Mark proposes to Linda, will she say, "Well, first we'll need our computer health card clearance, and then..."? How far-fetched does this sound? Well, it is not as far out as you might think. Birth registries are already in existence in many areas of North America, the United Kingdom, and Europe. Information obtained from birth certificates and medical records is entered into a computer. If, for example, the frequency of certain birth defects begins to increase sharply in a particular geographic area, the computer signals the increase.

Investigations can then be conducted to determine whether some mutagen or teratogen recently introduced into the environment might be the cause.

On an experimental basis, a few genetics centers have devised what is called a genetics record linkage system. Again, computers are used, this time to "link" members of a family together. Family histories are stored in the computer's memory bank along with data on possible genetically determined conditions. If the system were operative and, for example, an individual were diagnosed as having Huntington disease (HD), the physicians of all the relatives at risk of also having the gene for HD could be notified and genetic counseling advised.

Registries and computer storage and retrieval of genetic information are but two outgrowths of our increasing ability to "screen" for genetic disorders. In fact, genetic screening is becoming a fairly routine medical procedure for a number of conditions. The article titled "The Screening of Benjamin Miller" (page 87) describes the first genetic screening program ever carried out on an entire population—in this case, all or nearly all newborn babies. It also indicates how such screening programs got started.

The National Academy of Sciences has made it quite clear that genetic screening is different from most other types of medical screening, such as that for infectious diseases. Most children have "tuberculin" tests for TB and hearing and vision tests in school. These are all medical screening tests that are considered to be "nongenetic" (even though one must keep in mind that genetic factors play a role in susceptibility to infections and in the development

*Reprinted with permission from the *New England Journal of Medicine*, 291:15(803), 1974.

of many kinds of hearing and visual problems). The nongenetic disorders for which there are medical tests usually occur frequently. Genetic disorders, on the other hand, generally are rare by comparison. In nongenetic screening, an individual is tested for her or his own benefit. Genetic screening usually does little for the individual; the advantages are more often gained by offspring, siblings, or other relatives.

In some cases, genetic screening may create as many problems as it solves. Muscular dystrophy (MD) in males, for example, is reported in some studies as occurring two or three times more frequently than does PKU. A good, inexpensive screening test is available for MD. The diagnosis can be confirmed in newborn babies. Why, then, is the screening test for MD not done routinely, as is the test for PKU?

Part of the answer may lie in the fact that MD is, at present, untreatable. Most people, including medical professionals, are not yet ready to accept screening for a disorder that is not treatable. Knowing that MD is inevitable, for example, condemns a family to as much as a three-year wait until the boy develops this ultimately fatal disorder. Some advocates have tried to justify MD screening on the basis of the three-year wait. A couple could have one or even two more affected males before they found out that a son had the disease. Since the average number of children per couple in the United States is now slightly under two, about half of the boys who have muscular dystrophy will be the second child in the family. This boy's parents would not be likely to have another child soon, especially not after the onset of the disorder. So, the preventive aspects, while real, are not very urgent. Finally, put yourself in the position of the parents of an infant boy who has a *false* positive test. It might take weeks or even months before other tests establish that the initial result was not a *true* positive. One wonders how long it would take for those parents to be *sure* that their son really is unaffected.

A complex series of problems is emerging from the possibility of screening all pregnant women for the prenatal detection of neural tube defects, such as spina bifida. The test, which is already available, depends on the detection of alphafetoprotein (AFP), which leaks from the fetus to the amniotic fluid and eventually into the mother's blood *if* the brain and spinal cord of the fetus are not developing properly. If (a) all pregnant women were tested for AFP in their blood between 16 and 18 weeks of pregnancy, (b) a confirmatory AFP analysis were done on amniotic fluid, and (c) all fetuses identified as likely to have a neural-tube defect were aborted, 80% to 90% of the cases of this common group of birth defects would be eliminated. Currently, there are six to seven thousand babies with neural-tube defects born in North America every year.

But should such a screening program be instituted? If so, should it be mandatory or voluntary? First of all, how well do people really understand what a neural-tube defect is? The defects are so severe that over half of the affected infants die at birth or within a few days of birth. Of those surviving that time period, another half die before the end of the first year. However, of those who survive beyond one year, many, often as a result of modern surgical techniques, live happy and productive lives, with varying degrees of handicap. Some individuals with spina bifida have no handicap at all. The prenatal tests cannot distinguish between severe and mild cases.

And what about the question of abortion, which is unacceptable to many couples? At this time, the decision to terminate a pregnancy rests with the pregnant woman and her physician. However, some argue that the state, because it pays for the screening program and the care of institutionalized children, might legitimately make screening and abortion mandatory.

Recently, genetic screening has moved into the workplace. For example, there is evidence that large numbers of people have an inherited enzyme deficiency that makes their lungs very susceptible to damage from cigarette smoke, asbestos particles, and other atmospheric pollutants. Such individuals tend to develop chronic emphysema, a loss of elasticity in the lungs. Their lives are considerably shortened. The managers of an asbestos mining company, after being informed that it was possible to screen employees and prospective employees for this genetic predisposition, instituted company-wide screening. Susceptible miners were to be identified and retrained for other jobs in the company. New employees were to be screened so that susceptible applicants would not be hired. The union responded by taking legal action against the company, charging discriminatory labor practices.

Genetic screening, like many advances in science and technology, often creates new problems as it solves others. Some of the more obvious and difficult questions include the following:

1. To what extent should confidentiality be protected? For example, should the relatives of a carrier be told about the carrier status against the wishes of the individual?

2. What uses of information obtained from screening might constitute violations of human rights? What practices or procedures might be viewed as discrimination against individuals, families, or groups?

3. How much should society be permitted to do for a person's "own good"? On what grounds might laws be passed to limit individual choice in order to obtain some "public good"?

4. Is it just or unjust to withhold screening services from particular individuals or groups? Why? Is it just or unjust to withhold the information obtained? Why?

X-LINKED INHERITANCE

Human cells have 23 pairs of chromosomes—22 pairs of autosomes, and one pair of sex chromosomes. In human males, the pair of sex chromosomes is identified as the X and Y chromosomes. The Y chromosome is much smaller than the X chromosome. Human males produce two kinds of sperm. Half of them carry an X chromosome; the other half carry a Y chromosome. In human females, the pair of sex chromosomes is identified as the X and X chromosomes. All the eggs produced by the female carry an X chromosome. If an egg is fertilized by an X-bearing sperm, the offspring is a female (XX). If an egg is fertilized by a Y-bearing sperm, the offspring is a male (XY).

Not all kinds of animals have sex-determining sperm. In some species, such as birds, butterflies, and moths, the female has two kinds of sex chromosomes and produces two kinds of eggs. In these organisms, all sperm carry the same kind of sex chromosome. The chromosome of the egg, then, determines the sex of the offspring.

In still other species, one of the sex chromosomes may be missing entirely. In some grasshoppers, for instance, males have 22 autosomes (11 pairs) and one X chromosome. Females also have 22 autosomes, but they have two X chromosomes. Half the sperm have 11 autosomes. The other half have 11 autosomes and one X. The sex of the young grasshopper depends on the kind of sperm that fertilizes the egg. In this case, one X chromosome results in a male grasshopper.

In most plant species, the same plant produces both male and female sex cells. Sex chromosomes can be found, however, in plant species that do have separate male and female individuals. Such plants include holly, asparagus, willows, and cottonwoods.

X-Linked Inheritance Is Discovered

Around 1910, Thomas Hunt Morgan was raising thousands of fruit flies in the laboratories of Columbia University. Fruit flies found in nature, as far as was known, had dark red eyes. But in the course of examining fruit fly cultures, Morgan found a male fly that had white eyes. It was mated with a red-eyed female and all of the F1 generation had red eyes. This was not surprising, since Morgan assumed that the gene for white eyes was recessive.

Flies of the F_1 generation were then mated to each other. In the F_2 generation, a ratio of ¾ red-eyed flies to ¼ white-eyed flies was obtained. This ratio of eye colors also was expected. But all the white-eyed flies were males! This trait seemed to be linked to the sex chromosomes of the individual. Further experiments confirmed the finding.

White eyes in fruit flies are called an *X-linked trait*. Morgan's knowledge of meiosis led him to conclude that male fruit flies produce two kinds of sperm. Half of the sperm would carry an X chromosome and half would carry a Y chromosome. Each sperm also would carry one chromosome from each pair of autosomes. Females, on the other hand, would carry one X chromosome, plus one chromosome from each pair of autosomes. The Y chromosome apparently was inactive in the inheritance of eye color. Thus, in the fruit fly the gene for eye color is on the X chromosome.

Humans Also Have X-Linked Traits

Since human beings have a pair of sex chromosomes similar to the sex chromosomes of fruit flies, it is reasonable to expect that some human hereditary traits would turn out to be X-linked. A number of X-linked traits are now known in humans, including colorblindness, hemophilia, and one form of muscular dystrophy. Red-green colorblindness is the inability to distinguish red, green, or both of these from other colors. It is a rather common trait.

The distinctive patterns of inheritance associated with X-linked traits are apparent in pedigree charts like these for red-green colorblindness.

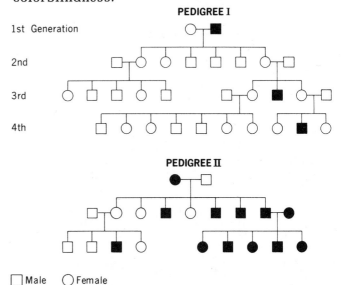

Figure 1. Two pedigrees for red-green colorblindness

Some study of these pedigrees should allow you to answer questions like

1. Is the allele for colorblindness dominant or recessive? How can you tell?

2. Is it X-linked or not? How do you know?

After you have answered these two questions, you should be able to predict the expected results of a mating between a colorblind man and a woman who is homozygous for normal color vision.

3. Among their male offspring, what fraction would have normal vision?

4. What fraction would be colorblind?

5. Among their female offspring, what fraction would have normal color vision?

6. What fraction would be carriers?

7. What fraction would be colorblind?

Repeat the calculations, this time for a mating between a carrier woman and a man with normal color vision.

8. Among their male offspring, what fraction would have normal color vision?

9. What fraction would be colorblind?

10. Among their female offspring, what fraction would have normal color vision?

11. What fraction would be carriers?

12. What fraction would be colorblind?

There are many more colorblind men than women. It is not difficult to see why this is so. If a man receives an X chromosome that carries the gene for colorblindness from his mother, he will be colorblind. This is because there is no allele on the Y chromosome to offset the recessive gene for colorblindness on the X chromosome. But in order for a woman to be colorblind, she must receive two X chromosomes that carry the gene for colorblindness, one from her mother and one from her father. Therefore, her mother would have to be a carrier and her father would have to be colorblind—an infrequent combination.

If one X chromosome in ten carries the gene for colorblindness, one male in ten will be colorblind. To find out how often females would be colorblind, apply the second principle of probability. This principle states: The chance that two independent events will occur together is the product of their chances of occurring separately. The chance of a female getting two X chromosomes, each carrying the colorblind gene, is the product of the two separate probabilities, 0.1×0.1, or 0.01. Thus, the frequency of women who are colorblind would be only about one-tenth of the frequency of colorblind men (1 in 100 for the female compared to 1 in 10 for the male). The actual frequency of colorblind men ranges from 5% to 9% in different populations.

The most common type of hemophilia is another X-linked trait in humans. It is a much more serious condition than colorblindness. Fortunately, it is very rare. Hemophilia is a condition in which the blood fails to clot after an injury or clots very slowly. Some males with hemophilia experience frequent and painful bleeding around the joints. Others are more mildly affected and have only increased bruising and prolonged bleeding if their skin is cut.

X-linked hemophilia is a genetic defect with a royal history. The trait appeared in a son and three grandsons of Queen Victoria of Great Britain. Because of frequent marriages among the royal families of Europe, the gene became rather widely spread. During the 19th and early 20th centuries, the course of history was affected by the gene for hemophilia, especially in Spain and Russia. For example, Rasputin, a Russian government official, claimed to be able to control the bleeding in the young Prince Alexis Czarevich, a hemophiliac. The fear of Rasputin's power apparently affected the Czar's decisions in certain matters of state. Figure 2 shows a pedigree of the distribution of hemophilia in Queen Victoria's descendants. Perhaps if the gene for hemophilia had passed to the Queen's grandson, who became Kaiser Wilhelm II, World War I might not have occurred!

Colorblindness and hemophilia have been used as typical examples of X-linked inheritance for many years. However, there are nearly 200 other known X-linked conditions. Not all of them are recessive. Some are dominant. For example, there is one condition in which the enamel of the teeth is very hard and its surface rough. The enamel is also very thin and cylindrical in shape. As the enamel surface becomes worn, the underlying dentin becomes yellow. This condition is called hereditary enamel hypoplasia, or inherited, poorly developed enamel. This type of tooth enamel is inherited as an X-linked dominant. Such conditions are seen much more frequently in females.

To date very few specific genes have been unequivocally assigned to the Y chromosome. Obviously, important male sex-determining genes, called H-Y antigen and testis-determining factor, are there, but other assign-

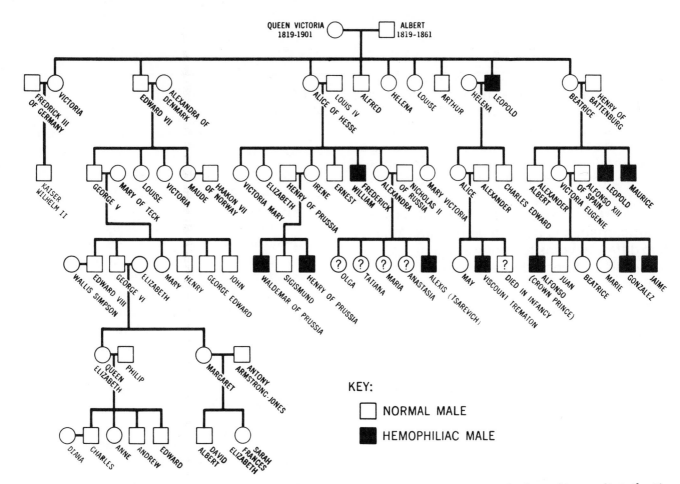

Figure 2. A pedigree of some of Queen Victoria's descendants, showing the hereditary distribution of hemophilia

KEY:

□ NORMAL MALE

■ HEMOPHILIAC MALE

ments are controversial. There is convincing evidence suggesting that hairy ears (hair growing on the fold of the ear lobe) is Y-linked, but in some families it appears to be autosomal. This trait is seen quite frequently in Eastern Asian, dark-skinned males. The pattern of inheritance for a gene on the Y chromosome is unique and easy to construct. Try it.

Hard Choices for Families

Whether a fetus has an X-linked, genetic disorder can, in many cases, be determined by prenatal tests done in the second trimester of pregnancy (see "Prenatal Diagnosis," page 68). Hemophilia, for example, can be detected by withdrawing a sample of fetal placental blood for analysis. But for most X-linked disorders, there is no specific prenatal test.

For the nondetectable serious X-linked diseases, the sex of the child can be determined prenatally through chromosomal analysis. When the doctor is reasonably sure that the mother is a carrier of the gene for X-linked muscular dystrophy, for example, the parents may be informed that there is a one-in-two chance of

their male children being affected. Female children have a one-in-two chance of being carriers, but none will have the disease.

Parents in this situation have to make some hard choices. First, they must decide whether or not to have the test and learn the sex of the fetus. If they choose to have the test and the fetus turns out to be female, their worries are ended. They should, however, inform their female children that they have a 50% chance of carrying the gene for MD.

What happens if the fetus is a boy? The chance is 50% that the child has MD. The chance is also 50% that the child does *not* have MD. Parents must decide whether to abort and risk losing a normal son or to continue the pregnancy and risk the birth of a son with MD.

Some people feel that abortion is wrong and that the test should not be performed in situations like this. Others feel that parents should be able to decide whether to have the test and what to do once they receive the results. Difficult choices like these depend on many factors, including religious views, laws, and personal values.

DEMONSTRATING X-LINKED INHERITANCE

More than 100 genes have been assigned to the X chromosome. They affect a wide variety of characteristics, many of which have nothing to do with sexual differentiation. Since the inheritance of these genes corresponds to the inheritance of the X chromosome, they are said to be X-linked. The inheritance of the X-linked characteristics is easy to demonstrate using two different coins (a penny and a nickel) and some sort of record-keeping chart such as Figure 1.

Father: Penny   Mother: Nickel

Heads: _____   Heads: _____

Tails: _____   Tails: _____

OFFSPRING	GENOTYPE	SEX	PHENOTYPE
1			
2			
3			
4			
5			
6			
7			
8			
9			
10			

Figure 1.   A table for recording data

Figure 2 lists just a few of the many characteristics that are determined by genes on the X chromosome. Capital letters stand for genes with dominant effects, and small letters stand for genes with recessive effects.

In order to understand X-linked inheritance, it is necessary to remember that if a gene is carried on the X chromosome in a human male, there is no homologous gene on the smaller Y chromosome. Therefore, a trait controlled by any gene on the X chromosome will be expressed, although just one gene is present. On the other hand, for a recessive trait to be expressed in a female, the specific gene must be present in both of her X chromosomes.

Use the following example to begin the demonstration:

1. The normal gene (allele) responsible for producing antihemophilic globulin (Factor VIII) is designated (**H**). The gene for hemophilia A has a recessive effect and is designated (**h**); it produces an abnormal factor VIII with very little clotting activity. Suppose the father—represented by the penny—carries the normal gene (**H**). His Y chromosome has no genes involved in blood clotting. The mother—represented by the nickel—is a carrier with one normal gene (**H**) and one recessive gene (**h**).

2. Assign the possibilities for egg and sperm cells as follows:

   Father: Penny
   Heads: X chromosome, **H** gene
   Tails: Y chromosome

   Mother: Nickel
   Heads: X chromosome, **H** gene
   Tails: X chromosome, **h** gene

   Now, through flips of the coins, demonstrate the sex, the genotype, and the phenotype of ten offspring this couple might have. record your findings on your copy of Figure 1.

3. Repeat the procedure using other characteristics and other possible genotypes in the parents. What patterns and trends can you discern?

CHARACTERISTIC	DOMINANT GENE	CHARACTERISTIC	RECESSIVE GENE
Normal blood clotting	H	Hemophilia A	h
Normal color vision	R	Red weakness (protanomaly)	r
Normal color vision	G	Green weakness (deuteranomaly)	g
Normal eye pigmentation	A_o	Ocular albinism	a_o
Normal G6PD enzyme	Gd	G6PD deficient	gd

Figure 2.   X-linked characteristics

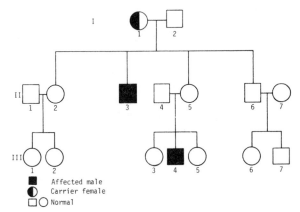

Legend:
■ Affected male
◐ Carrier female
□○ Normal

Figure 3. Pedigree for an X-linked recessive trait, G6PD enzyme deficiency

Interpreting the Results

1. If a man who is not a hemophiliac is married to a woman who is a carrier of the gene for hemophilia, what percentage of their male offspring are expected to be hemophiliacs?

2. The egg and sperm do not contribute equally to the genetic makeup of the embryo. Explain.

3. Colorblindness and hemophilia are both more common in males than females. Explain.

4. Figure 3 shows a pedigree for the X-linked recessive trait, G6PD enzyme deficiency.

   a. What is the genotype of female II, 5? How do you know?

   b. What is the genotype of female II, 2? How do you know?

   c. What is the chance that female III, 6 is a carrier? Explain.

   d. If male II, 3 married a female with two normal alleles for G6PD enzyme, what percentage of their sons is expected to be G6PD deficient? What percentage of their daughters is expected to be carriers?

THE LYON HYPOTHESIS

For many years, geneticists did not understand how a female, who was homozygous for mutant genes carried on her two X chromosomes was no more seriously affected than a male, who had only one such gene on his one X chromosome. Geneticists wondered why two "doses" of the gene seemed to have no greater effect than one.

A hypothesis that seems to answer these questions was offered by several groups of researchers in 1961. The first person to explain the hypothesis precisely and in detail was Mary F. Lyon, a British geneticist. The hypothesis is now called the "Lyon hypothesis" in her honor.

The Lyon hypothesis, also called the "X inactivation hypothesis," has four parts: (1) one of the X chromosomes is inactivated in each of the somatic (body or nonreproductive) cells of a normal female; (2) the inactivation is random—either the X from the mother or the X from the father may be inactive in any single cell; (3) once inactivation occurs in a cell in a developing embryo, the same X chromosome will be inactivated in all the cells that descend from that cell; and (4) the inactivation occurs early in the development of the embryo, at about 16 days after conception.

Several kinds of evidence support this hypothesis, although there are still questions as to the mechanism of inactivation and whether it is complete or totally random. Lyon began to formulate the idea when she observed female mice who were heterozygous for X-linked genes for coat color. These females had fur that was made up of patches of the different colors. Males did not show patchy coat color, and neither did mice having only a single X chromosome (the XO chromosomal makeup).

In 1949, Murray Barr and Ewart Bertram began to study a darkly staining mass that appears in the nucleus of certain cells. Although these bodies had been noted as early as 1909, Barr and Bertram were the first to show that they are normally present only in female cells. In human beings, these "Barr bodies" are found adhering to the inner wall of the nuclear membrane (Figure 1). Susumo

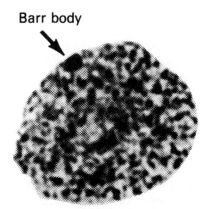

Barr body

Figure 1. A cell with one Barr body

Ohno, an American geneticist, suggested that the Barr bodies might be made up of materials from sex chromosomes. Recalling her mouse studies, Mary Lyon hypothesized that the Barr body is an inactivated X chromosome. This would explain the difference in "doses" between males, who have one X chromosome, and females, who have two X chromosomes.

The most convincing evidence in support of the Lyon hypothesis came from studies of an enzyme called G6PD. In humans, this enzyme is produced by an X-linked gene. Several investigators showed that there is no difference in the activity of the enzyme between normal males and females. And there are no differences among individuals with three or more X chromosomes. Thus, the "dose"—the number of genes present—does not seem to make any difference in the amount of the enzyme that is present or in the action of the enzyme.

Other studies were done on cells from heterozygous females who had two different alleles for different forms of G6PD on each X chromosome. In other words, one allele on one X chromosome coded for one form of the enzyme and the other allele on the other X chromosome coded for a different form. Biochemical tests can tell the difference in the enzymes that are produced. When cells from these heterozygous females were grown in cell culture, it was found that only one form of the enzyme was produced in the progeny of any single cell. Thus, it appears that only one X chromosome is inactivated. These results also suggest that the same X is inactivated in all the cells that descend from any single cell.

As far as is known, X inactivation occurs only when there are at least two X chromosomes present. It does not seem to occur in 46, XY or 45, X individuals. And all but one X chromosome will be inactivated in a cell. For example, males with Klinefelter syndrome—47,

XXY—will have one Barr body in each cell. Females who are 47, XXX will have two Barr bodies in each cell. How many Barr bodies would you find in the cells of an individual who is 48, XXXX?

The Lyon hypothesis helps us understand why X-linked conditions tend to have a highly variable expression in female carriers. Female carriers of hemophilia may be as severely affected as males, not affected at all, or have symptoms somewhere in between. Similarly, female carriers of muscular dystrophy have varying degrees of muscle weakness. In theory, the variability among carriers for X-linked alleles results from random inactivation of X chromosomes. Inactivation early in embryonic development of most of the X chromosomes that carry the gene for hemophilia or muscular dystrophy can lead to a female who exhibits mild or even no symptoms. Conversely, inactivation of most of the normal alleles can lead to the severe symptoms that sometimes are observed.

X inactivation also accounts for the relatively mild clinical effects of having one or more extra X chromosomes. Individuals who have an extra X chromosome may have few, if any, medical problems. The presence of an extra autosome, as with Down syndrome and other trisomies, produces much more serious effects.

Important questions about X inactivation still remain. Some researchers are working on the problem of whether the entire X chromosome is inactivated, or whether a part still remains functional. Others are looking at how "random" X inactivation really is in in any given cell. Some believe there may be a genetic mechanism that "selects" a particular X chromosome for inactivation.

GUEST EDITORIALS

GENETICS AND ETHICS: WHY STUDY HUMAN HEREDITY?*

Although it was first published in 1933, J.W.N. Sullivan's *The Limitations of Science*[1] had a great deal of influence in the 1950s and makes interesting reading even today. A glance at the book's "Table of Contents," not to mention the paperback cover, immediately informs the reader of the prestige that physics held over the other sciences in the 1950s. The paperback cover, for example, shows a compass encompassing a rose, surrounded by a model of a molecule. Ironically, the moon is a tiny speck awaiting exploration far off in the distance. The chapters "The Expanding Universe" and "The Mystery of Matter" are followed by chapters that consider themes such as the limitations and values of science. But strikingly important for today's students of biology and human genetics are Sullivan's closing remarks about biology, in contrast to the sciences of chemistry and physics:

> Biology, perhaps the least developed of the studies that truly deserve the name of science, is in a very different case. Its practical importance, although very considerable, is not at present overwhelming. A massacre of chemists would bring about the downfall of our civilization; a massacre of biologists would have unfortunate, but not disastrous results. Biology is not to be valued chiefly for its practical importance. Neither is it of any great consequence theoretically. It is seldom that we come across a biological idea that impresses us as a staggering intellectual conquest. Even the theory of natural selection does not reveal hitherto unsuspected resources of the mind. Indeed, it is difficult to resist the impression that on its theoretical side, biology is exceptionally inadequate. It seems to be quite surprisingly deficient in distinctive concepts.

If Sullivan was right at the time, he was not right for long. In 1953 Watson and Crick published the research that established the structure of the genetic material, DNA. The subsequent "cracking of the genetic code" opened the door for the solution of one of the fundamental biological problems—the molecular basis of inheritance.

Such scientific work challenged Sullivan's less than complimentary view of biology. First, the *theoretical importance* of biological concepts was rapidly being formulated and discussed. Second, biology was to have very *practical importance* for everyone. No longer could it be properly said that "there are very few general laws in biology" and that not one of these laws can be convincingly shown to have a universal application" (pp. 186-187).

If the publication by Watson and Crick in 1953 signaled our entrance into a new era in biology, it heralded also a new connection between science and ethics. For one thing, recent years have seen rapid and previously unimaginable advances in biology and medicine. Consider, for example, the following:

1. Advances in the effectiveness of the many available drugs and pharmaceuticals

2. Understanding of the structure, function, and influence of chromosomes and genes in nonhuman species and applications of those understandings in plant and animal breeding

3. The ability to control the processes of conception and reproduction

4. Recent successes with *in vitro* fertilization and the techniques required for successful embryo transfer to assist infertile women

5. Advances in the understanding, treatment, and prevention of the "major killers" such as heart disease and cancer.

6. An ever-increasing anticipation that human aging processes can be inhibited, or at least retarded, e.g., to reduce wrinkling of the skin and graying of the hair

7. An ever-increasing likelihood that fewer infants will

*This overview of genetics and ethics was prepared by Dr. Stuart Spicker, Professor of Community Medicine and Health Care, University of Connecticut, Farmington. Philosophy is his specialty.

be born with deformities, disabilities, and genetically determined disorders

All this "new biology" forces us to reconsider the traditional views of both science and ethics. Ethics may be defined as the study of the meaning and value of one's life. In the context of biology and genetics, one might even say that ethics is the study of the varieties of life, their individual significance, and their significance *for* each individual.

Human genetics is not just a scientific enterprise. Rather, questions are now raised that have never been formally stated before—except, perhaps, in the works of some science fiction writers. We who are alive today actually have the capacity to modify humankind. As Paul DeHart Hurd has suggested: "The rationale underlying the 'new' biology is a recognition that human beings are now largely responsible for directing their own evolution."[2] This responsibility is the result of a newly acquired power in human minds and human hands. How are we to assume this responsibility wisely enough to ensure that benefits are actually obtained—while disasters, of either the biological or ethical kind, are avoided?

One way to cross the boundary between science and ethics is to consider three *fundamental genetic concepts in terms of their ethical counterparts:*

Variability

Variability, as a biological term, is the divergence among individuals of a group; specifically, it is a difference between an individual and others of the same species that cannot be attributed to a difference in age, sex, or position in the life cycle. The variations that have been important in human evolution are those gene-controlled differences in phenotypes that conferred on the individual some adaptive advantage. Variations among individuals may be continuously distributed, for example, height or weight. Or they may be discontinuously distributed, as is the case with certain disease states. You either have the disease or you do not. No known "in-between" exists.

The notion of variability has, as its ethical analogue, the idea of *tolerance.* At the biological level, differences among individual members of a species are neither "good" nor "bad"; they simply exist. At the level of human conduct, or ethics, it is important to consider the full spectrum of variability in the human species. At one end of the spectrum we note that the majority of people have no particular dysfunction or disability that may appreciably affect their roles in the social world. However, there are a significant number who have had to cope with (or on occasion have succumbed to) various forms of dysfunction, disability, and disease. Although there has been a noticeable improvement in the way handicapped persons have been treated, much remains for us by way of understanding and appreciating the positive attributes of all people. *Tolerance,* a notion within a theory of *virtue ethics,* should bring this point home. (See "A New Look at the Handicapped, page 84.)

In the realm of human conduct, variability manifests itself in communities where many different interests, points of view, beliefs, customs, and heritages are found.

Such *pluralism* can sometimes cause tensions among different groups. The study of virtue ethics suggests that tolerance—the ungrudging acknowledgment of the existence of divergent appearances and behaviors and the willing acceptance and even encouragement of diversity—can do much to relieve such tensions.

From a discussion of genetic factors that influence variability, it is not too great a leap to discussions of the virtue of tolerance—the acceptance of both individual idiosyncrasy and group diversity. One should not presume that expressions such as "without regard to creed, race, color, and national origin" solve the problem. Such catch-phrases can falsely lead one to conclude that only specific groups are acceptable. This is one form of intolerance under the guise of tolerance.

Tolerance alone is not a cure-all for every social ill. But before we can talk intelligently about ways to achieve the common good, we may first have to acknowledge and even appreciate diversity. Just as the notion of variability is basic to biology, the idea of tolerance is basic to ethics. The first and most fundamental level of ethical analysis is the free and open consideration of biases, prejudices, fears, vices, and virtues.

Individuality

The notion of *individuality* in biology leads naturally to the conclusion that each organism is unique. Although there are family resemblances among closely related individuals, even so-called "identical twins" are not, strictly speaking, identical. The uniqueness or individuality of each organism is captured in the biological notion of phenotype. The phenotype is the result of the genotype (the genetic constitution of the organism) in conjunction with the environment, and is, therefore, the physical appearance and observable properties of an organism.

In ethics, the analogue of the phenotype is the actual conduct and decision making of each person. Such behavior is observable. We use it as a basis for judgment of praise or blame. We can call such behavior *responsibility*.

Moral action is freely chosen action. Whereas, the moral person must fulfill obligations that are said to be binding, the moral person must freely choose to carry out these obligations. *Humanistic* moral theory stresses human freedom and choice. It emphasizes determinations of right and wrong through rational inquiry and argument. *Authoritarian* moralists, in contrast, anchor obligations in some form of absolute power or supreme authority outside of humankind. Such absolute power has taken the form of the will of God, the sovereignty of the State, the paramount interests of society, or even biological laws. Whatever the authority, it is assumed to take precedence over the choices, decisions, and judgments of individuals.

Adaptation

Evolution theory shows that the adaption of a species to its natural environment is essential to survival. Adaptation has its ethical analogue in the social world, because the very survival of our species may be at stake if we fail to adapt to the new knowledge brought about by biology, technology, and medicine. We call this analogue *social responsibility*.

Given that our species has survived, it is clear, in retrospect, that we have successfully adapted to multipel and complex environments. But adaptation is not just a biological notion. It means more than surviving extremes of environment such as climate, natural dangers, or nutritional deprivation. We also adapt to the social forces and pressures that other human beings create for each of us. And we, too, serve as forces upon others. At times we even "apply" certain social "pressures" on others—friends, relatives, and acquaintances.

GENETICS: KNOWLEDGE OF HUMAN HEREDITY	ETHICS: HUMAN CONDUCT AND MORAL DECISION MAKING
WHAT DO I KNOW?	MORALLY, WHAT OUGHT I TO DO?
1. Variability	1. Tolerance vs. intolerance
2. Individuality	2. Personal responsibility for one's life vs. irresponsibility
3. Adaptation	3. Social responsibility for new knowledge and the survival of the species vs. egoism and the danger of extinction

New knowledge in human genetics has already exploded, and there is, no doubt, more to come. How will we as individuals and as a society control, monitor, and govern the uses of this new knowledge? We must once again adapt our species (and, indirectly, other species) to a world in which new power is in our hands. New knowledge requires new social responsibility: the very careful use of new knowledge to assure the survival of *homo sapiens*.

The Examined Life

We are living at a time when we may observe people's unwarranted expectations of science and medicine. Powers once attributed to the "gods" or "magic" are now transferred to the scientific and medical professions. There is a tendency to reject the unwelcome outcomes of human reproduction and to blame doctors for illness, insanity, and even aging. The public now tends to take health, sanity, youth, and perpetual joy as its due. Nothing less seems acceptable.

The common word for those who anticipate nothing short of perfection is arrogance. We live at a time, then, when an arrogance of unreasonable expectations can only serve to give false hope. The public will soon have to reconsider its demand that physicians and biomedical scientists provide perfect resolutions to all health problems.

The arrogance of unreasonable expectations can perhaps be counterbalanced by the virtues of prudence, temperance, tolerance, humility, and honesty. We should assume an attitude of rational skepticism in concert with these moral virtues as we take up the challenge posed by hard moral choices.

Rapid advances in our knowledge of human genetics

and our new abilities to intervene in nature's processes even justify that we be a bit anxious, as well as skeptical about the consequences of our endeavors. This is not to suggest that we adopt an attitude of fear, which surely incapacitates us. Rather, we should continually question the work and actions of the scientific community—while at the same time questioning our own conduct and actions. Ethics, after all, is nothing but the raising of questions about our conduct and actions toward one another. If we ask, "What is it to be moral?" perhaps the best answer is, "To know what one is doing." The moral person knows what he or she is about. The moral person is thoughtful, intelligent, self-conscious, conscientious, and responsible. To be moral is to be self-critical. To paraphrase Socrates, only the examined life—the critical life—is fit for human living.

References

1. Sullivan, J.W.N. *The Limitations of Science.* New American Library of World Literature, Mentor Books, New York. Originally published by Chatto and Windus, England, 1933, p. 185.
2. Hurd, Paul DeHart. "The Historical/Philosophical Background of Education in Human Genetics in the United States." *BSCS Journal,* 1(1):7, 1978.

A NEW LOOK AT THE HANDICAPPED

Personal Attitudes

How a person with a disabilty or disfigurement is regarded by others is largely determined by a phenomenon known as *"spread."* Spread is how a handicapped person's disability is perceived to affect—or "spread"—to other characteristics of that person.

Beatrice Wright, a professor of psychology at the University of Kansas, and other psychologists have gathered evidence on spread. They have found, for example, that our attitudes toward blindness *as a condition* tend to be more negative than are our attitudes toward blind people *as individuals.* Dr. Wright suggests that the way in which handicapped persons are seen and reacted to by nonhandicapped persons is strongly influenced by these two vastly different attitudes or frameworks. Dr. Wright calls these "coping" and "succumbing" attitudes.

Briefly, the *succumbing attitude* tends to highlight the difficulties and "tragedy" of being handicapped. The succumbing attitude, then, emphasizes what the person can't do. The *coping attitude,* on the other hand, tends to enable one to seek solutions to problems. Disabled persons are seen as actively attempting to lead their lives constructively, and not as passively destroyed by their limitations and difficulties. The coping attitude should not make us callous to the hardships of handicapped persons. Instead, it suggests that suffering has its limits and that despair is not a necessary outcome of the handicapping condition.

Public Responsibility

To begin to overcome the prevailing succumbing framework, we must alter the way we

Table 1. Contrasts between coping and succumbing attitudes

Coping	Succumbing
1. The emphasis is on what the person *can do.*	1. The emphasis is on what the person *can't do.*
2. Areas of life in which the person can participate are seen as worthwhile.	2. Little weight is given to the areas of life in which the person can participate.
3. The person is perceived as playing an *active role* in molding his or her life constructively.	3. The person is seen as *passive,* as beaten down by difficulties.
4. The accomplishments of the person are appreciated in terms of their benefits to the person and others (asset or intrinsic evaluation), and not primarily devaluated because they fall short of some irrelevant standard.	4. The person's accomplishments are minimized by highlighting their shortcomings (comparative evaluation, usually measured in terms of "normal" standards).
5. The negative aspects of the person's life, such as the pain that is suffered or difficulties that exist, are felt to be manageable. They are also seen as limited because satisfactory aspects of the person's life are emphasized.	5. The negative aspects of the person's life, such as the pain that is suffered or difficulties that exist, are kept in the focus of attention. They are emphasized and exaggerated and seen to usurp all of life (spread).

speak of handicapped persons, "for a person is not equivalent to the impairment."[1] Labels like "*the* deaf," "*the* mentally retarded," and "*the* wheelchair patient," tend to cause us to consider all persons with similar handicaps as a group, as if such persons were all the same. As we have seen, this is false at the genetic level and is no less false in the public and social context.

Public responsibility toward the handicapped is a topic of much debate. Recent events reveal that change may be in the wind. Modifications of buildings are now being made in many places to remove physical barriers. Discriminatory practices, such as refusing to employ a handicapped person when the person can do the job, are being made illegal. And suits have been filed against those who have allegedly denied housing to the handicapped. Such shifts in public policy may be indicative of a more widespread acceptance of the "coping" attitude than used to be the case. But the lines are not clearly drawn, as the following case study illustrates.

Charlene was born with various physical abnormalities. She was a low birth weight dwarf. Her eyes were, it seemed, too large, and her nose was "beaklike." Her facial features were unusual; her face was narrow and her lower jaw receded. In addition, her right foot was twisted.

The medical geneticist called in consultation recognized this condition as a specific form of dwarfism inherited as an autosomal recessive trait. In taking the family history, the geneticist learned that Charlene's parents were first cousins. Although Charlene's life expectancy was not likely to be shortened, the geneticist pointed out that all known patients with this condition are profoundly mentally retarded. It was assumed that institutionalization probably would be necessary.

Charlene's parents were of modest means. Charlene's father, recalling the severely retarded brother of his best friend at high school and what he termed the "devasting impact" on that family, had already decided that Charlene would not be cared for at home.

Charlene's parents lived in a state that does not provide any appreciable funds for the care of the retarded in institutions. Various legal actions were in progress that might require institutions to make improvements, but, generally speaking, these institutions were destined to remain inadequate in their provision of reasonable care to retarded residents.

From this case, some important questions may be raised:
1. Do health-care providers, doctors and nurses, tend to view people like Charlene with succumbing or coping attitudes?
2. What attitude did Charlene's father display?
3. Should Charlene's parents feel guilty, since conditions inherited as autosomal recessive traits occur more frequently as a result of consanguineous (blood-related) marriages?
4. What is our public responsibility for providing institutional care for retarded persons like Charlene?
5. How should a state decide what resources it should provide for the care of persons like Charlene? Is money a serious problem?
6. In our society, questions about public responsibility often translate into questions of taxation and allocation of tax revenues. How would you, as a citizen at a public meeting at Town Hall, argue for additional tax money to be spent on institutional care for persons like Charlene? How do you think people would react if you presented Charlene as a victim of her handicap? How would they respond if you portrayed Charlene as competent and productive?

Suppose that, instead of institutional care, you wanted tax money to be spent on education for people like Charlene. Would your approach differ? Why or why not? What are the long-range consequences of this approach?

SOME PROGRESS MADE ON NEUROFIBROMATOSIS

by Joan Beck, *The Charlotte News*, dist. Field Newspaper Syndicate, 1981. Reprinted with permission.

Suppose John Merrick, the grossly deformed central character of the movie and play "Elephant Man" lived here and now instead of 19th century England. Would he still be shunned and treated like an ugly freak by those who couldn't see his humanity because of his distorted face?

The answer is far from a resounding "of course not." What Merrick had was a little-known genetic disorder called neurofibromatosis. Probably 100,000 Americans have the same disease today. There is no cure. And the social and vocational rejection many victims encounter may hurt more than the complex medical problems they must endure.

A former college teacher talks matter-of-factly about the problems "we uglies" have in getting jobs and promotions. A young woman in her 20s wonders if "anyone will ever love me." The mother of a six-year-old fights for public understanding and research as essential to her son's future.

Out of the Cruel Closet

Perhaps this column can help pull elephant-man disease out of this cruel closet, with the aid of one of its victims, Frances Zapatka, the former teacher.

Neurofibromatosis is marked chiefly by skin discolorations and the uncontrollable growth of tumors on the nerves just under the skin— sometimes masses of little tumors, sometimes large ones. Tumors can also appear on the auditory nerves, causing deafness; on the optic nerves, causing blindness; and on the spinal cord and in the brain where they can be fatal. Sometimes the bones enlarge and become misshapen and the spine develops a severe curvature.

Plastic surgery can now usually prevent the severe disfigurement of a John Merrick, although the tumors often return and surgery sometimes seems to make them grow even faster. Zapatka has already had 130 operations and "of course" faces more. She says tumors are growing in the area of her upper palate, spreading and lifting the bone beside her eyes. It's painful, she acknowledges, but "the pain is not constant."

Neurofibromatosis is one of the most common of all hereditary diseases and is caused by a single, abnormal, dominant gene. So there's a 50-50 chance in each pregnancy that a baby will

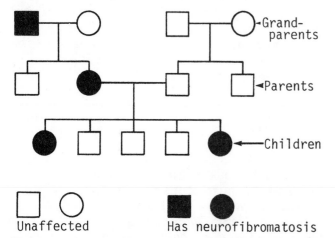

Unaffected   Has neurofibromatosis

Figure 1. Pedigree for a family with neurofibromatosis

inherit the disorder if even one parent has it. But symptoms vary greatly and occasionally don't start until middle age, after a parent has already unwittingly passed the disease on to a new generation.

No Explanation for Some

It can't be detected by biochemical testing or prenatally. Some cases appear to be new, spontaneous mutations, for which doctors have no explanation.

"My mother had four children before she discovered she had neurofibromatosis," Zapatka says. "She still has only minor symptoms." But Frances, the oldest offspring, began developing signs of the disease shortly after birth when tumors started to grow around her nose and "along the smile lines of my cheeks," and her eyelids began to droop. The diagnosis was made when she was two years old. She was treated first with radium and chemical injections, which were ineffective, and had the first of those 130 operations when she was eight.

A younger sister has much milder symptoms, little more than tiny acnelike tumors. "Otherwise she is very attractive, as I probably would have been," Frances comments. Three younger brothers have apparently beaten the genetic odds.

Tumors or not, Zapatka has had an energetic and productive life. After her father deserted the family when she was 11, Frances took over considerable responsibility for her younger brothers and sister while her mother went to work. Frances worked her way through college and graduate school and taught for 15 years at elementary, high school and junior college level, often taking tough classes no one else would handle. But when her medical problems increased and medical bills became almost as large as her income, she was forced on disability.

Foundation Set Up

In part because of "The Elephant Man," neurofibromatosis victims and families are beginning to go public about the disease. They've set up a National Neurofibromatosis Foundation, Inc. (340 East 80th St., 21-H, New York, N. Y. 10021) to encourage research, help families and spread understanding.

It takes a while to learn to cope with the public, Zapatka has found. "Most people experience uneasiness on meeting those with the form of neurofibromatosis I have. Some may be frightened. Some may consider it (us) obscene, leprous or contagious. Some see only our disfigurement. Others get to know us and enjoy us as persons."

That's some progress since the days of John Merrick. But it's not enough.

THE SCREENING OF BENJAMIN MILLER

My name is Ruth Shapiro. I teach tenth grade biology at Park Hill High School in Lincoln, Nebraska. My story is about what I learned from one of my students, Greg Miller.

Last November I noticed that Greg was terribly anxious about something. For two or three weeks, he seemed nervous, distracted, and unable to concentrate. But one Tuesday, I was relieved to see Greg happy and smiling in class and eager to share good news.

At lunch I joined the group of students around Greg. I was delighted to offer my congratulations on the birth of Greg's baby brother.

"What's special about Benjamin?" I asked brightly.

"Well, he doesn't, he doesn't have...have..." Greg became obviously upset again and seemed on the verge of tears. I put my arm around him and said gently, "You don't have to talk about it if you don't want to, Greg. But I've noticed that lately you've been upset about something. I've been wondering if it is anything I can help you with."

With that, the dam burst, and Greg told me the whole story. Greg's 20-year-old brother, John, is in an institution for the developmentally disabled. John is severely mentally retarded. He cannot walk and has frequent convulsions. Until John was five, the Millers took him from one doctor to another, trying to find out what was wrong. By the time the diagnosis was made, it was too late. John's brain was permanently damaged.

Greg had been very worried that the new baby might be sick like John. So far, so good. Benjamin had been tested for the condition and found to be unaffected.

That night, I called Greg's father to tell him about my conversation with Greg and to offer to help in any way I could. Clarence Miller turned out to be a life science instructor at Carroll Community College. He volunteered immediately to talk in Greg's class about genetic screening. He came one week later. His talk was recorded, and what follows is the abridged transcript:

"When our son, John, was born we were very happy. He appeared to be perfectly normal. When he was a little older, we marveled at his exceedingly light coloring. His blond hair was almost white. And his eyes were the bluest blue you've ever seen. His mother also noted that he had an unusual odor about him. I really didn't notice it, but it upset her a great deal. John was a healthy boy, but his development was slow. He didn't sit up alone until he was a year old, and he didn't walk until he was two. He learned to say 'mama' and 'dada' but not much more than that.

"Our doctor kept reassuring us the baby was normal—'only a bit slow.' And to make sure, he did a thyroid-function test, with normal results. I was in graduate school in those days and so poor we could hardly pay the doctor's bills. After five years, it finally occurred to me to take advantage of the university's family health service. A young pediatrician took one look at John, did a urine test, and made the diagnosis of PKU.

"The letters PKU stand for *p*henyl*k*eton*u*ria, an autosomal-recessive, inborn error of metabolism discovered by Folling in Sweden in 1934. The metabolic defect is a deficiency of the enzyme phenylalanine hydroxylase. This enzyme normally converts the amino acid, phenylalanine, to another amino acid, tyrosine. When no conversion takes place, excess phenylalanine accumulates in the blood to levels ten times greater than normal. The result is phenylalanine 'poisoning.'

"In the overwhelming majority of cases, this leads to severe mental retardation and all the other symptoms that occurred in our son. These include the fair coloring, odor, skin rash, and convulsions.

"As I mentioned, PKU is a recessively inherited condition. Our risk of having another child with PKU is 25% with each pregnancy. No prenatal diagnosis is possible. Some people in our situation think that is too high a risk. Others are willing to take the risk because the retardation is preventable.

"That's because scientists have developed a special diet as a form of treatment of the condition. Its mainstay is a formula made out of milk protein components from which phenylalanine has been removed with charcoal. The maintenance of the diet is easy during the bottle-feeding period, but difficulties arise later on. Keeping the older child on the special diet requires constant parental guidance, and the child must be taught to appreciate the importance of the diet. The diet is not attractive or very palatable. A 'low phenylalanine diet' usually means no meat, fish, cheese, eggs, normal bread or cake. It means small amounts of green vegetables, potatoes, and fruits. A specially prepared milk substitute, low protein foods, and special corn-starch products are the mainstay of the diet. One particular problem is that, as yet, there is no really good-tasting bread substitute. This complex diet plan must be followed. The child remains on this during the years the brain is still growing, or until at least age six. Studies are underway at the moment to see if the diet can be stopped then or should be continued until age ten. Some scientists believe the diet should be continued even beyond the age of ten. Available evidence indicates that people treated in such a manner have normal intelligence. The diet prevents the manifestations and complications of this condition.

"Problems arise when a successfully treated woman with PKU wants to become pregnant. More than 100 offspring of such women have been studied. Almost all are retarded and have minor anomalies. About one-fourth have major malformations, as well. A homozygous fetus of a carrier mother is protected from prenatal brain damage because its mother clears the fetal bloodstream of excess phenylalanine. But, in the case of the homozygous *mother*, all of whose fetuses will at least be heterozygous, the placenta maintains a higher level of phenylalanine in the fetus than in the mother. A fetus exposed to these high levels of phenylalanine during the entire nine months of pregnancy will be born with brain damage. To prevent this, the mother must be on a low-phenylalanine diet during the pregnancy. Distasteful as the diet may be, there is no getting around the fact that homozygous women contemplating pregnancy have to go back on the diet some time *before* conception occurs.*

"For the diet to be effective in a newborn with PKU, it should be started within the first two weeks of life. How do doctors determine who needs the diet? They do this by screening all newborn babies for this genetic disorder. What do we mean by genetic screening?

"Genetic screening is a search in a population for people with certain genotypes. These genotypes are (1) those already associated with disease or predisposition to disease, (2) those that may lead to disease in descendants, or (3) those that produce other variations *not* known to be associated with disease. PKU clearly falls into the first category, because successful detection through screening leads to effective treatment and genetic counseling to prevent recurrence. But what conditions must exist before a new screening program should be implemented on a statewide or regional basis?

"A committee of the National Academy of Sciences in Washington, D. C. reported that genetic screening, when carried out under controlled conditions, is an appropriate form of medical care when the following criteria are met:

a. There is evidence of sub-stantial public benefit and acceptance, including accep-tance by medical prac-titioners.
b. The feasibility of screening has been investigated and it has been found that benefits outweigh costs; appropriate public education can be

*USDHHS. *Maternal PKU,* DHHS Publication No. (HSA) 81-5299, USDHHS, Rockville, Maryland, 1981.

carried out; test methods are satisfactory; laboratory facilities are available; and resources exist to deal with counseling, follow-up, and other consequences of testing.
c. An investigative pretest of the program has shown that costs are acceptable; educa-tion is effective; informed consent is feasible; aims of the program with regard to size of the sample to be screened, the ages of the screenees, and the setting in which the testing is to be done have been defined; laboratory facilities have been shown to fulfill re-quirements for quality con-trol; techniques for com-municating results are workable; qualified and effective counselors are available in sufficient numbers; and adequate provision for effective ser-vices has been made.
d. The means are available to evaluate the effectiveness and success of each step in the process.

"The committee report was published in 1975. Screening for PKU began some ten years before that, however. Now, over 40 states have screening for PKU. Screening programs for PKU were instituted before the validity and effectiveness of all aspects of treatment, including appropriate dietary treatment, were tested thoroughly. Nevertheless, current assess-ment of these screening programs shows that the methods are reasonably ef-ficient, the means for moving from test to treatment are adequate, and the appropriate dietary treatment is harmless and effective.

"What happens in actual practice? Since blood phenylalanine levels rise only very slowly in a newborn, it is best to test the infant several days after birth. The doctor takes a drop of blood and puts it on a special kind of filter paper. These filter papers are sent to a testing lab where automated equipment handles many specimens at once.

"The test is quite ingenious. Dr. Robert Guthrie of New York developed it. The test is based on an increase of bacterial growth by excess phenylalanine. Facilitation of bacterial growth on the filter paper indicates an excess of phenylalanine in the infant's blood. When this happens, the physician is notified, and the lab does a more precise measurement of the blood phenylalanine level. If the blood level is high, the infant is presumed to have PKU. The doctor begins giving the child the special diet. After the blood phenylalanine level has dropped to a normal range, the diet is stopped. The doctor then gives the infant a large amount of phenylalanine to see how he or she responds. If the level of phenylalanine rises and the level of tyrosine drops, the diagnosis is considered confirmed. The child continues on the treatment program.

"For PKU, the cost of the test is quite small, and the treatment is highly effective. On the other hand, the cost of caring for a severely affected individual in an institution for many years is catastrophically high, both in emotional and financial terms.

"The average laboratory charge for the PKU screening test was between $2.00 and $2.50 in 1981. One case is likely to be found for every 15,000 to 16,000 infants screened. The cost of detecting one PKU case in 1981 was between $30,000 and $40,000. This seemingly high cost must be compared to what it costs to provide residential services for a mentally retarded PKU child or adult. It costs an average of about $7,500 each year to provide these services. On the average, a mentally retarded individual requires residential care for about 25 years. So for each child with PKU who is institutionalized, there is a projected lifetime cost of $187,500. When compared to the $40,000 detection cost, the savings are obvious. Thus, screening for PKU is cost-effective. It leads to prevention through correct diagnosis, treatment, and genetic counseling.

"Last Friday, we had a new baby boy at our house. As Greg may have told you, we waited for Benjamin's arrival with some apprehension. His mother is 38 years old and hadn't had a baby since Greg was born, over 15 years ago. So she had amniocentesis. This test ruled out the presence of a chromosomal defect, but it couldn't tell us anything about PKU. The PKU screening test given to Benjamin after he was born showed normal results, and his levels of phenylalanine and tyrosine remain normal.

"Benjamin has brown eyes and brown hair just like Greg. We are all very happy that he does not have PKU."

During our class break, we talked more about genetic screening and shared some snacks that Greg and Clarence Miller had brought in honor of Benjamin's birth.

Reference: National Research Council: Committee for the Study of Inborn Errors of Metabolism. National Academy of Sciences, Washington, D.C., 1975.

THE BOY WITH THE EXTRA X CHROMOSOME

Mr. Richard Row, a biology teacher at Jefferson High School, was using the copy machine in the school office. He saw Tom Benes, one of his tenth grade students, waiting behind him with two dimes and a letter to be copied. Mr. Row and Tom had become good friends. Tom had done a special project in genetics earlier in the year and in addition, Mr. Row was the school bandmaster and Tom played clarinet. Mr. Row had sensed for several weeks that something was bothering Tom.

"Let me have it, Tom; I'll copy it for you," offered Mr. Row. Tom declined the offer, but did not leave.

"Can I talk to you about something?" asked Tom.

"Sure, Tom. Can you come to my classroom during lunch hour?" Mr. Row suggested. Tom agreed.

Tom showed up at noon, but just picked at his lunch. He looked ill at ease. He was a very bright student and the best clarinet player the school had ever had. However, Tom had been seriously considering dropping out of the band because he was self-conscious about his height. At six feet four inches (183 cm), he towered over everyone else, and he felt that his band uniform fit poorly. To make matters worse, in spite of his height, Tom appeared immature. He had no beginnings of a beard and his voice was still high. He avoided sports because he was embarrassed about his undeveloped genitals.

The letter Tom had was from a pediatrician who specializes in inherited diseases. The Benes' family doctor had referred Tom and his parents for genetic counseling. The letter was from the Genetics, Clinic, Community General Hospital, East Rivertown, Ohio. Here is what it said:

Dear Mr. and Mrs. Benes and Tom:

This is the letter we promised to send to you following your visit to our clinic for genetic counseling on June 2, 1983. As you will recall, I told you that we prepare letters like this for most of the patients and families referred to us. Genetic conditions tend to be unfamiliar to most people. A letter like this usually helps our clients remember what we talked about. In addition, the copy we sent to your family physician, Hugh Johnson, will serve as a record of the consultation and as a source of information should you wish to discuss any of these things with him in the future. Of course, we have also sent Dr. Johnson the complete test results.

I will begin by reviewing the events that led to your being referred to "Genetics" in the first place. Tom, you have been and still are a healthy 16-year-old student doing well scholastically and socially. All three of you became a bit concerned when Tom went through the usual teenage growth spurt without showing any signs of voice deepening, beard development, or hair in the armpits and groin. At first, Dr. Johnson—quite correctly—was not concerned, since there's such a wide variation in the age at which sexual maturation occurs in both boys and girls. When he examined Tom, however, he noted that his testicles were smaller than expected for this stage of his development. For this reason, he ordered some tests to evaluate the level of male sex hormone in Tom's blood. He also ordered a chromosome analysis. When I phoned to give your doctor the results of the chromosome test, he decided to recommend that the three of you come to see us for genetic counseling.

Tom, I'm sure you recall my telling you that you are one of many individuals who has one more X chromosome than usual. Chromosomes are the structures in which genes are located. Each person has thousands of genes, usually in 46 chromosomes. Both our genes and our chromosomes come in pairs, one set from our mothers and one from our fathers. One pair of chromosomes, the X and Y pair, is concerned with sex determination. Because of an error in meiosis that occurred either in the egg or the sperm from which you developed, Tom, you ended up with that extra X.

About one out of every thousand males has this 47, XXY chromosome constitution, instead of the usual

46, XY. The books refer to the condition as Klinefelter syndrome and list a number of characteristics that may be associated with it. These include tall stature, some minor birth defects, small testicles and sterility, and even mental retardation. Obviously the most serious of these do not apply to you. Nor, in fact, do they apply to most of the rest of the many males in the world who are also 47, XXY. As best we can tell, the extra X chromosome does relatively little harm because it is inactivated! The idea that one X chromosome is inactivated is called the Lyon hypothesis.

Most men who are 47, XXY appear perfectly normal mentally and physically and many never find out they have an extra X. The only consistent findings have been sterility due to no sperm production and a tendency to be tall. Nearly all 47, XXY men mature sexually without any hormone treatments and most become sexually active.

At our meeting, we discussed marriage, infertility, and possible options for having a family, including adoption and artificial insemination. I believe it was you, Mrs. Benes, who wondered whether this obviously "genetic" condition was "hereditary." That very detailed family history we took, on both yours and Mr. Benes' side, failed to turn up any relatives with problems we might associate with 47, XXY or any other chromosomal disorder. This was as we expected, since there are no known examples of more than one individual who is 47, XXY in a family. I did mention, however, that there are families with an apparent tendency to repeated nondisjunction during meiosis— for example, a child with 47, XXY and another with Down syndrome. Were you and Mr. Benes to have another child, you might wish to consider amniocentesis.

I hope our counseling session and this letter have answered your questions. If not, please don't hesitate to contact me. I'd be happy to see you any time. I would also like to thank you for allowing the two medical students and the pediatric resident to join us for the session. It was an invaluable learning experience for them. They asked me to be sure to include their thanks in my letter.

Yours sincerely,
Robin Ramirez, MD

By the time his teacher had finished reading the letter, Tom felt a little more comfortable. "Mr. Row," he said, "I brought the letter to you mainly to thank you for making our sessions last fall on the sex chromosomes so clear and interesting. When the geneticist started talking about Klinefelter syndrome, I started to feel really bad. I felt embarrassed and upset until Dr. Ramirez started to talk about X inactivation and the Lyon hypothesis. I couldn't believe that I could remember anything when I was so nervous, but hearing something I knew about sure helped relieve the tension!"

"Tom, I'm delighted to hear that our work together helped you. Even from a quick look at this letter, I have learned a great deal. Tell me more about genetic counseling. I'm particularly interested in the presence of the medical students. Did they just appear with the doctor, or did you and your parents have some say in the matter?"

"I'm glad you asked that," Tom replied. "Before we went into the geneticist's office for the counseling, we talked quite a bit with her about what a new subject medical genetics is and how important it is for doctors to understand how people react to hearing about the facts, as well as the facts themselves. She said right off that she understood how nervous we were and that it would be perfectly okay if we decided not to have any students attend our session. Then she gave my parents and me all the time we needed to decide. Although I nearly freaked out when she started talking about such personal subjects— you know, one of those students was a girl and she didn't look much older than I am—the geneticist made things so interesting with pictures of chromosomes and by having everyone participate in the discussion, that before long we were *almost* relaxed"

"Tom, you said you wanted me to see the letter mainly to thank me and that's very gratifying. but is there anything else on your mind?"

"Yes, there is. I know I can call the geneticist or even go to see her again, but I have a couple of questions that I bet you can answer. I read in a textbook that the extra chromosome causes mental retardation and obesity. Are those things going to happen to me?"

"Well, that's a question you should ask Dr. Ramirez, but from my reading on the subject, I'd say definitely not. Among those few 47, XXY men who are mentally retarded, the retardation is present at birth and does not worsen as the person grows older. With regard to becoming overweight, every human being, no matter how many X chromosomes he or she possesses, has a genetically determined predisposition to accumulate varying amounts of fat. This predisposition even varies at different times in our lives. With only rare exceptions, we are able to control our genetic predisposition through diet and exercise. I feel confident that you will be careful about your food intake and get enough exercise to keep your weight in the normal range."

Tom then asked some very fundamental questions about gene action in the X chromosome. "If one of the two X chromosomes is inactivated in chromosomally normal 46, XX females, why don't all females have at least some of the features of the 45, X Turner syndrome (short stature, webbed neck, absence of secondary sexual characteristics, sterility, and other problems)? Along the same line, why do males with two or more X chromosomes have any problems at all?" Tom also wondered why the textbooks seem to indicate that most 47, XXY males have many physical problems and are mentally retarded, when we now know that, except for infertility, most are quite normal. Finally, he got up enough nerve to ask Mr. Row about artificial insemination. Is it available? Is it legal? Where do donors come from? How do you know they're normal?

Being a recipient of genetic counseling and knowing that he had an extra X chromosome could not change Tom's condition. But within a few months his beard and pubic hair began to appear. Understanding his problem helped him regain and further develop his self-confidence. When he stopped slouching his band uniform fit him perfectly.

PREGNANCY AFTER 35 HAS RISKS, BUT AMNIOCENTESIS CAN ALERT MOTHERS IN TIME, SAYS AN EXPERT

Reprinted from "In His Own Words," *People Weekly* magazine, January 14, 1979, by special permission; © 1980 Time Inc. All rights reserved.

As more women postpone childbearing until their mid-30's, often for career reasons, a new element of risk is added: Mothers of 35 and older give birth to nearly one-fourth of all babies with mongolism, although such women constitute only about 5% of all mothers. Risk of other genetic disorders also increases. In the past 15 years, however, a prenatal diagnostic technique has been developed which can alert mothers and physicians to chromosomal abnormalities in the fetus 15 weeks after conception. It is called amniocentesis.

A pioneer in the field is Dr. Aubrey Milunsky, 43, assistant professor of pediatrics at Harvard Medical School and medical geneticist at Massachusetts General Hospital. Since 1970 he has been director of genetics at the Eunice Kennedy Shriver Center for Mental Retardation in Waltham, Mass. Trained in his native Johannesburg, South Africa, Dr. Milunsky became a member of the Royal College of Physicians in London before emigrating to the U. S. in 1966 (he became a citizen in 1971). He is the author of six books, including *Know Your Genes* (Avon, $1.95), written for prospective parents. Recently he explained to Gail Jennes of *PEOPLE* why he believes that with prenatal testing, "Women who postpone babies need run no greater risks of having children with birth defects or genetic disorders than younger women."

What is amniocentesis?

The procedure consists of inserting a small needle through the abdominal skin into the womb, or uterus, from which a tablespoon or two of the liquid surrounding the fetus is withdrawn. Suspended in this amniotic fluid are cells, some living, which have been naturally sloughed off from the fetus. By analyzing them, many prenatal diagnoses can be made, including, incidentally, the sex of the unborn.

Do women ask for amniocentesis just to determine whether it's a boy or girl?

No; in more than ten years we have had only three such requests. We will not do amniocentesis for that purpose. Prenatal studies represent a scarce and expensive technology, and family planning is an inappropriate use of it.

How accurate is the procedure?

That depends on the expertise of the laboratory. In good laboratories, accuracy exceeds 99.4 %.

What risks do older mothers run?

The chance of having babies with chromosome defects, including Down's syndrome, or mongolism, becomes really significant at age 35, when the figure for genetic defects is close to 1%. At 40, the risk rises to 3% and at 45 to 10%.

Is amniocentesis itself risky?

It is not a test to be undertaken on a whim. There should be good reasons for it. There is a risk that the needle introduced into the body cavity may introduce infection or cause bleeding or a miscarriage.

What are the chances of losing the baby?

Very small. A National Institutes of Health study suggests a figure below 0.5% is reliable. In good hands, it's closer to 0.2% to 0.3%.

When during pregnancy should such a test be made?

At 15 to 16 weeks into the pregnancy. If the physician waits much longer—18 to 19 weeks—there is almost no time for preventive abortion to be initiated if a serious defect is found.

Who should perform the test?

A qualified obstetrician experienced in the technique. It is best done in a hospital with ultrasound facilities, which can determine the exact location of placenta and fetus.

Is an anesthetic necessary?

Some obstetricians routinely give a local anesthetic, others use none at all. Some argue that the patient says "Ouch!" and then the test is essentially over. It takes just a few minutes.

How long must a couple wait to know the results of the test?

There is a two-to-four-week waiting period while the cells are grown in a culture medium. They can then be examined under a microscope to determine if the correct number of chromosomes—46—is there. If the cell has an extra number, we can predict the genetic disorder. For instance, if there is an extra chromosome number 21, the offspring will have Down's syndrome.

Why do women 35 and over run greater risk in pregnancy?

It is not clear why. One theory suggests that both hereditary and environmental factors like X rays make the chromosomes more sticky at the point of division when conception occurs. An extra chromosome hangs in and the person is born with one extra chromosome in every cell.

Who should consider amniocentesis?

Couples with a child born defective or with a history of genetically transmissible disease. One example is spina bifida, an open defect of the spine which causes paralysis of both legs, no bladder control, and often retardation. Mothers of such children have said, "Never again!" But with the test they have had two or three more normal children.

So it eliminates fear that a baby will have certain defects?

Yes, and this is especially rewarding for a couple who have previously had a tragedy—a child with retardation or grotesque features. You can tell them for certain that their next baby does not have that condition.

How often does a couple face a decision to abort?

Only about 2% or 3% even have to consider the question.

Who makes the decision to abort?

I believe this is the parents' choice, not the doctor's. Physicians should not direct or coerce them. I believe parents have the right to know all the available information, and then they themselves should determine whether to continue or abort the pregnancy.

Can the father's age be a problem?

Yes, in certain genetic disorders. For example, fathers of circus dwarfs tend to be older—beyond 45. But the evidence in other chromosome disorders is contradictory.

Suppose the husband and wife disagree about abortion?

On these rare occasions, the courts have recognized that the woman has all the legal rights in this matter and that she can determine what to do.

What about those who say, "Many families have been advanced and enriched by having a defective child?"

For more than 20 years I have cared for families who have children with major birth defects and genetic disorders. The chaos, grief, and economic shambles of such families are legion. It is not myth. It is real and devastating, not only for the parents but for the siblings, let alone the unbelievable suffering of the actual child.

How much does amniocentesis cost?

Nationally, costs range from $250 to $500, which includes laboratory tests, counseling, and ultrasound. As a result, until recently, this tool has been for the upper-middle to high income group. You discover to your horror that the poor basically have few opportunities to have this test.

How many such tests are done?

The tardiness of the new technology is remarkable. In Massachusetts I would estimate close to 17% to 20% of women who need amniocentesis have it. Most states have a figure closer to 5%.

Why are the figures so low?

Lack of information provided to patients, and lack of information on the part of their own doctors. Physicians who graduated before 1960 had little formal genetic training and even in 1970 many medical schools did not provide full courses.

What about law cases in which the mother of a mongoloid child has sued, claiming her doctor did not inform her of the risk or about amniocentesis tests?

I am involved in at least a dozen lawsuits as an expert witness. I've been called both by plaintiffs and by defendants. The most common complaint is that physicians do not tell patients that these tests exist.

The test is a minor surgical procedure, yet certain physicians, because of religious or other bias, warn patients that the procedure kills babies. This is a serious ethical problem.

What is the cost of rearing a defective child?

The lifetime care of a mongoloid child is estimated at $500,000. It is fallacious to argue that home care is the simple answer. In practice, the vast majority of severely defective people ultimately become a burden to the taxpayer.

Where should a woman go if she does not live near a major medical center?

She should speak with her obstetrician and if necessary seek a second opinion from a university medical center's department of obstetrics or genetics. It is worth traveling any number of hours for that advice and to travel that route one more time for the test. It may spare a lifetime of grief.

When will treatment inside the womb be possible?

There is only one case of a biochemical genetic disorder where the fetus was treated through the mother by the administration of vitamin B^{12}. The fetus and subsequently the child developed normally. With new genetic engineering tools we may ultimately talk about not only treatment of genetic disease but cure. But we are a long way from that state.

GENETIC COUNSELING

Elizabeth Middleton is a genetic counselor at Colorado General Hospital in Denver, Colorado. She tells us about her work:

After I graduated from high school, I went to Montana State University in Bozeman and majored in psychology. In our human genetics course, we had a visiting speaker who was a pediatrician-geneticist from a hospital in Missoula. She talked so enthusiastically about her work that I got very interested. I read a lot about genetics and called several more people working in the field. Then, I decided to go to the University of Wisconsin for graduate studies in genetic counseling. Four years ago, I graduated with a master's degree in medical genetics. Right away, I got the job at Colorado General Hospital, where I have been ever since. I've found that genetic counseling is indeed a wonderful profession with a tremendous future. It is very satisfying work.

Genetic counseling is the *giving of information about a genetic condition*. This includes information on diagnosis, cause, what the future holds for the person with the condition (giving a prognosis), the chance of it recurring in the next pregnancy or in a future generation, and so on.

Genetic counseling occurs in many different settings. Our most important setting is the general and pediatric genetics clinic. The most common situation is when a child has a condition that is suspected to be genetically caused or predisposed. The child is brought in for diagnosis and counseling for parents. At times, the condition turns out *not* to be genetically caused, as in cases where the mother drank too much alcohol during pregnancy. Or, the child's problem may represent interaction between a maternal disorder and the fetus during prenatal development, as in the malformed child of a mother with diabetes. In some cases, a child may have suffered brain damage before, during, or after birth.

There are many disorders that "look" genetic but are "sporadic." This means that they occur only once in a family. Their cause is unknown, and the risk of recurrence in future pregnancies or generations is very low. Sometimes, a child may have died from a genetic disorder and the parents have just learned of the possible risk of recurrence. Also, parents sometimes ask about their chances of having an affected child because a relative has a particular disorder.

Most cases we see are *single* cases in a family. Most people do not come in with a history of several other affected relatives to identify it as an obviously inherited condition. We do not have descriptions of all genetic conditions, and we frequently are unable to make a diagnosis. This can make counseling difficult.

What are the conditions we see most often? In our clinic, they are mild to moderate mental retardation; malformations such as spina bifida, cleft lip, cleft palate, clubfoot, dislocated hips, and scoliosis; chromosomal abnormalities such as Down syndrome; and disorders due to gene mutations such as cystic fibrosis, hemophilia, and muscular dystrophy. There are special clinics for the last three conditions in our hospital. We go to these clinics to counsel.

We also spend a lot of time at the prenatal diagnosis clinic. We see women who are 35 years old or older and are at an increased risk of having a child with Down syndrome or women who have had a child with spina bifida and are at risk of having another. We also talk to women who are at risk of having a child with a gene mutation that can be diagnosed before birth or someone who has a complication of pregnancy that may indicate an abnormal fetus. Besides counseling before and after the prenatal diagnosis procedures, the two most important activities in this clinic are amniocentesis and ultrasonography.

Ultrasonography is a way of examining internal organs by "bouncing" sound waves off

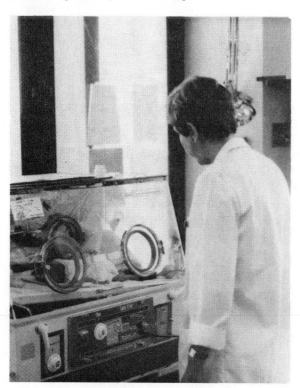

these structures and viewing their patterns on a screen. We can examine in considerable detail the fetus and its organs using this technique. We also can determine the location of the placenta. Using ultrasound, we have been able to diagnose kidney, brain, spinal-column, and abdominal-wall defects.

In amniocentesis, the obstetrician uses a local anesthetic. Then she or he inserts a needle into the uterus. The doctor must carefully avoid the placenta to prevent placental bleeding. About 10 to 15 milliliters of amniotic fluid are withdrawn and the fluid is sent to the lab. The procedure usually is done at about 16 weeks of pregnancy. In competent hands, it is quite safe. It has only about 1% risk of complications such as infection, spontaneous abortion, or fetal injury.

The two most important lab jobs done in prenatal diagnosis are chromosome analysis and alphafetoprotein determination. The amniotic fluid contains cells that have been shed by the fetus. These cells are used in a chromosome analysis to determine if the fetus has Down syndrome or some other chromosomal defect. Alphafetoprotein usually is produced only by fetuses and only during a certain stage of their development. Excessive leakage of this protein into the amniotic fluid indicates an open developmental defect somewhere. It may be an open spina bifida, absence of brain (anencephaly), open body wall, or some other defect.

In 96% of the cases we examine prenatally, we can reassure the mother that the fetus does not have a defect such as Down syndrome or spina bifida. Among the other 3% to 4% who receive a positive diagnosis, some elect abortion and some do not. Some just want the facts, so they can better prepare themselves for the birth of their baby. Because of prenatal diagnosis, many fetuses that might have been aborted—because a genetic disorder was possible—are saved.

Some people think prenatal diagnosis and abortion are the same thing. But they are not. In fact, many people can have children they really want, but might otherwise be afraid to have, because prenatal diagnosis is available. Nevertheless, feelings are strong, and the issue is beginning to show up in state legislatures. For example, on February 25, 1981, the state senate in Utah voted to prohibit pregnant women from obtaining amniocentesis. The bill is, of course, far from becoming law; but the implications for law makers and citizens are clear.

We have three other regular activities connected with genetic services at Colorado General Hospital. We have a clinic with obstetricians, gynecologists, urologists, pediatricians, and endocrinologists. These specialists examine infants with abnormally formed genitalia, infertile couples, and couples who have experienced repeated spontaneous abortions. They try to determine if there are genetic causes for these conditions.

We also work with the Mental Retardation and Child Development Center. We diagnose and counsel in cases of mental retardation and other learning disabilities not caused environmentally. That is also where we see all children with genetic metabolic defects like PKU. In addition, we hold almost 50 visiting clinics each year in 12 different towns in the state. We try to solve problems locally, but when a case requires more extensive work, we refer people to the clinics at Colorado General Hospital.

Our team of workers includes the secretary, doctors, lab experts, a clinic nurse, a social worker, and myself. The secretary receives calls, gives messages, and makes appointments. I coordinate all clinic activities. I contact each family to find out what their expectations are. I tell them about us, our staff, our facilities, and about what we can and cannot do. I prepare them carefully for what probably will happen during their visit. Then I get a family history and gather all the necessary data, such as medical records and X rays. I make a preclinic summary of the case and present it to the entire staff at our weekly conference. We may be able to decide on probable lab tests, X rays, or other consultations during that meeting.

When the family arrives, I introduce them to the staff and make sure they understand what will happen. The physicians then complete their examination before a counselor sits down to talk to the family. By that time, we have had several hours with the family and are able to talk with them comfortably. With the family, we look at the facts, the probabilities, and the options they have for dealing with their particular situation.

As you can see, genetic counseling is, in large part, a teaching job. I try, initially, to convey the facts about a condition. I sometimes use a chalkboard or prepared diagrams. Sometimes, I provide additional reading material. Informing and teaching clearly, correctly, and effectively are very important, but they are by no means the only important aspects of genetic counseling.

People are very strongly affected after having a child with a genetic disorder, which usually happens without forewarning. They also must face difficult choices that may conflict with the views of their spouses, churches, relatives, or the community. The best of counseling skills are required to assuage grief and guilt, to strengthen the ability to cope with the problems, and to restore the ability to make well-informed and carefully considered decisions.

Sometimes, as the bearer of bad news, I receive the brunt of the family's anger. A counselor must encourage people to express their feelings openly and freely. I do not take these outbursts personally, but I try to respond sympathetically and professionally.

It's not that counselors don't have feelings. Sometimes I have very strong feelings about what a family should do. But I work very hard *not* to impose my values on people. My job is to help people make their own decisions.

Three principles guide the genetic counselor. The first is "above all, do no harm." I must avoid doing anything that might hurt anyone—in any way. The second principle is that the counselor must allow and support grieving, healing, reconciliation, and acceptance. Finally, it is my job to strengthen and safeguard the integrity of the decision-making processes of the individuals and couples who come to me. They must make their own decisions, without being told what to do or not to do.

I have found that most people, faced with tragic situations and difficult decisions, rise to the challenge. They seem to deepen in character and to grow in strength and compassion. Many parents have told me—somewhat wryly—after our first contact, "This has been a great learning and growing experience, but I would not wish it on my worst enemy!"

There are many other ethical issues that I face in my work. For example, suppose an infant needs a blood transfusion. The parents are typed to see if one of them might be a compatible blood donor and the "father" is found not to be the father of the child. Whom do we tell? Where do we record the fact, knowing that all records may be subpoenaed for legal purposes?

Recently, a young man of 18 approached one of the physicians on our team. He had found out that Colorado General Hospital conducted a genetic evaluation on him years ago, before he was adopted. He wanted to know about his natural family. We pulled his files and found that he was the result of father-daughter incest. What should we tell him? Does he have a "right" to facts that might do him severe psychological harm?

We now have a reliable screening test for muscular dystrophy in affected males, even newborns. After screening several thousand newborn males, we found four that had a strongly positive test, although they appeared to be perfectly normal. On further testing, they were found to have the condition. It may take two or three years for the disorder to become evident. Here is another difficult ethical question. Should we tell the parents and let them suffer the agony of knowing their presumably normal infant will gradually develop a deadly, untreatable disorder? Or, should we not tell them and expose them to the risk of having another boy before the present infant's condition has been diagnosed?

I recently prepared a family history in a case of hemophilia. The mother was a carrier. She had several sisters who were at a 50% risk of being carriers. All were in their child-bearing years. The mother adamantly refused to divulge their names, and she warned me not to upset her family by trying to make contacts. In this case, I worried a great deal about how my duty to protect privacy and "above all, do no harm" could be balanced against my responsibility to try to prevent genetic disorders and greater suffering. Doctors and lawyers are not obligated to contact someone who is evidently in need of service. Does this maxim also guide genetic counselors?

At our last staff meeting I learned about a boy with an X-linked condition. He has symptoms of mental retardation, cerebral palsy, and self-mutilation. The genetic counselor assigned to the case learned confidentially from a social worker that the boy's mother and maternal grandmother are carriers. Each had several illegitimate daughters who were put up for adoption. The daughters are all at 50% risk of being carriers. So far as we know, none was ever told that she was adopted. What should a genetic counselor do in a situation like this?

Just last week, I told a couple of their 5% chance of having another child with a severely handicapping condition. I added, routinely, that that means they have a 95% chance of *non*-recurrence. But the parents had read that the disorder occurs as frequently as once in 2,000 live births. They reasoned that, if only 5% of parents with one affected child had another affected child, several hundred additional affected children would be born each year in the U. S. They saw this as adding a very large burden of handicap, grief, and expense to society. They were reluctant to add to that toll, even though they'd wanted another child and the chances were greatly in their favor. I had a hard time deciding what to tell them next.

Whenever I talk with people about problems like these, I warn them not to come to any firm conclusions too quickly. I also remind them of their fundamental right to change their minds tomorrow, and—if new developments warrant—to change it back on the next day. To remind myself of this, I have a poster on my wall that quotes Mark Twain: Beware of friends who agree with you—they might be wrong, too.

DID YOU KNOW THAT—

1. Genetic disorders are *not* rare.

2. Very few inherited disorders are the result of extra or missing chromosomes.

3. Scientists are a long way from cloning humans; they may never be able to do it.

4. Genetic counseling centers are located in almost every state.

5. Many genetic diseases can be treated.

6. Not all genetic disorders are birth defects.

7. Some genetic disorders can be prevented.

8. Most inherited characteristics do not follow Mendelian patterns.

9. Everyone carries some genes that could result in disorders in them or in their children.

10. The availability of amniocentesis encourages many people to have children who might otherwise be afraid to do so.

11. You cannot "catch" a genetic disorder.

12. Inherited traits for intellectual giftedness do not skip a generation.

13. Down syndrome is not caused by trisomy X.

14. Only males in a family being affected does not necessarily indicate an X-linked disorder.

15. A one-quarter probability does not mean one in four children in a family.

16. Not all birth defects are genetic disorders.

17. If you toss 19 heads in a row, your chances of tossing a tail on the twentieth flip is still one-half.

18. Some genetic disorders, such as Huntington disease, usually do not appear until midlife.

19. Many of our most common killers, such as heart disease and cancer, are thought to have a genetic base.

20. Human genetics is of interest to ethicists, philosophers, and theologians, as well as to scientists.

CAREERS IN GENETICS

Genetics is a rapidly growing branch of biology. It offers many and varied career opportunities now and will continue to do so in the future.

Agricultural Genetics

The most impressive early achievements of genetics were in plant and animal breeding. These accomplishments have led to tremendous improvements in crop productivity and in livestock. Because serious food shortages occur in many areas of the world, improvement in productivity of crops is a serious concern of biologists. As the world's population continues to grow, food shortages are likely to become more severe.

Agricultural geneticists are working to develop new plant strains that are more resistant to pests and disease, higher in nutritional value, and capable of higher yields. Newly developed strains yield billions of dollars in cash crops each year.

Selective breeding of cows and other livestock has produced animals that are more resistant to insect diseases and capable of producing a better quality and quantity of meat.

Although genetic research has improved the quality and yield of crops and livestock, much more work is needed to meet the world's ever-increasing demand for food.

Schools and colleges of agriculture are associated with a number of state universities. Those interested in entering agricultural genetics as a career should contact one or more such schools for more information.

Human Genetics

Human genetics is the study of human variability. Normal human variability sometimes is included under the broad field of anthropology. In the U. S., anthropology has become separated from genetics. However, in certain European countries, professors of human genetics are also professors of anthropology, so a close link is maintained between the two.

The study of normal human variability has only begun. Hundreds of different human population groups await closer characterization of physical attributes. We need more information about such things as height, head size and shape, functional characteristics (strength, endurance, lung capacity, and liver functions), blood groups, serum proteins, enzymes, and other characteristics.

Career opportunities in both agricultural and human genetics are improved through graduate studies leading to master's or doctoral degrees.

Additional post-graduate study in a special field also is an advantage.

Medical Genetics

Medical genetics is the study of abnormal human variability. This includes conditions due to chromosomal anomalies, multifactorial gene-environment interaction, and mutations. New methods of chromosome analysis have led to the discovery of hundreds of additional syndromes that are due to structural changes in chromosomes. Most genetic conditions are multifactorial disorders, just as most normal characteristics are multifactorial. These disorders account for most birth defects as well as a large number of diseases of adults.

Other areas of human genetic biology are expected to expand considerably in this century. These include immunogenetics, biochemical genetics, pharmacogenetics, and behavioral genetics.

For those wanting to pursue a career of research in these fields, graduate study toward a PhD and post-doctoral studies are recommended. For those wanting to do clinical genetics—that is, using the practice of medicine to help people with genetic defects—medical school and post-MD training, including residency and post-doctoral fellowship, are recommended.

Genetic Counseling

Recently, a new group of professionals has arisen in response to the enormous demand for genetic services. These are the genetic counselors. Many genetic counselors have master's degrees with special training in genetic counseling. Some are physicians and some have PhD degrees in genetics. They provide a wide range of services in clinics and hospitals. Demand for well-trained and experienced genetic counselors is outstripping supply. And the demand probably will increase. Genetic counselors now serve on the staffs of institutions for the retarded, blind, and deaf. They work in schools and in state offices such as bureaus of maternal and child health. They are employed in city and county nursing and social service departments, large hospitals, and many other institutions.

Professional Qualifications

Recently, the American Board of Medical Genetics was formed to assure highest standards of training and knowledge for those who work in clinical genetics or genetic counseling. Board examinations are given to four groups: genetic counselors with master's degrees; clinical geneticists who are physicians; PhD human geneticists; and PhD (and/or MD) laboratory geneticists. This last group includes cytogeneticists, biochemical geneticists, and immunogeneticists. All of these groups will be expected to keep up with changes and new knowledge in their fields. The U.S. plan is similar to the plan already established in Canada.

Other Career Opportunities

For those not wishing to go beyond a four-year college education, there are many other career opportunities—particularly as trained and certified laboratory technicians to work in immunogenetic, biochemical, and cytogenetic labs. Those who are interested in careers in genetics should contact local hospitals, clinics, colleges, or universities for information on the subject.

GENETICS IN HISTORY: GREGOR MENDEL

Figure 1. Gregor Johann Mendel

The life and the accomplishments of Gregor Johann Mendel, the Augustinian monk whose experiments with garden peas and flowers form the basis of modern genetics, are often romanticized. He tends to be portrayed as a simple monk who almost stumbled onto the laws of heredity as he tended the monastery garden. With no intention of diminishing the extraordinary contributions of this brilliant man, we feel that it is important to realize that very few major advances occur "out of the blue." The majority of successul investigators are well-educated, hard-working, and familiar with the related work of their predecessors. They are innovative individuals whose work builds on data obtained by others. Mendel was no exception.

Gregor Johann Mendel was born on July 22, 1822 in Heinzendorf, an agricultural district of present day Czechoslovakia. The son of a peasant, Mendel received much of his early education from the vicar of a neighboring village. Mendel's early education included horticulture as well as elementary subjects. Mendel's outstanding ability was recognized at an early age and his parents were advised to send him to the secondary school in Leipnik. He was later sent to the Gymnasium (secondary school) in Troppau.

During Mendel's fifth year at Troppau, his father became seriously ill and was forced to retire. Mendel began private tutoring to pay for his education. Weakened by the strain of long hours, Mendel became very ill and was forced to leave the Gymnasium for several months. He later recovered, completed his studies, and enrolled at the University of Olmutz. Beset by illness again, Mendel left the university and spent a year recuperating at his parent's home. With the aid of his younger sister, who gave him a part of her dowry, Mendel was able to complete his education at Olmütz.

On the recommendation of his physics teacher, Mendel entered the Augustinian monastery. The decision to enter the monastery at Brno was a matter of necessity rather than choice. At the monastery, Mendel was able to continue his studies without the financial worries that had plagued him during the previous years. During his stay at the monastery, Mendel studied agriculture and sheep breeding, as well as philosophy and natural science. He was later placed in charge of the experimental gardens run by the monastery.

When Mendel completed his theological studies, he was assigned duties at a neighboring hospital where he ministered to the sick. Mendel was so overcome by the condition of the patients that he began to experience severe depression. The abbot transferred him to Znojmo in Moravia where he served as a substitute teacher.

Mendel was so successful and popular as a teacher, it was suggested that he take a university examination for teachers. Mendel took the examination but failed it. On the advice of the physics professor, Mendel was sent to the University of Vienna.

After returning to Brno, Mendel taught at the Brno Technical High School. During this time, Mendel began his work on garden peas. In May of 1856, he attempted to take the university examination for teachers for the second time. Unable to handle the stress associated with the examination, Mendel broke down and did not complete the examination. He returned to Brno very ill. He served as a substitute in the Brno Technical School until 1868, when he was elected abbot of the monastery. He served in this capacity until his death in 1884.

At about the same time Mendel was beginning his plant hybridization experiments, he began a careful study of weather. He quickly achieved a reputation as an authority on meteorological phenomena. He published numerous meteorological reports beginning in 1863. He suggested, as early as 1870, that the collision of conflicting air masses produced tornadoes. Although Mendel's weather studies received less recognition than his plant hybridization experiments, they demonstrated the same research methods that characterized his plant experiments.

Mendel's plant experiments were unique for several reasons. First, he bred many plants with identical traits. He later made hundreds of crosses for each trait. Second, Mendel used the mathematics of probability to analyze his data and to arrive at hypotheses that would explain his results. Third, Mendel did not try to study every characteristic of an offspring at once. Instead, he limited his study to a single trait at a time.

During Mendel's time, chromosomes were unknown and scientists had no knowledge of the processes of cell division. Using only the results of his breeding experiments, Mendel provided the first clear explanation of the nature of heredity.

Although Mendel published his results in 1865, it was not until 1900 that his paper was "discovered" by three scientists working independently on similar problems. All three recognized that the report of an almost unknown Augustinian monk preceded their reports by over three decades. Mendel had already laid the foundation for the study of heredity.

GENETICS IN LITERATURE: POETRY CORNER

from "Ode (Intimations of Immortality from Recollections of Early Childhood)"

...

Ye blessed Creatures, I have heard the call
Ye to each other make; I see
The heavens laugh with you in your jubilee;
My heart is at your festival,
My head hath its coronal,
The fullness of your bliss, I feel—I feel it all.
Oh evil day! if I were sullen
While earth itself is adorning,
This sweet May-morning,
And the children are culling
On every side,
In a thousand valleys far and wide,
Fresh flowers; while the sun shines warm,
And the babe leaps up in his mother's arm—
I hear, I hear, with joy I hear!
—But there's a tree, of many, one,
A single field which I have looked upon,
Both of them speak of something that is gone:
The pansy at my feet
Doth the same tale repeat:
Whither is fled the visionary gleam?
Where is it now, the glory and the dream?

...

William Wordsworth (1770-1850)

"Leaf after Leaf.,,"

Leaf after leaf drops off, flower after flower,
Some in the chill, some in the warmer hour:
Alike they flourish and alike they fall,
And earth who nourished them receives them all.
Should we, her wiser sons, be less content
To sink into her lap when life is spent?

Walter Savage Landor (1775-1864)

"Signpost"

Civilized, crying how to be human again: this will tell you how.
Turn outward, love things, not men, turn right away from
    humanity,
Let that doll lie. Consider if you like how the lilies grow,
Lean on the silent rock until you feel its divinity
Make your veins cold, look at the silent stars, let your eyes
Climb the great ladder out of the pit of yourself and man.
Things are so beautiful, your love will follow your eyes;
Things are the God, you will love God, and not in vain,
For what we love, we grow to it, we share its nature. At
    length
You will look back along the stars' rays and see that even
The poor doll humanity has a place under heaven...

Robinson Jeffers (1887-1962)

"Tell Me, Tell Me..."

Tell me, tell me, smiling child,
    What the past is like to thee?
"An autumn evening, soft and mild,
    With a wind that sighs mournfully."

Tell me, what is the present hour?
    "A green and flowery spray,
Where a young bird sits gathering its power
    To mount and fly away."

And what is the future, happy one?
    "A sea beneath a cloudless sun—
A mighty, glorious, dazzling sea,
    Stretching into infinity."

Emily Jane Bronte (1818-1848)

From "The Repetitive Heart"

III

All clowns are masked and all *personae*
Flow from choices; sad and gay, wise,
Moody and humorous are chosen faces,
And yet not so! For all are circumstances,
Given, like a tendency
To colds or like blond hair and wealth,
Or war and peace or gifts for mathematics,
Fall from the sky, rise from the ground, stick to us
In time, surround us: Socrates is mortal.

Gifts and choices! All men are masked,
And we are clowns who think to choose our faces
And we are taught in time of circumstances
And we have colds, blond hair and mathematics,
For we have gifts which interrupt our choices,
And all our choices graps in Blind Man's Buff:
"My wife was very different, after marriage,"
"I practise law, but botany's my pleasure,"
Save postage stamps or photographs,
But save your soul! Only the past is immortal.

Decide to take a trip, read books of travel,
Go quickly! Even Socrates is mortal,
Mention the name of happiness: it is
Atlantis, Ultima Thule, or the limelight,
Cathay or Heaven. But go quickly
And remember: there are circumstances
And he who chooses chooses what is given,
And he who chooses is ignorant of Choice,
—Choose love, for love is full of children,
Full of choices, children choosing
Botany, mathematics, law and love,
So full of choices! So full of children!
And the past is immortal, the future is inexhaustible!

Delmore Schwartz (1913-1966)

LOOKING TO THE FUTURE

GENE MAPPING

Cathy Glenn was starting her sophomore year of high school. She was excited about the prospect of taking biology. She had done very well in her earlier science courses and was looking forward to the beginning of the school year.

During the first class session her teacher, Mrs. Mayes, assigned a science fair project. Although Cathy had received good grades in junior high school science, she had never done a science fair project before. She had no idea of where to begin. After school, she went back to Mrs. Mayes' office to ask for some suggestions. Mrs. Mayes gave her some tips on getting started and suggested a number of topics, including gene mapping.

Cathy found several books on genetics in the local library but discovered that some of the material was so technical that it was hard to understand. Cathy decided to stay after school and discuss gene mapping with Mrs. Mayes.

Mrs. Mayes told Cathy that the subject would make a fascinating science fair project because it is such a good example of how what appears to be rather "far-out" research has real value for many people and their families.

"For example, consider Huntington disease," Mrs. Mayes said. "This very serious disorder is caused by a dominant gene on an autosome. Any child of a parent who has HD has a 50% risk of developing the disease. Usually, symptoms do not develop until a person is 35 or even older. Right now, there is no way to determine who has the dominant gene until the symptoms actually appear."

Mrs. Mayes continued, "Suppose we knew that the gene for Huntington disease was right next to the ABO blood group gene locus. Imagine also that, in a particular family, the individuals with the disease were all blood group B. Thus, we would know that the chromosome with the Huntington gene also contained the gene for blood group B. Under the right circumstances, we could identify the individuals who would develop Huntington disease long before they developed any signs of it, simply by determining their blood group. This simple pedigree (Figure 1) is an example. The father has the disease and has passed the Huntington gene to his son and one of his two daughters. Obviously, the blood group could be determined any time after birth. The actual signs of the disease wouldn't occur until many years later. This is, of course, not a fact at all. But it is a simple way of showing how gene mapping could be applied to the solution of real problems."

In order to understand the recent advances in gene mapping, Mrs. Mayes went on to say, Cathy needed to remember that genes are organized along the length of a chromosome. Genes on the same chromosome are said to be "linked." Thus far, scientists have not been able to comprehend the system that accounts for the location of specific genes or groups of genes in specific places in specific chromosomes.

Mrs. Mayes explained that during meiosis, when the chromosomes come together in pairs—no. 1 with no. 1, no. 2 with no. 2, and so on—crossing over sometimes occurs, and chromosome segments are

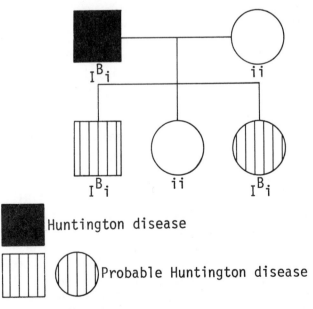

Figure 1.   Hypothetical pedigree to illustrate the use of linkage

101

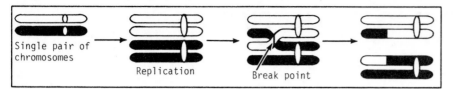

Figure 2. Crossing over during early stages of meiosis

transferred (Figure 2). As a result, genes located on the same chromosome in one generation of a family may *not* be transmitted together to the next generation. The closer together two genes are on a chromosome—or, in other words, the more closely they are linked—the more likely they are to stay together. Thus, they are less likely to be separated by crossing over.

Mrs. Mayes, noticing a confused look on Cathy's face, asked if she had any questions. Cathy responded, "How does all of this information help scientists locate the position of genes on chromosomes?"

Mrs. Mayes explained that, until recently, pedigree studies were the only methods available to scientists for assigning genes to chromosomes. Although studies of family trees have allowed geneticists to assign hundreds of genes to the autosomes and nearly 200 to the X chromosome, the work is painstaking. People today tend to have relatively few children. Only rarely are even three generations available for study. Even if we had huge families to study, we could never figure out which of the 22 autosomal chromosomes any gene is on.

The discovery of cell fusion in cell culture dishes was an important achievement in cell biology. Since the intial recognition of spontaneous cell fusion, various methods have been developed that not only increase the frequency of cell

fusion but also the survival rate of the resulting cells. These new methods provided scientists with exciting new information in many areas of cell biology. Mrs. Mayes then explained to Cathy some of the details of the research on gene mapping using these cell fusion methods.

"In 1967, Weiss and Green successfully fused human cells with mouse cells. After the fused cells had grown for a few weeks in culture dishes, Weiss and Green made an extraordinary observation. In the "hybrid" cells derived from one mouse cell and one human cell, the mouse chromosomes were still there. But 75% to 95% of the human chromosomes were gone! It was as if the mouse cell was able to kick the human chromosomes out! Suddenly the door to mapping human chromosomes was thrown open."

Mrs. Mayes went on. "The procedure is a bit tricky, but it's so fascinating that you'll enjoy working through it. Just keep your eyes on the diagram (Figure 3) and it will all make sense. We start with specially chosen mouse and human cells. The mouse cells come from a mouse with a genetic defect, a deficiency of the enzyme thymidine kinase, which will be represented by the symbol TK⁻. The human cells come from a person with a different genetic defect that we'll refer to as HGPRT⁻. You'll see why we chose those particular cells for our fusion experiment in just a moment.

"The first step is to mix the mouse and human cells and add the fusing agent. Believe it or not, antifreeze (ethylene glycol) is the best cell fuser available. Apparently, it makes cell membranes sticky. After the cells grow for awhile, we have a mixture of unfused human and mouse cells; human cells fused with human cells; mouse with mouse; some "giant cells" with many nuclei. Finally, there are the ones we want: cells that come from one human and one mouse cell—the hybrid cells."

At this point, Cathy asked, "How can scientists tell one cell from the other? How can they isolate the hybrid cells to do mapping studies?"

Mrs. Mayes explained: "This is where those genetic defects come in. The original TK⁻ mouse cells and HGPRT⁻ human cells grow just fine in regular culture medium. But we have a special medium called 'HAT' which omits three components that are essential for making new DNA. Cells that have both TK and HGPRT (TK⁺ and HGPRT⁺ cells) can make their own precursors or building blocks. TK⁻ and HGPRT⁻ cells can't and they just don't grow. Thus, when we put our fused cell mixture into 'HAT' medium, cell colonies begin to grow. The cells in those colonies must all be hybrids. Why? Because the TK⁻ mouse cells supply HGPRT and the HGPRT⁻ human cells supply TK. Only the hybrid cells have the ability to make both chemicals. (The 'giant cells' have so many nuclei that they cannot divide, so they just sit there.)

"Now the scientists can pick off the hybrid cell colonies, grow them for several weeks, check the chromosomes period-

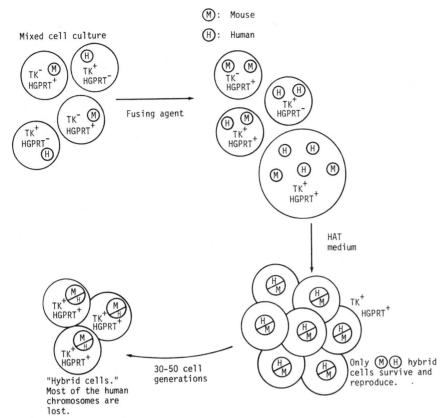

Figure 3. Steps in cell hybridization

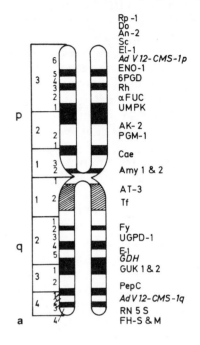

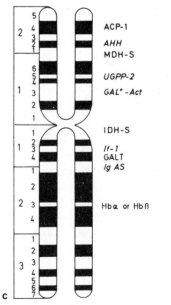

Figure 5. Human chromosome 1

From A. P. Mange and E. J. Mange, *Genetics: Human Aspects*, Saunders College, Philadelphia, 1980, Figure 12-14.

Human chromosomes | Mouse chromosomes

Figure 4.

and Y. In addition, consistent segments within chromosomes have been identified and categorized. Improvements in banding methods, used in conjunction with other methods, permitted the assignment of gene loci to specific chromosome bands (Figure 5).

ically, and watch the human chromosomes disappear. It's easy to tell the human chromosomes from the mouse because the mouse chromosomes have a distinctive shape. The centromere (Figure 4) is located at one end of the chromosome and there are no short-arm chromosome segments extending beyond the centromere. Here's where the mapping comes in. It was Weiss and Green again who did the first autosomal gene assignment. They noted that all of the hybrid cells that were able to grow for a long period of time in the HAT medium had one specific human chromosome. It turned out to be number 17. They concluded that the human gene for TK must be on chromosome 17, because the cell could not grow in HAT medium without it. This was the first assignment of a human gene to a particular chromosome on a biochemical basis.

"From this beginning, there has been an explosion of information on the human gene map. Another major step forward was the introduction of banding methods for human chromosomes in 1970. These methods made it possible for scientists to progress from simple assignments of chromosomes to groups, by size and location of the centromere, to identification of each specific chromosome from 1 through 22 plus X

"Today specific genes have been assigned to every human chromosome. The number of assignments is increasing almost monthly. A typical example is shown in this diagram of human chromosome 1. The abbreviations are mostly for proteins. There are a couple of diseases: RP-1 is one form of retinitis pigmentosa. Rh is the blood group gene.

"You may wonder how the scientists go about getting the genes in the right order. It takes time and a bit of luck and depends on chromosome abnormalities. For example, if we found in a hybrid cell a chromosome 1 with a specific piece missing (a chromosome "deletion"), and the human AK-2 and PGM-1 enzymes were also missing, we would know that the genes for AK-2 and PGM-1 are located in that region of the chromosome. All sorts of deletions and other chromosome rearrangements are found naturally. Many more can be induced in the laboratory using mutagenic chemicals, viruses, and ionizing radiation."

Mrs. Mayes then told Cathy about some newer methods for locating genes on chromosomes. Among these is *in situ* (in place) hybridization. *In situ* hybridization involves the use of radioactively labeled messenger RNA or labeled DNA to determine the location of repetitive DNA fractions on chromosomes. Since the labeled messenger RNA only combines with its complementary DNA, the position of the DNA may be detected by autoradiography.

Cathy asked what practical value all this work on mapping might have. Mrs. Mayes answered that there are many possible applications. Mrs. Mayes said, "Look at this gene map for the X chromosome (Figure 6). You can see that the

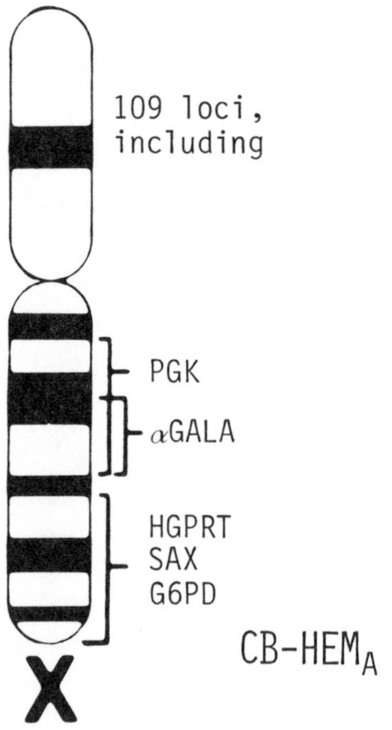

Figure 6. Map of some of the genes on the human X chromosome

From F. Vogel and A. G. Motulsky, *Human Genetics: Problems and Approaches*, Springer-Verlag, New York, N. Y. , 1979, p. 119.

gene for glucose 6-phosphate dehydrogenase (G6PD) and the gene for hemophilia (HEM$_A$) are closely linked on the long arm of the X. It is unlikely that these two genes would be separated during crossing over. There are two major types of G6PD. The different types can be detected in cells extracted during amniocentesis. If a female carrier of hemophilia were heterozygous for G6PD types, it could be determined which type was linked with the gene for hemophilia. Prenatal diagnosis on cells from a male fetus, using the G6PD type as the key piece of information, would determine with a high degree of accuracy whether the

fetus was affected with hemophilia.

"Gene mapping has also been used to study the evolutionary relationship among different species. A great deal of work has been done on mapping the location of genes in primates, such as the chimpanzee and the gorilla. It is assumed that the more similar the gene maps between two species, the more closely related they are. The banding patterns of the chromosomes of the chimpanzee, gorilla, orangutan, and humans are quite similar. The chimpanzee and *Homo sapiens* also share the same structural genes on chromosomes 1, 2, 11, 12, 17, 21, and X.

"Gene mapping, especially in microorganisms, has also led to a new understanding of how genes are organized on the DNA molecule. It was originally thought that a gene was specified by a continuous string of DNA. But gene mapping studies have shown that some genes overlap others. Some genes occur in pieces, with large segments of uncoded DNA between them. There are even some segments of DNA—called "transposons" or "jumping genes"—that can move from one place to another. It is expected that gene mapping techniques will shed more light on gene function and regulation, leading eventually to better understanding and improved treatment for diseases of all kinds."

Cathy looked at the clock and realized that she had become so involved in the conversation that she had forgotten about her basketball practice. She thanked Mrs. Mayes for her help and assured her that she now had a better idea of how to begin her science fair project.

WHAT IS OUR RESPONSIBILITY TO FUTURE GENERATIONS?

An interview with Sheri Berenbaum, U. S. Senator, a member of the Senate Committee on Health and Human Services.

Interviewer: Well, Senator Berenbaum, I certainly appreciate your taking time from your work on the Senate Committee on Health and Human Services to discuss your views with us today.

Senator Berenbaum: My pleasure. I welcome the opportunity to discuss health issues with you.

I: I know that you are very interested in improving the health of the citizens of your state. And you have been particularly active in legislation regarding genetic screening programs of both adults and newborns. Now, tell me, senator, are we making progress in eradicating genetic diseases?

SB: First of all, I think you are a bit confused about what is meant by genetic disease and by our goals for the programs I have worked hard to fund. There is not just one genetic disease. There are many, and they are inherited in different ways. Some are recessive—cystic fibrosis, for example—and some are sex-linked. Others are dominant. Disorders that show predictable patterns of inheritance are the ones we know most about. Other diseases are much less predictable. They may have a genetic component, but they also are influenced by environmental factors. Second, I'm not sure what you mean by "eradicate."

I: I mean cure. Isn't that what we want to do?

SB: Well, there again, that sounds too simple to me. When you talk about curing a genetic disease, do you mean providing treatment or preventing it from occurring?

Great progress has been made in the last 20 years in both prevention and treatment of genetic disorders. PKU is a good example of a success story due to treatment. If PKU is detected soon after birth, the child can be placed on a complicated special diet that is low in phenylalanine and high in tyrosine. As a result, phenylalanine does not build up to poisonous levels and tyrosine is available in adequate amounts. The child does not develop mental retardation. In most states now, infants are screened for PKU a few days after birth. I think this is a good example of an important improvement in public health.

I: How much does it cost to screen all infants?

SB: Actually, the taxpayer is saving money with this program. By detecting PKU infants and arranging for dietary treatment, we prevent the severe mental retardation these children would develop without the treatment. Without treatment, 90% of these children would have I.Q. scores of less than 50. These treated children don't have to be institutionalized. The taxpayer now pays only about one-third of the cost that used to be associated with this disease.

I: So you say we have eradicated one genetic disease, PKU.

SB: There you go again, using that word "eradicate." It's true we have learned how to diagnose and treat PKU children so they can live normal lives. But the result actually is a slow increase in the genes responsible for PKU.

I: Are you saying that by treating genetic diseases *today* we are affecting the genetic makeup of future generations? Will these genes spread through future populations? Will everyone have to grow up on a special diet?

SB: That question is not as simple as it appears. The answer depends on the type of inheritance pattern a particular disorder follows and on how common it is.

For a rare disorder that has a recessive pattern of inheritance, we see a slow increase. For example, if the disorder appears in 100 people out of every million today, it will increase very slowly. After 2,000 years of medical treatment, only 121 people out of every million will have the condition (Figure 1).

I: Are dominant traits different?

SB: Very different. Look at this chart (Figure 2). A very rare dominant condition may occur in only 20 individuals out of a million. Successful treatment of a dominant condition results in a rapid increase in the number of people who need to be treated. After 2,000 years, 2,018 people in every million will require the treatment.

I: Is PKU inherited as a recessive or a dominant?

SB: PKU is a recessive (Figure 1). It will increase very slowly in

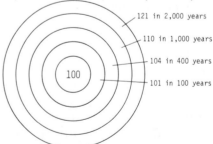

Figure 1. Increase in the frequency of a rare recessive trait due to successful medical treatment of those people diagnosed as homozygous recessive. (Source: Victor A. McKusick and R. Claiborne, *Medical Genetics,* Hospital Practice Publishing Co., New York, 1976, p. 277, portion of figure)

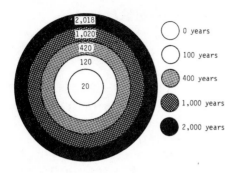

Figure 2. Increase in frequency of a rare dominant trait due to successful medical treatment of those people with the trait. (Source: Victor A. McKusick and R. Claiborne, *Medical Genetics,* Hospital Practice Publishing Co., New York, 1976, p. 277, portion of figure)

our population. Today, the number of babies with PKU is about 100 in every million babies in the U.S. If we continue to screen and treat for PKU, in 2,000 years about 121 in every million babies born in the U.S. will have PKU.

I: Is that fair to future generations? Maybe we should have laws that prohibit individuals with PKU from having children.

SB: This is a difficult problem. It may not be terribly important right now for a rare recessive such as PKU with a slow rate of increase. For a dominant, this may be a very important question. But I will not introduce any legislation prohibiting certain people from having children. At this point, people have to decide for themselves what is their responsibility to future generations.

I: But government has been heavily involved in medical research that results in screening to identify affected individuals. Taxpayers' money also goes for treatment of these individuals. Doesn't government, therefore, have responsibility for protecting future generations?

SB: You make it sound as if government is some mysterious

entity with power over the lives of all citizens. I thought this was a government "of the people, by the people, for the people." I was elected to represent those citizens. And I don't think my constituents favor laws prohibiting certain people from having children.

I: Have you asked them?

SB: My staff is writing a questionnaire to send to voters in my state. We will include some questions on these issues. However, most people know very little about human genetics. So many new developments have occurred in the last ten years that it's not something people learn about in school. How do you ask someone what they think about responsibility to future generations when they don't know what the long-term effects of treatment can be?

I: What can you tell us about efforts to prevent genetic disorders?

SB: Prevention is an important part of the programs I have supported in the U.S. Senate. One method of prevention is amniocentesis. The prenatal screening of a fetus at risk for Tay-Sachs disease can inform the parents if the child-to-be will develop the disorder. The parents then can decide whether to terminate the pregnancy or have the child. In the case of Tay-Sachs, most decide to terminate the pregnancy. There is no treatment for the disease, and the child usually dies before reaching age five.

I: This means that the genes of the child with Tay-Sachs never get passed on to future generations. So, this sort of program should not affect people living 2,000 years from now.

SB: No. Even this sort of program may have some effect on future generations. Those

parents who decide to terminate a pregnancy because of an affected fetus usually have other children. Because the parents are both carriers of the Tay-Sachs gene, their normal children have a 67% chance of being carriers. Therefore, the number of carriers may be very slowly increasing. This, then, may generate a need for more prenatal screening in the future. As in other areas of our culture, we may be increasing our dependence on what some call "high technology." If we use that technology, many people may be hurt. But medical genetics is only one of the many technologies we depend on today.

I: Thank you, Senator. I enjoyed our conversation, and I'm sure our reders will have more to think about regarding future generations.

RECESSIVE GENES AND THE GENE POOL

What happens to the frequency of the recessive gene in the gene pool generation after generation? To answer this question, one can set up a population model, make random matings, predict probability of offspring, and compare real data to expected data. To try it for yourself, you will need a pencil and a copy of Figure 1, 80 red and 120 white beads of the same size and material, string or wire, a box, and a calculator, if you have one.

1. The Hardy-Weinberg principle shows that the frequency of a recessive gene is the square root of the frequency of homozygous recessive individuals in the gene pool. Therefore, if 36% of the population is homozygous recessive for the gene for PTC tasting (that is, they cannot taste PTC and have the genotype **tt**), the frequency of the gene in the gene pool is $\sqrt{.36}$ or 0.6. The frequency of the dominant allele is 1 - 0.6, or 0.4.

2. A model of this population can be set up by wiring beads together in pairs. Use red beads to represent the **T** allele and white beads as the **t** allele. Tie or wire beads together to make a population of 100: 16 pairs of two red beads (homozygous tasters **TT**); 48 pairs of one red bead and one white bead (heterozygous tasters **Tt**); and 36 pairs of two white beads (homozygous nontasters **tt**).

3. Place these 100 pairs of beads in a box, mix them thoroughly. Have one person at a time withdraw, at random, two pairs of beads. These pairs represent matings. Record each mating on a copy of Figure 1 in the column marked "Number of Crosses."

4. Repeat the mating procedure 50 times. Return the beads to the box after each mating.

5. Assume that each pair of "parents" produces four "offspring" and that the genotypes of these four progeny are those that are *theoretically possible* in single gene pair inheritance. Tally the offspring from each of the 50 matings: then total the number of **TT, Tt,** and **tt** offspring.

6. Calculate the genotype frequencies of the offspring. Then calculate the frequencies of the alleles in the gene pool of the offspring.

Interpreting the Results

1. How do the genotype and gene frequencies of the "offspring" in your matings compare with the genotype and gene frequencies of the "parents"? Discuss and explain your results.

2. Why are physical and mathematical models like this one such important conceptual tools in biology?

3. In this population, no forces of natural selection were operating against any of the genotypes. And all genotypes were capable of reproduction. What do you think would have happened to the gene frequencies if these conditions had not been met? Why?

POSSIBLE CROSSES	NUMBER OF CROSSES	NUMBER OF OFFSPRING	EXPECTED GENOTYPES OF OFFSPRING TT	Tt	tt
TT x TT					
Tt x Tt					
TT x Tt					
tt x tt					
TT x tt					
Tt x tt					
TOTALS	50	200			

Figure 1. A chart for recording data

SELECTION AND THE GENE POOL

"Recessive Genes and the Gene Pool" (page 107) illustrated what happens to the frequencies of genes and genotypes when all genotypes have an equal chance to reproduce. Selection results in *unequal* reproduction of genotypes. What would happen to the frequencies of tasters and nontasters if individuals with one or the other genotypes had a greater or lesser chance of survival and reproduction? To find out, you will need four copies of Figure 2 and one copy of Figure 3, a pencil, the pairs of red and white beads you wired together for the "Recessive Genes..." exercise, a box, and a calculator, if you have one. You will need more red-red (**TT**) and red-white (**Tt**) combinations than you used before. You can make these pairs in advance or as you need them.

1. The original population in the "Recessive Genes and the Gene Pool" activity (which we will symbolize by G_0) had genotype frequencies of **TT** = .16, **Tt** = .48, and **tt** = .36. The gene frequency was **T** =.4 and **t** = .6. When 50 crosses were made with this G_0 population and the genotypes of the 200 offspring (the G_1 population) were calculated, you probably found very little, if any, difference in the frequencies.

2. Now, take this original population and introduce a new factor. Suppose that, through a spontaneous mutation, all the homozygous recessives in the G_0 population are sterile. On the basis of this new information, determine what the effect would be on the G_1 population. Put the G_0

population in the box and draw out 50 matings. Record the matings and the offspring on a copy of Figure 2. Return the beads to the box after each mating.

3. After you have determined the genotypes of the offspring in the new generation, calculate the genotype and gene frequencies and record your answers in the space provided. Now, empty the box and establish this new generation as the breeding population. Label a fresh copy of Figure 2 and proceed as before.

4. Repeat this procedure until you have generated data for four generations of offspring (G_1 through G_4).

5. Summarize the genotype and gene frequencies for all five generations (including G_0) on your copy of Figure 3.

Interpreting the Results

1. What is happening to the frequency of the recessive gene?

2. In which genotype in G_4 are most of the recessive genes found?

3. How does this compare to G_0?

4. Compare your data from the "Recessive Genes and the Gene Pool" activity to the data in this activity. Is selection enough to explain the differences? Explain your answer.

5. Even under extreme selection, can a recessive gene be eliminated from a gene pool?

GENERATION NUMBER ____

POSSIBLE CROSSES	NUMBER OF CROSSES	NUMBER OF OFFSPRING	EXPECTED GENOTYPES OF OFFSPRING TT	Tt	tt
TT x TT					
Tt x Tt					
TT x Tt					
tt x tt		0	0	0	0
TT x tt		0	0	0	0
Tt x tt		0	0	0	0
TOTALS	50				

Genotype frequencies in the new generation   TT _____   Tt _____   tt _____

Use these for matings in the next generation.
Gene frequencies t _____   T _____

Figure 2. A table for recording data

GENERATION	GENOTYPE FREQUENCIES TT	Tt	tt	GENE FREQUENCIES T	t
G_0	0.16	0.48	0.36	0.4	0.6
G_1					
G_2					
G_3					
G_4					

Figure 3. A table for summarizing frequencies of genes and genotypes

THE MIRACLE OF SPLICED GENES

Scientists call it "the construction of biologically functional bacterial plasmids *in vitro*." To laymen, what it means is the creation of new forms of life.

The technology, popularly known as recombinant DNA, is only about seven years old, but it has already become almost routine. In laboratories all over the world, biologists are taking genes from one organism and planting them into another. So far, the gene splicers have succeeded in inducing bacteria to make human insulin and several other hormones. And that's only the beginning. Someday, bacteria will be turned into living factories. They will churn out vast quantities of vital medical substances, including serums and vaccines, to fight diseases ranging from hepatitis to cancer and the common cold. "Anything that is basically a protein will be makable in unlimited quantities in the next 15 years," says David Baltimore of the Massachusetts Institute of Technology.

Revolution

The impact of genetic engineering on the world's economy could almost equal the recent revolution in microelectronics. Single-celled organisms might yield the proteins that now come from cattle, which would help alleviate world food shortages. Implanted genes could increase the yield of alcohol from corn. Genetically engineered bacteria are being designed to eat their way through oil spills and to extract scarce minerals from the soil. "There has been a golden age of chemistry and a golden age of physics," says Peter Farley, president of Cetus Corp., one of the young companies organized to capitalize on recombinant DNA's potential. "Now it's biology's turn."

As pure science, recombinant DNA represents the most significant step in genetics since James Watson and Francis Crick discovered the double helix in 1953. It will enable scientists to identify each and every one of the 100,000 genes in the human cell. This knowledge might be used to replace defective genes with healthy ones and overcome such genetic diseases as hemophilia and sickle-cell anemia. Some technologists even suggest that the breakthrough will enable science to fashion "better" human beings. By harvesting genes at will, researchers also hope to find the answer to baffling biological questions. How do cells with the same genes differentiate into skin, muscle, and nerve? What makes a normal cell turn malignant? "Recombinant DNA will not only let us understand diseases such as birth defects and cancer, but will also help us understand ourselves," says molecular biologist Phillip Sharp of MIT.

All scientific revolutions—from Galileo's observations of the planets to the splitting of the atom—evoke the cry of heresy. Recombinant DNA is no exception. From the dawn of the recombinant era, many laymen have wondered whether scientists have gone too far by mixing genes that nature ordained to live apart. Among the first to challenge the new technology were scientists themselves. They feared that bacteria containing noxious genes could burst out of the lab and spread the earth with a man-made plague of untold horror.

While they pondered such scenarios, scientists imposed upon themselves a moratorium on most recombinant studies. Expanded research programs began in 1976 only after the National Institutes of Health issued guidelines imposing strict safeguards in the laboratory. Fortunately, no real-life Andromeda Strain has emerged, and most scientists agree that their worst anxieties were unfounded. "There was an overreaction from the beginning," says Howard Goodman of the University of California, San Francisco. "The concern exceeded the hazards, which were all theoretical." In January, the NIH relaxes its guidelines to facilitate research.

Locked Drawers

Now the scientists have other concerns. They worry that the pristine realm of pure science may become contaminated by the tantalizing economic promise of the new DNA research. They fear that exclusive patents may become as coveted as Nobel prizes. A California researcher was accused by university colleagues last year of taking chemicals vital to a recombinant project to a commercial firm. Because of such incidents—some real, some rumored—scientists worry that the free exchange of information traditional to science will give way to closed notebooks and locked drawers. "With millions of dollars coming into labs, suddenly scientists aren't scientists anymore," complains one prominent biologist.

Faustian bargains between the scientist and the entrepreneur have been struck before. But in this deal, the item for sale is nothing less than the fundamental chemical blueprint for life—the gene. The form and function of every living plant and animal are determined by molecules of deoxyribonucleic acid (DNA), formed into the famous double helix described by Watson and Crick. Whenever cells divide, the DNA duplicates itself, passing on its genetic inheritance to the next generation of cells. DNA also guides the cell in the manufacture of proteins essential for life, including hormones like insulin, antibodies to fight disease, hemoglobin to carry oxygen and enzymes that carry out chemical reactions.

DNA resembles a spiral ladder. The sides are formed of sugars and phosphates. The rungs are formed by pairs of the four chemical bases, adenine (A), guanine (G), cytosine (C), and thymine (T). To form a rung, A always joins with T and C with G. The sequence of bases running along a strand of DNA forms a code that tells the cell what protein to make. Proteins consist of amino acids hooked together like the cars of a train. A specific three-letter sequence of DNA bases orders up a particular amino acid that, after a series of intermediate steps, takes its place on the protein the cell is assembling. The sequence CAT, for example, calls for the placement of the amino acid, valine; TAC dictates the addition of another amino acid, methionine. Three-letter codes of bases exist for each of the 20 amino acids that living cells use to make proteins.

Fragment

In recombinant technology, DNA is spliced from one type of cell to another (diagram). Researchers take bacteria, viruses, animal cells, or plant cells, break them apart and extract the DNA. They use enzymes to cut the DNA chemically at specific points along its length. They can then pull out a DNA fragment with the particular array of bases they want to study. This gene is linked to the DNA of one type of *Escherichia coli*, a bacterium that normally flourishes harmlessly in the intestinal tract.

E. coli contains rings of DNA called plasmids. The researchers remove a plasmid, open the ring with a cutting enzyme, and insert the new fragment of DNA. They close the ring with an annealing enzyme and put the plasmid back into the bacterium. Each time the bacterial cell divides, it will pass the new gene along to the next generation and, in a matter of hours, the researchers have thousands of bacteria containing the hybrid DNA. The new colony, a genetic clone, will produce the specific protein determined by the inserted gene. In the pioneering experiment described in 1973, Stanley Cohen and Annie Chang of Stanford and Herbert Boyer and Robert Helling of UCSF inserted a gene into *E. coli* that makes the salmonella germ resistant to the antibiotic streptomycin. The *E. coli* then become resistant themselves.

Potent Poisons

The possibility of accidentally spreading genes that make bacteria resistant to antibiotics was one of the concerns that triggered the debate over the safety of recombinant research.

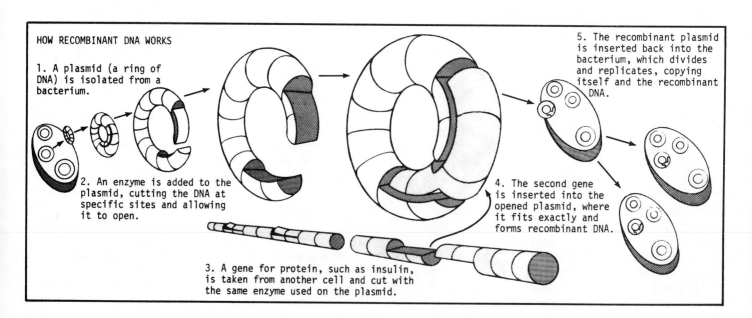

HOW RECOMBINANT DNA WORKS

1. A plasmid (a ring of DNA) is isolated from a bacterium.

2. An enzyme is added to the plasmid, cutting the DNA at specific sites and allowing it to open.

3. A gene for protein, such as insulin, is taken from another cell and cut with the same enzyme used on the plasmid.

4. The second gene is inserted into the opened plasmid, where it fits exactly and forms recombinant DNA.

5. The recombinant plasmid is inserted back into the bacterium, which divides and replicates, copying itself and the recombinant DNA.

And under the new NIH guidelines, research on resistance genes remains largely restricted. Also under tight controls are experiments involving the DNA of disease-causing bacteria or viruses, and genes for the synthesis of potent poisons. Such research must be carried out in top-security "P4" labs, in which workers must change clothes and shower before leaving, and handle their bacteria under sealed hoods to ensure containment. No such research is going on now. Under the revised guidelines, nearly 80% of recombinant research can be done with the sterile procedures that normally prevail in any hospital lab. These include decontaminating items before disposal and a ban on food at the workbench.

Scientists revised their thinking about the hazards of recombinant work after achieving a better understanding of the bugs they were working with. The K-12 strain of *E. coli* used in most experiments has lost its capacity to survive for long outside the laboratory and spread dangerous genes. Human genes, moreover, differ so much from the genes of their bacterial hosts that they function only under conditions controlled by the researcher. "People worried about inadvertently creating something dangerous," says Walter Gilbert of Harvard. "But scientists now know they could not even deliberately create something dangerous."

Still, some researchers believe that the safety issue is being swept under the rug. "For the first time, biologists have a chance to get rich, so there is very strong peer pressure to go along," says Richard Goldstein of Harvard. Allegedly, some researchers have lost their jobs for voicing their concerns too publicly. One safety question that remains is the potential hazard to workers in plants where protein-producing *E. coli* are grown in vat-size quantities. "At such levels, you might have a direct toxic effect," says Baltimore.

Chains

Among the first recombinant products to be manufactured in enormous quantities will be human insulin. Insulin is a protein consisting of two chains of amino acids. In 1978, researchers at City of Hope National Medical Center, Duarte, Calif., took the first step by making chemically some fragments of the gene for insulin. Scientists at Genentech, Inc., of South San Francisco, another of the new firms set up to exploit recombinant research, assembled the fragments and inserted the synthetic genes for each of the two insulin chains into *E. coli* plasmids. Alongside, they implanted a regulatory mechanism called the lac operon, which serves as an "on-off" switch to activate the insulin genes. Once the plasmids were put back into *E. coli*, the insulin genes responded and the bacteria began turning out insulin chains. The insulin now used by diabetics comes from cattle or pigs and contains impurities that can cause allergic reactions. Once full-scale production begins, human insulin made by bacteria promises to provide a cheaper and safer alternative.

Recombinant techniques have started to produce other important human proteins. Two months ago, researchers at the University of Zurich and Biogen, S.A., of Geneva reported inducing *E. coli* to make interferon, a natural virus fighter. Interferon may help prevent flu, hepatitis, and other viral infections and is now being tested against cancer. The quantity of interferon that could be made available through bacteria is significant. Interferon research has been hampered by the fact that the substance can now only be extracted in small amounts from such sources as white blood cells. Costs of a single course of treatment run as high as $50,-000. Pituitary growth hormone necessary for the treatment of certain types of dwarfism is also scarce and costly, but researchers have begun producing it through recombinant methods. Some day, they may use the same techniques to make Factor VIII, the blood protein that victims of hemophilia need to prevent bleeding.

Scientists are also using recombinant methods to unravel basic mysteries about genes. One is how genes are regulated. All cells, except eggs and sperm, contain a complete set of genes, but most of them don't do anything until they are somehow "turned on." At least one type of gene regulation has now been explained by Mark Ptashne and his colleagues at Harvard, using a standard lab virus called "lambda."

Lambda readily invades *E. coli*, where it adopts either of two radically different life-styles. In one, lambda DNA takes over the machinery of the bacterium and forces it to make more lambda viruses. The *E. coli* bursts, releasing the new lambdas, then dies. In its other mode, the lambda DNA remains harmlessly quiescent as the bacteria reproduces generation after generation.

Message

How the lambda genes behave, the researchers showed, depends in large part on "repressor" molecules (diagram). Normally, DNA sends messages for protein syntheses with the aid of a "transcribing" enzyme. But if a repressor molecule lies on a gene, the enzyme can't pick up DNA's instructions, and the gene remains inactive. Ptashne

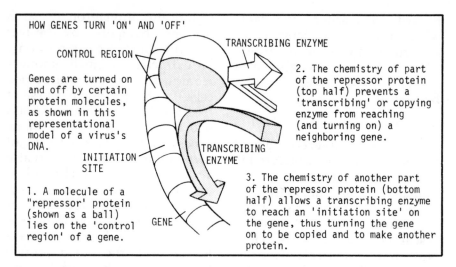

HOW GENES TURN 'ON' AND 'OFF'

CONTROL REGION

TRANSCRIBING ENZYME

Genes are turned on and off by certain protein molecules, as shown in this representational model of a virus's DNA.

INITIATION SITE

TRANSCRIBING ENZYME

GENE

1. A molecule of a "repressor" protein (shown as a ball) lies on the 'control region' of a gene.

2. The chemistry of part of the repressor protein (top half) prevents a 'transcribing' or copying enzyme from reaching (and turning on) a neighboring gene.

3. The chemistry of another part of the repressor protein (bottom half) allows a transcribing enzyme to reach an 'initiation site' on the gene, thus turning the gene on to be copied and to make another protein.

discovered that the same repressor molecule can also turn genes on. Depending on how the repressor is positioned within the "control region" of the DNA, it can either attract the transcribing enzyme, thus turning on the genes for viral reproduction, or deflect it, thus keeping the genes turned off. This work uncovered principles of gene regulation that may let scientists insert genes of higher organisms into bacteria, and also switch them on.

Scientists now can also determine both the exact sequence of bases in a piece of DNA and the precise locations of genes within chromosomes. There are hundreds of thousands of possible combinations of sequences within genes. Because researchers have the ability to produce genes in enormous quantities, they can finally study enough genes to map the bases.

Similarly, biologists can tell how the total of more than 100,000 human genes fit into the 46 chromosomes. To accomplish this, scientists clone a gene and mix it with chromosomes whose DNA spirals have been split down the middle. The DNA bases of the "test" gene automatically find their natural partners in the appropriate split chromosome, A to T and C to G. Thus, researchers will learn both which chromosome the gene

naturally fits into and where on the chromosome the gene normally rests. This "gene mapping" might make possible the cure of inherited diseases like sickle-cell anemia and hemophilia, which result from defects in a single gene. If scientists locate the proper chromosome, they could repair the defective gene or insert a properly functioning new gene into the cell.

Clue

The new DNA research could even help cope with the riddle of cancer. J. Michael Bishop and his colleagues at UCSF have cloned genes of viruses that cause tumors in chickens and isolated those that turn cells malignant. One of the tumor-causing genes instructs the cell to make an enzyme that transfers phosphate molecules to proteins. "Our hypothesis is that this transfer of molecules causes cancerous growth," Bishop says. So far, the hypothesis has not led to the development of a therapeutic strategy.

Scientists have also found that the tumor genes that invade the cell are virtually the same as genes that already inhabit it. Bishop suggests this may indicate how cells grow and differentiate. If the invading gene causes cancer by making cells proliferate uncontrollably, its harmless counterpart might

normally control growth and differentiation. Thus, the study of cancer, a medical problem, may lead to a better understanding of the science of cell differentiation.

Now that gene splicing is so relatively easy, scientists find they can reexamine old genetic dogmas. Until recently, for instance, microbiologists assumed that the genes of bacteria were just like those in higher organisms. But scientists led by Sharp at MIT and Philip Leder of NIH independently discovered a startling difference. All the bases in bacterial DNA are read by enzymes three by three and translated directly into amino acids. But in viral and mammalian DNA, they found, the elements of DNA that code for amino acids that are used to make protein are separated by sequences that don't seem to get translated into any protein at all.

The discovery of these intervening sequences, or "introns," alters the conventional picture of how human genes work (diagram). DNA bases are copied into a molecule of ribonucleic acid (RNA). But before the appropriate information is carried to the region of the cell where amino acids are assembled to make proteins, enzymes must first process the RNA. They must cut the introns out of the RNA and splice the remaining coding segments together. "This discovery is the biggest thing yet to come out of cloning DNA," wrote John Rogers of UCLA.

If genes are divided into pieces, nature must have a reason. Harvard's Gilbert thinks that piecemeal genes may have helped man evolve. Words separated by spaces can be moved around to form meaningful new sentences with less confusion than if words were strung out in an uninterrupted line. Similarly,

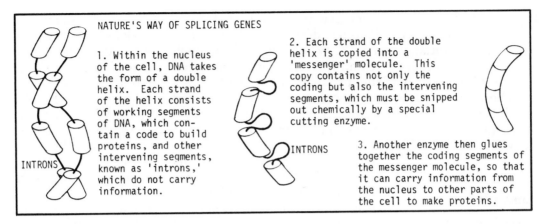

Gilbert suggests, the messages of DNA can be shuffled more easily into new combinations that make new genes if they are separated by introns. These fresh combinations of DNA might change the character of a cell and give the organism a selective advantage.

Another surprise came from the lab of Alexander Rich at MIT. Rich and his colleagues made crystals of DNA and found that they didn't look anything like Watson and Crick's graceful spiral. The pioneers of the double helix propounded their model from studying vague X-ray scattering patterns. Rich's crystals yielded sharp pictures that showed individual atoms in DNA for the first time. The crystallized DNA formed a zigzag shape that twisted left instead of a smooth curve twisting right. It is still uncertain why or when it takes that configuration at times.

Ideal Human

Rich thinks that the "Z-DNA," as he calls it, may possibly be involved in cancer. Cancer-causing chemicals could more easily reach the exposed bases. The smooth spiral of DNA can change into the Z form at special sequences of bases, so a small number of such transformations could attract carcinogens and trigger the start of cancer. Rich also believes that genes may change from smooth to Z-DNA

to turn themselves off in certain circumstances. "It's still like a new baby," he says. "We don't really know yet what it will grow up to be."

At the extreme of the new genetic research is the question of whether gene splicing could be used to create the ideal human being. Reputable scientists regard that prospect as fantasy. It is one thing to understand the basic blueprint written in the genes; it is quite another to translate the blueprint into an individual. In the formation of any organism, many gene products interact, and the circuitry is staggeringly complex. Besides, the final product of the genes—be it an Einstein or an idiot—is also shaped by environment. "Because of these complexities," says Jonathan King of MIT, "attempts to modify human beings through genetic manipulation is a policy of false eugenics. It will do more damage than it will anything else."

There is much that scientists don't know about DNA, and one tangential element of their rapidly advancing research troubles many of them. They fear that the commercial potential of their findings may hamper the flow of information that helps make research succeed. Traditionally, many important scientific ideas have arisen from free and informal contacts among researchers. The Cohen-Boyer collaboration that led to

the first recombinant-DNA breakthrough began over sandwiches during a lunch break at a biology symposium. "Scientists go off in the evenings and kick ideas around," says MIT's Sharp. "People who are being secretive won't participate and they'll suffer for it."

Ethics

The tantalizing lure of profits from recombinant DNA has already intruded on the sanctity of the academic lab. Scientists were shocked last year when Peter Seeburg, an assistant of John Baxter's at UCSF, left for Genentech and took with him some material to be used in producing growth hormone. Some researchers questioned the ethics of Seeburg's action, but he maintains that he had started the project and was entitled to the material and a share in any patent rights that might come from it.

The role of commercialism in DNA research may be decided soon by the U. S. Supreme Court. Last year, the Court agreed to decide whether new forms of life can be patented. If they can, a scientist and a company would be entitled to sell the resulting product exclusively for 17 years. Should the Court rule against patents, some scientists fear that their colleagues will resort even further to secrecy.

"I hope we will be able to go

the patent route and publish freely," says a university biologist who is also associated with a private firm. But others find no benefit in this manner of exclusivity. "There is enough potential in the field that it doesn't need patent protection to stimulate activity," says MIT's Baltimore.

Research Standards

DNA research has attracted so much attention from the public and from investors, that it has generated still another anxiety—what researchers call "science by press conference." Instead of presenting their work in traditional fashion to a scientific journal, where it can be "refereed" or evaluated by authorities before it is published, some scientists now rush their findings directly to the media. The City of Hope-Genentech team, for example, announced the production of insulin at a press conference before it had done the additional—and necessary—work to show that the hormone actually functioned. (Only about nine months later did Eli Lilly and Co. show that the bacteria-created insulin really worked.) Such premature announcement of results could reduce scientists' credibility and lower the standards of research. But many scientists remain confident that pure science and industry can work together. "Biologists have been unworldly," says Rich. "Chemists have been living in the commercial world for 50 years and still do exciting research."

To good scientists, research is exciting for its own sake. That's why they split atomic nuclei, listen to electronic impulses from the galaxies, and fiddle with strands of DNA in the first place. Whether their discoveries simply add arcane footnotes to the scientific literature or launch whole new fields of industrial endeavor remains of secondary concern. The burgeoning gene research promises to do a great deal of both. It will lift the curtain further on the ultimate secrets of life on Earth. And it will also enrich the lives of the planet's restless inhabitants.

MATT CLARK with SHARON BEGLEY in Cambridge, Mass., and San Francisco, and MARY HAGER in Washington

BOOK REVIEWS: FICTION

The Boys from Brazil, Ira Levin, Random House, 1976.

Ninety-four men have to die on or near certain dates in the next two and a half years. They're 65 years old, or will be when their dates of death come around. They're family men, stable, civil servants, mostly—men of minor authority.

Why have these harmless, aging men been marked for murder? What is the hidden link that binds them? You get the answer to these questions when you read this book. You also read an exciting adventure thriller in which a genetic tool—which is, in reality, only an idea—is put into practice in this work of fiction.

The 94 men are the adoptive fathers of 94 boys who are as alike as twins. When you meet the professor of biology, Numberger, you begin to get an idea of the diabolical plot that has been created by a hard core of Nazis still living in South America.

The theory is intriguing: With a single hair from Mozart's head, someone with the skill, equipment, and women to act as mothers could breed a few hundred infant Mozarts.

In the right environments, perhaps five or ten of them would develop their talents and the world would have a lot more beautiful music. Substitute Hitler for Mozart and you have a most interesting plot.

Although the actual technology to carry out the theory has not been developed—and may never be—this book presents a very interesting idea.

Altered States, Paddy Chayefsky, Bantam Books, 1978. Paperback, $2.25.

Edward Jessup is a 34-year-old professor of physiology at Harvard Medical School. He begins a unique search for the evolutionary roots of human development and behavior. His journey takes him to Central Mexico. He learns first-hand the power of the hallucinogens used by the old Indian brujos—priests-medicine men. He journeys through "the crack between the nothing" to the "unborn souls." Then, he returns to the isolation tank at Harvard Medical School. He floats for hours in warm water, in total darkness, with no external stimuli. He learns to guide his mind through regressions that allow him to view his primitive, primordial self, as he was—and as all humans were when they first emerged from the forests of equatorial Africa.

Jessup—and the reader—know that he must ultimately combine the two experiences. His sessions in the tank, under the influence of the drug, become more frequent and prolonged. And more frightening. He directs the genetic, anatomic, and physiologic regression of mind and body to an earlier stage of human development. His final confrontation with his genetic and behavioral origins is the hair-raising climax of this novel.

Chayefsky provides the reader with current information from many fields of biomedical research—genetics, molecular biology, biophysics, neurology, and psychology. And he restructures it into an entertaining story of the search for our ultimate roots.

BOOK REVIEWS: NONFICTION

A Double Image of the Double Helix,
Clifford Grobstein, Freeman, 1979,
$5.95.

When recombinant DNA research
became a reality, scientists and citizens
alike were concerned. Two serious issues
were raised: whether public health and
welfare were threatened by recombinant
DNA research; and, perhaps more basic,
whether research itself needs greater public
regulation. The concern started in the
scientific community with several con-
ferences, one of which led to a book,
Biohazards in Biological Research in 1973.
Public concern began in 1975, rose to a
climax in early 1977, and began to subside
in 1978.

The Asilomar Conference held in
California in February, 1975, brought
together 150 scientists *not* to discuss
science, but to talk about the possible
necessity for *controlling* it. The par-
ticipants achieved an uneasy consensus.
They agreed to limit their own freedom of
research, even though they had no certain
proof that the need for limitation existed or
that the consequences of it would be
positive. It is a remarkable account of the
uncertainty that frequently surrounds
science.

This book also explores the issue of
public concern. Various governmental
agencies got involved. The City Council of
Cambridge, Massachusetts, home of Harvard University and M.I.T., conducted a
series of open hearings in June and July of
1976. The hearings and their results are
well worth reading about.

The first controlled DNA recom-
binations were performed in 1973. The
National Institutes of Health developed
guidelines for this type of research in 1976.
Statutory regulation of the research was
proposed but dropped by the Ninety-Fifth
Congress. Public policy for regulating
research that might be biohazardous is not
clear-cut. This book leaves us some
unanswered questions. But that is a thread
that runs through all science: You may get
a few answers, but you usually end up with
many more questions.

Journey, Robert and Suzanne Massie,
Alfred A. Knopf, 1975.

This is the story of the long struggle of a
husband and wife against their only son's
hemophilia. The book describes how that
struggle tested their education, their
philosophy, and their religion.

The story begins with the happiness and
high hopes that a new baby brings. But the
joy is brief: The boy is a hemophiliac.

From that moment on, the reader is caught
up in the days, the crises, and the
stratagems of a mother, a father, and a
child fighting to make a life for themselves
in the face of a fearful, chronic disease.

From the mother we learn of her son's
struggle for physical survival and the
family's efforts to keep him growing, to
find doctors and schools and to help him
take command of his own life. She also tells
of her own battle to overcome bitterness
and self-pity. The father relates his struggle
to understand his son's illness and to find
the money to pay for medical care. These
are everyday people who help their son
grow up psychologically strong.

Rosalind Franklin and DNA, Anne
Sayre, Norton and Company, 1975.

You should read this book *after* you
read James Watson's *The Double Helix*.
Watson refers to a character named
"Rosy." Anne Sayre says that Watson's
"Rosy" represented, but did not really
coincide with, a woman named Rosalind
Franklin whom Sayre knew, admired, and
liked. No one will dispute Franklin's
contribution to the discovery of the
structure of DNA. Had she lived until
1962, the Nobel Prize Committee would
have been required to consider the
legitimacy of her claim to a share in the
honors divided among Watson, Crick, and
Wilkins. Franklin died on April 16, 1950,
at the age of 37. *The Double Helix* was
published ten years later. Sayre feels that
there is another side to the DNA story, and
she tells it in an interesting and exciting
manner.

This book is partly a biography.
Perhaps more important, it is also the story
of a great working scientist. Franklin's
work was X-ray diffraction—a
photographic technique for examining the
structure of molecules. Her work played a
key role in the development of the model of
the structure of DNA.

Franklin was a human being. She was
also a woman. Franklin saw Wilkins as a
man who did not like to have women
around. In fact, up to 1971, all the students
supervised by Wilkins were men. In this
uneasy atmosphere, this woman scientist
and sensitive human being did her X-ray
diffraction work and developed a set of
data that made possible one of the
century's greatest scientific developments.

The Case of the Midwife Toad, Arthur
Koestler, Random, 1973.

The midwife toad, *Alyles obstetricians*
is different from most other toads and

frogs. It mates on land. The female releases
her eggs in long strings of jelly. The male,
after having fertilized them, winds these
beads of eggs around his hind legs until the
eggs hatch—thus, the name "midwife
toad." Unlike the midwife toad, those
species that mate in water develop blackish
swellings on their palms and fingers. These
help a male hold onto a slippery female in
the water so that whenever she releases her
eggs, the male can be right there to fertilize
them. The male midwife toad has no
nuptial pads, no need to hold a slippery
female in water.

Paul Kammerer, a brilliant Austrian
scientist, claimed that by forcing these
toads to copulate in water, like other toads,
they eventually (after six generations)
developed nuptial pads as an acquired
hereditary trait. This was in the early 1900s,
when Mendel's papers had recently been
discovered. The notion that acquired
characteristics could be inherited was very
appealing to some scholars, especially to
educators. If what a student learned
(acquired) could be passed on to his or her
children genetically, without the new
generation having to study as hard,
education would be much easier.

Arthur Koestler describes the bitter
scientific controversy surrounding this
case, for Kammerer was accused of
falsifying his data. We meet many of the
early Mendelians in these pages and get a
taste of how unscientifically some
judgments are made. History is replayed
when Bateson, the English proponent of
Mendelian inheritance, "refused to look in
the telescope." And even after Kammerer's
suicide in 1926, we wait for Koestler to set
the story right in 1971. It is an exciting, but
very sad, story because it really happened.

**Genetic Politics—The Limits of
Biological Control,** Marc Lappe,
Simon and Schuster, 1979, $9.95.

To what extent does our biological
heritage control human behavior and
development? How heavily should we rely
on pronouncements that genetic influences
underlie tendencies toward violence,
alcoholism, mental disease, cancer, and
heart disease? What are the hidden costs
and pitfalls of genetic screening? What are
the dangers in assigning genetic causes to
IQ scores, obesity, or behavioral disorders?

The author examines these questions
and offers evidence that the possible roles
of genes in our lives may have been
overstated and oversimplified. He traces an
overreliance on a "scientific" explanation
for complex human attributes to a psychological and cultural urge to control and

simplify all the forces that impinge on our lives.

The damaging political and social consequences of this drive are revealed, beginning with the mass abuse of sterilization in the 1920s, to the genocide seen in Nazi Germany. It culminates in the less visible, but significant, consequences of assigning genetic labels—and expectations—to the current generation.

The author suggests that scientists, physicians, and politicians have misinterpreted data in an attempt to express complex phenomena in simplified terms and policies. He reviews the human costs of these errors. He acknowledges that the genes we inherit do play a role in human behavior and health. But this role, in his view, is more subtle and complex than most people realize.

This is a controversial book. It interprets historical events as evidence of frequent, unsuccessful attempts to use science wisely. Whether the reader agrees with Lappe's views or not, the book provides much food for thought. Science is not always "right." This book will help its readers develop a healthy questioning of scientific findings and reports.

Altered Destinies—Lives Changed by Genetic Flaws, William Stockton, Doubleday, 1979, $9.95

This book stresses the importance of communication between doctor and patient. The medical profession traditionally obligates physicians to teach. It is not enough to teach only in medical schools. The public, especially those with genetic defects or those with children with genetic defects, need the doctor as a teacher. Why do doctors fail to teach the public? Stockton gives four possible reasons:

1. It is difficult for doctors to translate technical jargon into everyday language.
2. It is easy to hide the ghastly truth behind technicalities, because the truth is as frightening to a physician as it is to a patient or parents.
3. Doctors are afraid that—if they simplify the subject for the public—their colleagues will accuse them of superficiality.
4. Professional acclaim is another possible reason. Doctor's derive greater acclaim from their colleagues by writing and talking to them in their technical language than from writing and talking to the public in simpler language.

In ten case studies, the author demonstrates how some health care providers have overcome communication problems. In Stockton's view, the key element in the medical care of victims of hereditary conditions and their families is

understanding how they feel. The families who seemed to deal best with their disease were those who developed an open and healthy relationship with a doctor or a genetic counselor and who received as much attention as they needed. Families who did not have a readily sympathetic ear coped less well, sometimes with sad results.

This book deserves attention. The reader not only experiences the trials and tribulations of individuals and families with genetic problems (and maybe cries a little with them) but also rejoices to see them triumph over their adversity.

The Double Helix, James D. Watson, Atheneum, 1968.

In this book, the reader can experience first-hand one of the critical discoveries in the history of genetics. Three young scientists—Francis Crick, James Watson, and Maurice Wilkins—worked together using data from chemistry, physics, and biology to construct a hypothetical model of the structure of DNA. Since the early 1940s, scientists had thought that DNA (deoxyribonucleic acid) was the genetic material of all life. That piece of information was valuable. But how DNA might control the genetic process could not be imagined until the structure of DNA was determined. How the three young scientists unraveled the mystery of the DNA structure reads like a detective story. Indeed, some of the methods and clues discovered and used would do credit to Sherlock Holmes himself.

The author, a member of the team that received the Nobel Prize for Medicine and Physiology in 1962 for their DNA hypothesis, gives an interesting first-hand account of the work. He also explores the work of many other scientists whose preliminary findings gave insight and direction to the search. He recaptures some of his original excitement. He also relates some of the boredom of tedious experiments. He tells of the many blind alleys they traveled. There were frequent mistakes, miscalculations, and wrong ideas.

Watson also describes the intense competition—among people, laboratories, and theories. Several scientists working in different laboratories and with different theories in mind were looking for the key to the structure of DNA. Watson, Crick, and Wilkins knew of their competitors. In particular, they knew that Linus Pauling, a biochemist from California, was very close to unlocking the mystery of DNA structure. Being first with a most acceptable hypothesis was extremely important. Watson seems to feel that a strong competitive drive moves science just as it does athletes who excel in their sport.

The Double Helix is not meant to explain genetics. Instead, it gives some valuable insights into scientists as people

and how science works. Watson destroys the stereotype of scientists as white-coated recluses locked away in smelly laboratories and dusty libraries. As the story unfolds, we see that scientists are human beings with all the strengths and weaknesses other people have. Watson and his friends walk along rivers, marvel at nature, worry about money, enjoy fine wine and good food, and argue about politics. Join James Watson in this book. You'll be glad you did.

The Genetic Connection—How to Protect Your Family Against Hereditary Disease, David Hendin and Joan Marks, William Morrow, 1978, $8.95

A reader who wishes to learn more about genetic counseling will find a great deal of information in this book. In a well-written and easy-to-understand fashion, the authors take the reader through prenatal tests, laboratory studies, physical examination, review of family history, and many new techniques. Although the book is written primarily for parents, young people who are not yet considering having families also can benefit.

There are two appendices of great value. Appendix I is "Where To Get More Information About Specific Genetic Disease," and II is a "State-by-State Listing of Genetic Counseling and Treatment Centers." There is no need for anyone to be ignorant about genetic disorders. This book will help improve the understanding of genetics that is so important to everyone.

ABOUT THE AUTHORS

DONNA DAY BAIRD

Donna Baird first became interested in biology when she attended a small liberal arts college in St. Paul, Minnesota. After working in a medical laboratory for a year and in welfare departments for three years, she went back to school at the University of Minnesota. She studied the behavior of a population of small grassland rodents and taught ecology classes. She also earned a doctoral degree. She enjoys gardening, backpacking, jogging, and racquetball. Two of her long-term goals are to become an expert GO player and to run a marathon. She is currently working toward a second doctorate, in epidemiology.

RONALD G. DAVIDSON

Ron Davidson was born in Hamilton, Ontario, Canada. He earned his MD degree at the University of Western Ontario and then trained as a pediatrician in Vancouver, British Columbia, and Boston, Massachusetts. He specialized in genetics at Johns Hopkins University in Baltimore and in later studies in England. He finally went to work at the Children's Hospital of Buffalo, New York, as chief of the Division of Human Genetics. When a new and unique medical school was opened at McMaster University in Hamilton, his hometown beckoned. He now directs a program in human genetics at McMaster, where he does genetic counseling, directs a biochemical genetics research project, and teaches. The medical school has pretty much eliminated lectures and labs. The medical students start solving clinical problems from their first day. They work together in tutorial groups of five. The school has even abolished exams! Ron Davidson was once introduced at a genetics research meeting as "the best golfer among human geneticists in North America." He also skis and plays (a miserable game of) racquetball.

H. EDWARD DREXLER

Ed Drexler is a biology teacher and the director of curriculum for Pius XI High School in Milwaukee, Wisconsin. He received a B.S. degree from the University of Wisconsin in 1950 and an M.A. from Ohio State University in 1964. His favorite pasttimes are reading, listening to classical music, hiking in the Rocky Mountains, and riding his bicycle. Ed's love for bicycling led him to ride all the way from Milwaukee to Denver, Colorado, in the summer of 1974. He carried everything he needed in a backpack and camped along the way. Next to bicycling, Ed likes teaching best.

BENNIE LATIMER

Bennie Latimer is a biology teacher at Cooley High School in Detroit, Michigan. She received her B.S. degree from Wayne State University in 1964 and her M.A. from the same university in 1974. She teaches the accelerated program at Cooley High and sponsors the medical career club. In college, she was an officer in Sigma Gamma Rho, and she is still active in that sorority. She enjoys cake decorating, interior and floral design, painting, silk-screening, photography, and reading.

JOHN M. OPITZ

John Opitz was born in Hamburg, Germany. He was trained as a pediatrician and clinical geneticist at the Universities of Iowa and Wisconsin. His first loves were natural history and zoology, and he maintains a broad range of interests in comparative anatomy, embryology, and evolution. Presently, he is coordinator of the Shodair-Montana Regional Genetics Program at Shodair Children's Hospital in Helena; a clinical professor of pediatrics and medicine (medical genetics) at the University of Washington, Seattle; and adjunct professor of medicine, biology, and of history and philosophy at Montana State University, Bozeman. He was founder and is editor of the *American Journal of Medical Genetics* and is a managing editor of the *European Journal of Pediatrics.* His hobbies are the history of biology and theology, natural history, and gems and jewelry making.

STUART F. SPICKER

Stuart Spicker graduated from the Bronx High School of Science in New York City in 1955, where he first became interested in various theories of evolution and their compatibility with differing ideas in theology. He went on to complete a B.A. in philosophy at the City University of New York at Queens College and an M.A. in social psychology at the New School for Social Research in New York. In 1968 he received a doctorate in philosophy from the University of Colorado at Boulder. He is co-editor of the book series *Philosophy and Medicine* and serves on the advisory boards of the *Journal of Medicine and Philosophy* and *Metamedicine.* His special interests are the philosophy of medicine and bioethics. He is presently Professor of Community Medicine and Health Care and Director of the Division of Humanistic Studies in Medicine at the School of Medicine, University of Connecticut Health Center at Farmington. He spends his free time at the jazz piano.

TED K. TSUMURA

Ted Tsumura teaches biology, health, and physiology at George Washington High School, Denver, Colorado. He is president of the Colorado Biology Teachers Association and was Colorado Teacher of the Year in 1976. He holds a doctoral degree in health education. Ted also is a member of the advisory committee for genetic screening, education, and counseling for the Colorado Department of Health. He has co-authored a health textbook. His favorite sport is basketball, and he holds a black belt in karate. Ted says of his teaching, "My goal each day is to watch for faces that light up. I know I have been successful when there is a warm glow in my room."

ADVISORY COMMITTEE

Back row (l ro r): Robert Burt, Jerry Resnick, Audrey Heimler, Betsy Simon. Front Row: Rosemary Park, Marshall Kreuter, George Henry

Robert A. Burt, JD
Professor of Law
Yale University
New Haven, Connecticut

Audrey Heimler, Genetic Counselor
Division of Human Genetics
Long Island Jewish-Hillside Medical Center
New Hyde Park, New York

George Henry, MD
Reproductive Genetics Center
Denver, Colorado

Marshall Kreuter, PhD
Chairperson, Health Science
College of Health   Division
University of Utah
Salt Lake City, Utah

Rosemary Park, PhD
Los Angeles, California

Jerry Resnick
Sheepshead Bay High School
Brooklyn, New York

Betsy D. Simon
Coordinator, Health Education
Baltimore City Public Schools
Baltimore, Maryland

Acknowledgment

The authors wish to thank Dr. Laurence B. McCullough for his thoughtful review of "Thinking about Ethical Questions," "A New Look at the Handicapped," and "Genetics and Ethics: Why Study Human Heredity?" Dr. McCullough is Associate Director and Senior Research Scholar, Kennedy Institute of Ethics, Department of Community and Family Medicine, Georgetown University School of Medicine, Washington, D.C.

BE AN ACTIVE PARTICIPANT

You now have some understanding of genetics and some of the genetic disorders that affect humans. If you want to learn more or do something to help someone, here are some suggestions:

1. If you live near a university medical center or a major metropolitan hospital, you may find an active genetic services unit. Contact them and let them know of your interest in genetics. Try to state a very specific area of interest. If you are too vague or general, busy professionals may not want to take the time to work with you. Visit the unit or department and find out what they do.

2. Check to see if there is any volunteer work in your community that is related to genetics. Your local hospital might need your help with health care activities involving children or adults with genetic disorders. Nursing homes, day care centers, nursery schools might have people with genetic disorders. They probably would be grateful for your help. Many groups need you as a volunteer, and your experiences as a volunteer will teach you a great deal.

3. Get involved with one or more of the many genetic voluntary organizations. There is much you can do for them: clerical work, telephone work, active participation in fund raising, and organizing fund-raising activities—walkathons, bikeathons, runathons.

If you don't know where to start, contact one of these agencies. Tell them what you would like to do. They will direct you to an agency that will be glad to have your help.

GENERAL ORGANIZATIONS

The National Easter Seal Society for Cripple Children and Adults
2023 West Ogden Avenue
Chicago, Illinois 60612
Deals with all types of physical handicaps. Produces a journal, bibliographies, and many publications. Write for their publications list.

March of Dimes Birth Defects Foundation
1275 Mamaroneck Avenue
White Plains, N. Y. 10605

11,000 local units. Concerned with the prevention of all birth defects. Write for publications. "Birth Defects—The Tragedy and the Hope" and "Genetic Counseling" are free and good reading. Mention a specific disorder if you are interested in one condition.

National Genetics Foundation
9 West 57th Street
New York, N. Y. 10019

Promotes a genetic counseling network. Can put you in touch with specialists and genetic counselors. Write for brochures, "How Genetic Disease Can Affect You and Your Family" and "Can Genetic Counseling Help You?"

ORGANIZATIONS FOR SPECIFIC CONDITIONS

Cleft Parent Group
P.O. Box 6215
San Jose, California 95150

Cooley's Anemia Blood and Research Foundation
Graybar Building, Suite 1644
420 Lexington Avenue
New York, N. Y. 10017

Cystic Fibrosis Foundation
6000 Executive Bldg., Suite 309
Rockville, Maryland 20852

Down Syndrome Congress
P.O. Box 1527
Brownwood, Texas 76801

National Foundation for Jewish Genetic Diseases
250 Park Avenue
New York, N. Y. 10177

National Hemophilia Foundation
25 West 39th Street
New York, N. Y. 10018

Committee to Combat Huntington Disease, Inc.
250 W. 57th Street
New York, N. Y. 10019

Muscular Dystrophy Association
810 Seventh Avenue
New York, N. Y. 10019

National Neurofibromatosis Foundation
340 E. 80th Street
New York, N. Y. 10021

PKU Parents Group
518 Paco Drive
Los Altos, California 94022

National Retinitis Pigmentosa Foundation
8331 Mindale Circle
Baltimore, Maryland 21207

National Association of Sickle Cell Disease, Inc.
945 South Western Avenue
Los Angeles, California 90006

Spina Bifida Association of America
343 South Dearborn, Room 319
Chicago, Illinois 60604

National Tay-Sachs and Allied Diseases Association
122 East 42nd Street
New York, N. Y. 10017

And many others